THE MULTIFAMILY MILLIONAIRE
VOLUME I

The
MULTIFAMILY
MILLIONAIRE

*Achieve Financial Freedom
by Investing in Small
Multifamily Real Estate*

Volume I

BRANDON TURNER
AND BRIAN MURRAY

BiggerPockets®
PUBLISHING
Denver, Colorado

Praise for
Brandon Turner's Books

How to Invest in Real Estate:
Winner of Indie Press Awards 2019
First and Second Place CIPA EVVY Awards 2019

"An insider's perspective, full of encouragement and resources for newcomers... Interested readers will find the book substantially useful as a starting point."

—Kirkus Review on *How to Invest in Real Estate*

"I only wish this book had been written in 2005 when I was starting my real estate investing journey!"

**—Ken Corsini of HGTV's *Flip or Flop Atlanta*
on *How to Invest in Real Estate***

"There are very few books that provide a detailed, step-by-step framework for accomplishing real estate success. Brandon Turner's *[Rental Property Investing]* does that and does it in a way that puts financial freedom through real estate within reach of anyone who wants it."

—J Scott, Author of *The Book on Flipping Houses*

"I wish I had *[Managing Rental Properties]* before I made all of my expensive property management mistakes! Brandon and Heather Turner have covered the biggest challenges for landlords and solved each one with step-by-step systems."

—Chad Carson, Author of *Retire Early with Real Estate*

Praise for Brian Murray's Crushing It in Apartments and Commercial Real Estate

---

Gold Award Winner,
Nonfiction Book Awards

Gold Award Winner,
2018 Robert Bruss Real Estate Book Awards

"A strong choice in a crowded category."

—*Publishers Weekly*

"Newbies and professionals alike will benefit from this volume, which is chockfull of insight and solid investing advice."

—BlueInk Review

"The mistakes he names can be learned from, and his transparency makes his stories of success both exciting and inspiring."

—Foreword Clarion Review

The Multifamily Millionaire, Volume I: Achieve Financial Freedom by Investing in Small Multifamily Real Estate
Brandon Turner and Brian Murray

Published by BiggerPockets Publishing LLC, Denver, CO
Copyright © 2021 by Brandon Turner and Brian Murray
All Rights Reserved.

Publisher's Cataloging-in-Publication Data

Names: Turner, Brandon, author. | Murray, Brian Harold, 1968-, author.
Title: The multifamily millionaire , volume I : achieve financial freedom by investing in small multifamily real estate / by Brandon Turner and Brian Murray.
Description: Includes bibliographical references. | Denver, CO: BiggerPockets Publishing, 2021.
Identifiers: LCCN: 2020946077 | ISBN: 9781947200944 (Hardcover) | 9781947200432 (pbk.) | 9781947200951 (ebook)
Subjects: LCSH Residential real estate--Purchasing. | Real estate investment. | Apartment houses. | House buying. | BISAC BUSINESS & ECONOMICS / Real Estate / General | BUSINESS & ECONOMICS / Real Estate / Buying & Selling Homes | BUSINESS & ECONOMICS / Investments & Securities / Real Estate
Classification: LCC HD1382.5 .T87 v.1 2021 | DDC 332.63/24--dc23

Printed on recycled paper in the United States of America
10 9 8 7 6 5 4 3 2 1

Dedication

The Multifamily Millionaire, Volume I,
is dedicated

by Brandon to Heather

and by Brian to Tricia.

*Our success would not be possible without your
continued support and sacrifice. There are no words
that can adequately express the depth of our gratitude
for all that you do.*

TABLE OF CONTENTS

PREFACE

I (Brandon Turner here—and anytime you read "I" throughout the book, it's me!) carefully unfurled the clump of bills and counted the money. It wasn't that I didn't trust the disheveled 20-something standing in front of me. He was, in fact, one of my best friends. Besides, I knew where he lived: about fifty feet from where I lived at the other end of that dirt driveway. He was handing over more cold hard cash than I had ever held in my hands: $650. This was a big deal for a 21-year-old making just above minimum wage.

After a few moments of small talk, I said a quick thanks and walked back home. Even though I had just walked out my front door less than two minutes earlier and had traveled less than twenty feet down the driveway, I returned to my domain with a skip in my step and my head held high.

It worked.

Something fundamental had changed in me. My tenant had just paid me $650 for the right to rent out the second unit on that small lot on that small street in that small town. I was, officially, a landlord.

On that day, two striking realities hit me at once:

First, I realized that my mortgage payment on that property was only $620, including taxes and insurance. I held $650 in my hand and soon that would be in my bank account, with the surplus being mine to spend as I saw fit. In other words, I had achieved profit. Cash flow. Success. Sure, that $30 would be eaten up by other costs associated with owning that rental (which you will become especially familiar with by the time you finish reading this book), but the fact remained: I had done it. I had made the leap.

I had invested a tremendous amount of time on education, networking, searching, analyzing, and making offers over the previous six months. I felt excited, nervous, ambitious, scared to death, optimistic, pessimistic, and every other emotion a person could feel. Then I repaired and rebuilt and rewired and rejuvenated and reimagined until the property was something I could be proud of. It had been an arduous journey—and it was complete.

The property was rented.

I had created a real money-making business that built "passive income." Of course, any landlord reading this story can point out half a dozen or more fundamental rules of landlording that I violated in this transaction—all of which you will learn through this book. (e.g., don't rent to friends and don't accept rent in cash). Regardless, I had accomplished what most only dream of. I was a real estate investor.

It is often said a person goes bankrupt in two phases: slowly, and then all at once. A person becomes a real estate investor in those same two phases. And on that warm first day of September back in 2007, after a slow phase of learning and growing, I became a landlord all at once. No, I didn't quit my day job that afternoon. I didn't post a photo on Instagram of me and my Lambo. (Instagram did not exist, and a Lamborghini would have been stolen in that neighborhood.) But I had changed. I had faced and defeated a giant. The mountain had been climbed. The battle had been won.

The second thing I realized as I clutched that cash in my paint-splattered hands was this: If I could do this once, why not do it again? After all, if I could cover my expenses on this property with the rent from one of the units and, effectively, live for free, why not buy more properties like this one and generate even more profit?

This was the day when it finally clicked—my *aha* moment: the incredible, alluring, very real power of multifamily real estate. This small duplex, located in a blue-collar neighborhood in a blue-collar town, was the spark that set a fire ablaze in my life. I decided, then and there, my future would be in multifamily real estate. I would collect units the same way my dad collects classic cars and my mother collects sand dollars. Because each and every unit I collected would get me one step closer to my goal of financial independence—the ability to work for the joy of it rather than a paycheck.

Fast-forward ten years. I sipped my subtly pretentious and unnecessarily expensive tall peppermint hot chocolate outside my local Starbucks, basking in the rare Pacific Northwest sun. The slight shaking in my hands wasn't from the sugar or the fully loaded log trucks rumbling by. My hands shook because there, on the page in my pen's blue ink, was a number I had only dreamed of being able to attain: $1 million.

In fact, it was slightly more. This document showed the difference between all my assets and liabilities, and it was meant to convey one simple thing to the bank: my net worth. And just like that, at age 30 and after a decade of investing in real estate, I was a millionaire—on paper anyway. And it was all due to that decision, on that fateful September day ten years earlier, to focus on investing my time, energy, and money in multifamily real estate.

This book is about that journey.

Not my journey, but *yours*!

Right now you may have dreams that seem as unattainable as a million-dollar net worth seemed to me when my biggest concern was what the neighbors thought of that in-person cash exchange.

Maybe your goal is to be a millionaire. Maybe you don't want to drive to a nine-to-five job anymore, spending your time making someone else wealthy. Perhaps the idea of traveling around the world in luxury is more up your alley. Or waking up whenever you feel like it, sipping coffee the way it was meant to be sipped: slowly and with intention. Maybe you want to watch your children grow up, not from the bleachers but on the field with them for every play of the game. Maybe you just want to stick it to all those kids in middle school who called you "the Window Kid." (Long, embarrassing story there. Stick around—I'll tell you later.)

Whatever your dream, we believe real estate investing can be your path to achieving it. And if your goal is to get there in a relatively expeditious manner, we believe multifamily real estate is the key. If you think it's not possible or that in order to become a multifamily millionaire you need to already be wealthy or come from a rich family, we can tell you from personal experience that's not true.

I was on a path that would have landed me in eighty-plus-hour work-weeks and miserable commutes as a lawyer when I inadvertently discovered the power of real estate investing. My life changed and I began to collect units, starting with that duplex I mentioned, at age 21. From there, I bought duplexes, triplexes, fourplexes, a five-unit property, and eventually a twenty-four-unit apartment building, which finally gave me enough cash flow to quit my job at age 27. That's when I began *The BiggerPockets Podcast*, on which I interviewed real estate investors about their journeys, while also writing books and blogs about my experiences on BiggerPockets.com.

At 30 I crossed the million-dollar net worth line, but I didn't stop there.

I continued growing my real estate portfolio. Eventually I got into buying large mobile home parks across the country, partnering with several exceptionally bright and experienced real estate investors, including the one and only Brian Murray, whom I met in 2015 when he first appeared on my podcast. Brian was a teacher when he acquired his first investment property as a side hustle in 2007. Without raising any outside capital, he bootstrapped his way from newbie investor to founder and CEO of Washington Street Properties, a commercial real estate investment company that owned more than $50 million in real estate and was ranked on the Inc. 5000 list of the nation's fastest-growing private companies for five years in a row. After building Washington Street Properties, Brian started investing in large multifamily syndications before partnering with me in 2019.

Today Brian and I work together at our company, Open Door Capital, to buy distressed mobile home communities and other multifamily commercial assets, purchasing more than fifty million dollars' worth of real estate and becoming one of the top 100 mobile home park operators in the country during our first year.

How This Book Is Different

This book was born on a volcano.

Brian had flown halfway across the world from his home on the East Coast of the United States to Maui, Hawaii, where I live. On our drive up the side of Haleakala, one of the largest (dormant, I hope!) volcanos on the planet, we began discussing how instrumental multifamily real estate had been to both of us in our journeys—and how we would not be millionaires without it.

We both had written books on real estate investing, but my previous books focused on a much more general approach to real estate. I saw the need for a be-all-and-end-all book on multifamily real estate—specifically about the unique nature of small multifamily. Brian, on the other hand, saw the need for a be-all-and-end-all book on large multifamily, and voiced concern over the number of investors attempting to get into multifamily real estate who lacked the whole picture and, as a result, faced difficulty and failure.

That day, on the side of a Hawaiian volcano, the idea for this book was born. But after just a few minutes of excited brainstorming, we realized that it should be not *one* book, but *two*. That's because the approach to buying small multifamily properties (something I've focused heavily on over the past decade and a half) is very different from the approach to buying large multifamily properties (something Brian has been focused on for the same amount of time). However, learning about *both* is vital to the long-term success of someone who wants to become a millionaire through real estate. And so *The Multifamily Millionaire* was born.

These books offer what very few others do: the concrete, step-by-step knowledge needed to actually become a millionaire. We recommend beginning with Volume I, the book you are holding. It will give you the foundation to building wealth through investing in multifamily real estate. Inside, you'll learn:

- How multifamily can help you achieve financial freedom in less than five years through The Stack (Chapter Two).
- The importance of carefully establishing your five-point crystal-clear criteria and how a few simple decisions can help you improve your deal flow, become an expert quickly, and inspire others to assist you (Chapter Three).
- The best way to pick a market—whether in your own backyard or thousands of miles away (Chapter Five).
- Two never-before-seen algorithms designed to take the guesswork out of estimating expenses on your multifamily property (Chapter Eight).
- Eight tips for getting multifamily property leads that no one else knows about (Chapter Eleven).
- Eleven property features to investigate while touring a multifamily property (Chapter Thirteen).
- How to legitimately invest in multifamily deals for little-to-no money down (Chapters Sixteen and Seventeen).
- Sneaky tricks for getting your multifamily offer accepted (Chapter Eighteen).
- And a whole lot more.

As you read through this book, make it your own. Underline, highlight, snap photos with your e-reader. Don't just read—digest this information. Read it as if you were going to be forced to teach the topics to someone else tomorrow. (True story: Studies show this technique may be the best way to remember what you read!) In the words of the late, great personal development speaker Jim Rohn, "Life doesn't get better by chance. It gets better by change." We believe this book has the potential to change your life, but it's not going to happen unless you truly dig in.

With that said, let's get started. It's time to turn you into a multifamily millionaire.

Brandon Turner

Chapter 1

AN INTRODUCTION TO MULTIFAMILY PROPERTIES

"A decision is what a man makes when he can't get anyone to serve on a committee."

—FLETCHER KNEBEL, BEST-SELLING AUTHOR

There are a *lot* of ways to invest in real estate, such as:
- Buying single-family houses
- Buying storage units
- Buying office buildings
- Buying mobile homes
- Flipping houses
- Building skyscrapers
- Buying/building large apartment complexes
- Buying/building small multifamily real estate

And you know what? There are many highly successful people in all these niches. That's the great thing about real estate—the plethora of choices. But that's also the dangerous thing about real estate: *so many choices!*

As business author Seth Godin once said, "In a world where we have too many choices and too little time, the obvious thing to do is just ignore stuff." When faced with the hundreds of different paths one can take to build a life of wealth and happiness, many people simply ignore them all, give up on their dreams, and go back to doing what they know: watching television, eating bad food, and hoping the government takes care of them in the few years between retirement and death.

But not you.

After all, you're reading a book on buying small multifamily real estate, so the topic obviously pulls at you—and for good reason! Multifamily real estate is one of the greatest investments someone can make and one of the best ways to begin building serious wealth and long-term income.

This book is designed to help you do just that. But first, let's get on the same page.

Defining Multifamily Properties

Multifamily. Multi-unit. Multi-dwelling unit. Apartments. Complexes. Flats.

Many different names, but they all refer to a type of real estate that we'll call "multifamily" throughout this book. A multifamily property is a singularly owned property that contains two or more residential housing units. Each residential area contains, at minimum: a bathroom, a kitchen, and a place for a bed.

Multifamily, therefore, could refer to a five-hundred-unit apartment complex in the suburbs, a duplex in the city, or a fourplex in the country. Multifamily properties come in all shapes and sizes: large buildings, small buildings, and even separate buildings on the same lot. My first multifamily property, the one I mentioned in the preface, contained two single-family houses located on one city lot, separated by a driveway and some dirt and grass.

I also own a three-unit and a four-unit with similar setups. Additionally, I have a five-unit that is located in one giant square building. Then there is the triplex I bought with one unit upstairs, one unit on the main floor, and one in the basement with a completely separate vacation-rental unit in the backyard.

Or take, for example, a property I own that contains fifty different mobile home units, each home independently owned by a resident but each "lot" that the home sits upon owned by me. Or the 126-unit apartment complex Brian Murray owns in New York. Or the house my friend and business partner Ryan Murdock owns that was once a large single-family house but has been carved up and remodeled over the past 140 years and now houses four separate families.

As you can see, multifamily is a broad niche. To cover the full spectrum of opportunities and provide as much value as possible, we are going to divide multifamily investing into two tiers. This book, Volume I of *The Multifamily Millionaire*, with writing led by me (Brandon), focuses on what we call *small* multifamily real estate. Volume II, with writing led by Brian Murray, focuses on what we call *large* multifamily real estate. But that begs the question: What is large, and what is small?

Oftentimes people draw a simple line between small and large properties: four units. They consider anything with four units or fewer to be small and anything five units or more to be large. And when it comes to *lending*, they are not wrong. As you'll learn later in this book, getting a loan on a single-family house, duplex, triplex, or fourplex is different from getting a loan on anything with five units or more.

However, aside from financing, in the real world, buying a fourplex is not all that different from buying a five-unit property. But buying a two-hundred-unit property is *very* different from buying a fourplex. So where do we draw the line? We want to make sure that someone reading this book is equipped to buy a five-unit, an eight-unit, or even a twenty-unit if they so desire. Because it's not that difficult—you *can* do this—even if you're just starting out.

Rather than making a strict distinction between small and large based on a specific *number* of units, we have decided to draw a softer boundary between small and large based on *approach*.

You see, the approach to buying a duplex is not that different from the approach to buying an eight-unit. They require similar processes, people, and skill sets.

There are many different processes, people, and skill sets involved when buying a two-hundred-unit apartment complex. That type of purchase likely involves tens of millions of dollars and the expertise of teams of professionals, with much of the work taking place around long mahogany tables. In practice, investing in large apartment complexes is more akin to buying, owning, and selling a business. Quarterly meetings and quarterly returns. Hierarchies of employees. Fund-raising webinars. Mission statements and business plans. We're certainly not saying large multifamily isn't within reach for small investors who want to go big—because it is—but it requires a different approach. Patience, Grasshopper: We'll get there in Volume II.

Purchasing a duplex, triplex, or something similar, on the other hand, is a simpler process. You'll be using your own cash, a bank loan, a partner, and/or some other more creative methods to finance the deal. You'll be managing the property yourself or hiring a small, local property manager to assist. You won't be forming companies inside companies inside companies. The property will likely be in your own name or the name of an LLC. Small multifamily real estate investing is something an individual can easily do independently with the help of various independent contractors (such as title companies, attorneys, and property managers) brought in to handle specific aspects of the job.

To help clarify how that differs from large multifamily real estate, here's a side-by-side breakdown of some of the differences between investing in small multifamily real estate (which we're focusing on in this volume of *The Multifamily Millionaire*) and large multifamily real estate (which is the focus of Volume II):

SMALL MULTIFAMILY REAL ESTATE	LARGE MULTIFAMILY REAL ESTATE
Likely financed by a local bank	Likely financed by large commercial lenders with assistance of mortgage brokers
Down payment probably self-funded	Down payment probably funded by raising money from investors
Typically managed by owner or small local property manager	Typically managed by large, third-party property manager
Usually local, though long-distance is entirely possible	Usually long-distance, but local is entirely possible
Owner likely knows tenants' names	Owner unlikely to know tenants' names
Repair work to units done by owner or handymen hired by owner	Repair work to units done by contractors or on-site employees
Property rehabs performed by owner or local contractors who handle small-scale projects	Property rehabs performed by contractors who handle large-scale projects
Bank's decision on whether to fund typically based on owner's borrowing strength	Bank's decision on whether to fund typically based on property's business strength
Owner usually involved in daily operation of investment	Owner usually not involved in daily operation of investment

Of course, these are general guidelines. It's entirely possible to see the owner of a two-hundred-unit apartment complex show up in overalls to do their own work. It's also entirely possible to see the owner of a duplex in a suit and running their business entirely as a business, without ever engaging in the daily operations of the property. However, the distinctions above tend to hold true, so we've divided our coverage into two volumes accordingly.

Will the information in this book help you invest in duplexes, triplexes, or fourplexes?

Definitely.

Will it help you take down that twenty-unit you've been driving past for years?

Absolutely.

Will it help you raise $6 million in a 506(c) Reg D Fund with a 65/35 LP/

GP split and an 8/15 percent tiered waterfall for distributions? Eh... for that, you'll want to read Volume II. But start here anyway! This book will give you the *foundation*. The lessons you learn in this book about small multifamily real estate will give you the tools, knowledge, and confidence to eventually move into the big leagues if you want.

And, of course, you don't have to move to the big leagues. Maybe buying giant apartment complexes doesn't sound appealing. That's fine by us. You can build massive wealth and financial independence not only for yourself but also for your children and their children just by effectively buying and managing small multifamily real estate. This book will show you how.

Eight Reasons to Love Small Multifamily Real Estate

We titled this two-volume set *The Multifamily Millionaire* because we believe multifamily real estate is the greatest way for the average person to become a millionaire. It's that simple. Millions of people, for generations, have become millionaires thanks to real estate—even people with less intelligence, fewer connections, and less capital than you.

There are far too many benefits to investing in small multifamily properties to list them all here, so we'll just highlight eight of our favorites.

1. Cash Flow

Let's play a quick grade-school math game. Becky sells cookies. She earns $10 at the bake sale. Go, Becky! But Becky had to spend money on baking supplies. In total, she spent $7. Therefore, how much profit did Becky actually earn? Three dollars. That is Becky's "cash flow," the profit earned after paying all of a business's bills. Becky's cash flow is hers to spend on whatever she wants. The same is true for your cash flow, and it's one of the reasons we love small multifamily real estate so much: It offers the opportunity to earn *a lot of cash flow.*

When purchased at the right price (which you will learn to do) and managed correctly (which you'll learn to do), small multifamily real estate tends to generate substantial monthly cash flow. Collect enough of these properties and you'll be able to quit your job sooner than you ever thought possible. It doesn't take that many small multifamily properties to give you the financial resources to live an incredible life; it just takes the *right* ones. This book is going to teach you exactly how to find, buy, and manage the right ones.

2. Simple and Low-Cost Financing

A few moments ago, we mentioned that when it comes to lending, banks and lenders draw a line between small and large multifamily properties. Let's discuss that a bit more in depth here. Properties with one, two, three, or four residential units are generally covered by a field of lending known as residential lending, while properties that contain five or more residential units (such as apartment complexes) are covered by commercial lending. Although both types of lending provide a similar service—loans that allow you to purchase real estate—there are some minor, and major, differences between the two. Residential lending often offers better interest rates, less money down, and longer loan terms.

Additionally, commercial loans often contain a provision known as a balloon, which means there is a date by which the loan's remaining principal balance must be paid back, regardless of the term. For example, let's say you have a 5.5 percent interest rate on a $100,000 commercial loan, and it's spread out over twenty-five years. Your monthly payment would be roughly $614. However, even though the loan is spread out over twenty-five years, you might have a seven-year balloon payment, meaning the entire remaining balance of the loan is due at the end of year seven, even though the loan hasn't been paid off. This would require you to either sell or refinance (get a new loan) before that deadline.

Residential financing tends to be much more simple and straightforward, not to mention cheaper, than commercial financing. Thus, another benefit of small multifamily real estate investing is the ability to obtain residential financing—as long as your property has four units or fewer.

3. Abundance of Opportunities

Most markets contain small multifamily properties. As a result, you aren't necessarily looking for a needle in a haystack. In fact, in Chapter Four, we're going to lay out seven different types of small multifamily properties you can look for, including monster houses, cottages, and up-and-downs. Of course, some locations tend to have more small multifamily properties than others, but the bottom line is that you can invest in small multifamily properties just about anywhere.

4. Less Competition

Although you can find multifamily properties in almost any market, most real estate buyers are not looking to buy a small multifamily property; most are looking for a single-family property to call home. They aren't concerned with cash flow or any other financial metrics. Logic and math play second fiddle to the emotional draw of a cute kitchen, a cute front porch, and a cute street for their cute kids to play in.

Therefore, when you invest in single-family real estate, you are competing with buyers who will pay more than they should because emotion tells them to. Emotion is tough to compete against when you're trying to find good investments. (That's not to say single-family houses never work as investments. However, the competition for those that do can be fierce, forcing investors to focus on off-market acquisition strategies and major rehab projects.)

Although you'll face significantly less competition when shopping for large multifamily properties, that competition will be much *savvier*. You'll be going up against teams of well-trained, well-financed, well-educated professionals.

Small multifamily real estate is wedged between those two highly competitive sectors. Armed with the knowledge in this book, you'll be perfectly positioned to take advantage of this real estate sweet spot. You'll be savvier than the average person who's shopping for a home, and you're looking to buy deals that are simply too small for most professionals to consider. As the law of supply and demand dictates, where there is less competition, better deals can be found. Those lucrative small multifamily deals can be your ticket to financial freedom, *fast*.

5. Growth Potential

Imagine being able to wake up each morning when you *want*, not when you *have to*. Imagine spending as much time as you desire with your kids, with your spouse, with your dog. Imagine not feeling guilty when you go to the gym because you have more than enough time. Imagine working hard on work that you love, that energizes you, that allows you to take bigger risks. Never again will you have to watch the clock, waiting for the small breaks your office allows.

These are not pipe dreams. This is real life for Brian and me, and for millions of other people who have successfully invested in real estate. Maybe your idea of financial freedom is different. But that's the best part about financial freedom—you get to choose! Let's be honest: You'd like to have financial freedom (however you define it) sooner rather than later, right? Whether you love your job or want to quit tomorrow doesn't matter. The freedom to choose how to live your life, unrestricted by the conventional need for money, sounds pretty amazing to almost everyone. And here's the thing: With multifamily real estate, you can get there *faster*.

When you invest in multifamily real estate, your portfolio grows more quickly than it would if you were collecting single-family houses. Yet the surprising truth is that it's not twice as difficult or expensive to buy a duplex versus a single-family home. Similarly, it's not four times as difficult or expensive to buy a fourplex versus a single-family home. In fact, it takes about the same amount of work.

If speed is important to you, investing in multifamily real estate will get you to the finish line faster. In Chapter Two we'll delve into a concept we call The Stack, which is perhaps the most effective strategy for scaling a real estate business faster than you could ever imagine. Stay tuned!

6. Opportunity to Buy from Bad, Burned-Out, or Checked-Out Landlords

People get into real estate for a variety of reasons, and many don't have the same level of excitement as you do. In fact, plenty of current landlords never wanted to be a landlord, or have long since discovered they just don't enjoy it. They may have inherited a property and have no idea what they are doing. Perhaps some bought into the idea that real estate investing was a quick and easy way to strike it rich, but have been unwilling or unable to do what is necessary to make the investment work.

Regardless of *why*, many landlords are burned out. The reason is that owning rental properties is *not* an entirely passive activity, especially at the beginning. It requires skills, knowledge, and persistence. It may also require you to make difficult decisions, miss important events, and continually educate yourself on best practices and legal changes, among other things. But this doesn't mean you shouldn't take the plunge. On the contrary, some of life's most worthwhile pursuits are found on the road less traveled. The easy path isn't always the right path, and the right path isn't always the easy one.

Now, we don't say this to scare you. Landlording can eventually become passive, and there are many ways to make it simple and easy.

Just like in sports, mastery comes after significant and continual personal improvement. If you read books, create systems, make and learn from mistakes, and do it all over and over, in time, landlording becomes easier and even fun. But for the many, many landlords out there who have not put the time into becoming good at their job, it can be hell and cause burnout.

One landlord's burnout is another landlord's opportunity. In fact, most of the properties we have purchased over our careers have been from failed landlords. Whether the landlord failed completely and the property was foreclosed, or the landlord simply gave up and sold the property at a discount to get out from under it, our best deals have come from burned-out or neglectful landlords. There are many opportunities for the ambitious real estate investor to buy these deals, turn them around, and make a killing.

7. House Hacking Potential

One of the best ways for new investors to get started in multifamily real estate investing is through a strategy we call "house hacking." House hacking means that the homeowner lives in one unit and rents out one or more units of their property so they can live there more cheaply than normal—maybe even for free. The story from the preface was based on house hacking. The income from the rented units can sometimes cover your entire mortgage payment and more, allowing you to essentially live for free. This is the power of house hacking, and small multifamily properties make it possible.

Now, why would anyone choose to invest in a rental property where they have to live in one of the units? What makes this option so appealing to new investors? Three words: low down payment. Earlier, we talked about the differences between residential and commercial lending, including how residential lending tends to be cheaper and easier to obtain. To take this concept a step further, residential lending becomes even better when the borrower is planning to live at the property. In the United States (and many other nations), homeownership is strongly encouraged, with the government even assisting in making this dream a reality for many people.

The U.S. Government does this through lending programs that offer loans with very low down payments. The most common example is the Federal Housing Administration (FHA) loan, which requires the borrower to put down only 3.5 percent of the purchase price. On a $200,000 purchase, that could be just $7,000 down. In addition to the FHA program, many banks now offer other loan products with low down payment options that have some unique advantages over the FHA program for just a slightly higher down payment.

Compare that to a residential loan for a property the owner is not living in. Down payment requirements could be as high as 30 percent on those non-owner-occupied loans, meaning that same $200,000 purchase could require up to $60,000 as a down payment! (Don't worry if you don't have that kind of money to invest in your next property. Later we'll discuss several different strategies for financing multifamily real estate, no matter how much you currently have in your bank account.)

Furthermore, although these owner-occupied loans are obviously designed for an owner to live in the property, the owner doesn't have to live there forever. Generally, the house-hacking owner must intend to live in the property for at least one year. After a year, you can move on to bigger and better things, but—get this—you get to keep the loan in place. In fact, after a year of living in that small duplex and collecting rent from my friend, I moved (into another duplex, actually) and began renting out my former home for $550 per month. Fourteen years later, I still own that property, which continues to provide significant monthly cash flow to my bank account. And it all started with a house hack.

8. Gateway to Larger Deals

We've already established that building a portfolio is important and the sooner you build a large portfolio, the sooner you become financially free. Therefore, perhaps one of the most important reasons to invest in small multifamily real estate is that those small multifamily deals become a *gateway* to larger deals.

Some real estate personalities advise their followers on social media to never buy a small deal, ever. "Start with fifty or a hundred units," they say. But that's like telling a brand-new runner to just sign up for the Boston Marathon! Starting with large multifamily real estate can be dangerous if you do not have the knowledge, experience, contacts, or capital to compensate for all the things you do not yet know. When first building a portfolio, you will make mistakes—no matter how closely you follow the advice in this book. However, would you rather go 10 percent over budget on a $20,000 rehab or 10 percent over budget on a $2,000,000 rehab? The former mistake ($2,000) might make you dip into your savings or spend some nights and weekends painting a property to recover those costs. The latter mistake ($200,000) could cripple you.

Small multifamily real estate is an excellent training ground for building your empire. It gives you the knowledge you need to ask the right questions on the big deals. It gives you the experience to walk into a bank and apply for a larger-than-average loan. It gives you the credibility to raise millions of dollars from people in your network. It gives you the confidence to make an offer on a property whose monthly water bill is more than you earn in a year. And it gives you the capital to invest in hiring the professionals who will make up your team if, and when, you head to the big leagues.

Small Multifamily Real Estate Frustrations

At this point, maybe you're thinking, "Great! Small multifamily sounds amazing! But what's the catch? What aren't these guys telling us?" As with most things in life, there are pros and cons. Specifically, we want to point out the five primary frustrations that small multifamily investors may encounter, along with some advice on how to overcome them.

1. Bleeding Money

Small multifamily real estate investors often discover that the profit never materializes after purchasing what they thought was going to be a fantastic investment. They look at the basic math and say, "Well, the total rent should be $3,000 a month on this triplex and the mortgage payment is $2,000, so I should be making $1,000 per month in profit. Where is it?" When the actual profit fails to live up to the projected profit the culprit is almost always the same: bad math.

Plenty of real estate investors (small multifamily or otherwise) do not know how to accurately analyze an investment, so they base their purchasing decisions on math no more complex than that in the above paragraph. What's so wrong with that math? The problem is that there are many more expenses besides the mortgage payment. In Chapter Eight, arguably the most important chapter in this book, we will delve into the world of analysis. You'll learn the difference between phantom cash flow (which the above math demonstrates) and pure cash flow, which is the secret to your long-term success and early retirement. We'll also examine the most common expenses you'll encounter while owning rentals so you can accurately estimate the future profitability of a property before spending a dime on it.

2. Property Management

Many small multifamily real estate investors are frustrated by the level of tenant management needed to maintain a profitable business. Managing multifamily properties is much more demanding than managing single-family rentals. In my experience, multifamily tenants tend to have lower incomes than single-family renters, which may lead to issues with consistent, on-time rent payments. Your systems must be set up to accommodate slightly more frequent interaction with tenants for rent collection and higher turnover rates. Ultimately, your skill as a landlord will be tested more than when dealing with single-family rentals.

This is not to say that there aren't really amazing, hardworking, responsible tenants who live in multifamily properties. In fact, the vast majority of our multifamily tenants are exactly that. They pay on time, don't cause issues, and are a joy to deal with. Still, if the idea of managing tenants worries you, stick with us. By the time you finish this book, you'll have all the necessary skills to handle whatever situation a tenant throws at you.

3. Shoddy Properties

As you begin shopping for small multifamily properties, you may notice that there are a lot of shoddy properties out there—especially at the lower price points. You see, when an individual owns the home they live in, they usually take extra special care of it. They'll make sure that higher-quality repairs are usually performed when they should be. Conversely, a good number of small multifamily landlords (many of them terrible) focus more on profit than quality.

- *Pipe leaking? Wrap it in duct tape!*
- *Hole in the wall? Fill it with toothpaste! (Not kidding.)*
- *Need more space? Slap up some plywood outside of the house and you've got a brand-new bedroom!*
- *Permit? What's a permit? You only need a permit when you get caught!*

When you combine the lack of quality repairs with the old age of many such buildings, you have the recipe for a money pit. Every time a tenant moves out (and many times while they still are renting the unit), this shoddy work needs to be fixed, and it can be expensive.

Does that mean all multifamilies are like this? Of course not. We've owned some previously well-maintained properties, and also made a lot of money fixing up properties that were neglected by prior owners. However, you should always get an inspection before buying a property, so you know what you're getting into. You should also fix up properties as well as you can when you buy them and do quality, long-lasting repairs and rehabs with qualified, vetted repair professionals (and get permits!). This early investment will help guard against ongoing problems. Finally, you should account for the added cost of maintenance when you do your math. And don't worry if you feel you're not an expert on this yet. You will be. Keep reading.

4. The Slumlord Factor

If you needed an animal to plow a field, would you choose a workhorse or a show pony? A workhorse, of course! But if you wanted to win an equine beauty contest, you'd probably pick a show pony. The type of horse you pick depends on your goal. Most small multifamily properties are the workhorses, not the show ponies, of real estate investing.

You won't be driving your friends past the property hoping for their *oohs* and *aahs*. You won't land a starring role on HGTV either. That's because your small multifamily real estate investment is meant to do one thing: generate cash flow. If you're looking for beautiful houses to impress your girlfriend's father, single-family homes might be more up your alley. When you invest in small multifamily properties, get ready for friends and family to joke about you being a "slumlord"—no matter how nice your properties are.

5. More Variable Expenses

Another downside to owning multifamily versus single-family proper- ties is the variable nature of some of the expenses, specifically the water bill, and potentially the heating, garbage, and electric bills, depending on the property and location. When you, the landlord, are responsible for paying certain utility charges that can go up and down and be hard to predict, those expenses have the potential to negatively affect your bottom line.

We've both had tenants deliberately *not* call to report a water leak just because they don't want anyone coming into their unit to repair it. They'd rather have a constant trickle of water (costing the landlord potentially hundreds of dollars per month) than have someone enter their home for a repair. The same applies to heat and electricity. When the landlord is footing the heating bill, it's not uncommon for a tenant to blast their heat all day while leaving their windows open in the dead of winter. If they were paying that bill, you can bet they wouldn't be so wasteful.

As a multifamily owner, what can you do? There are several options. Our preference is to shift the responsibility for the bill from the landlord to the tenants of each unit, but sometimes this is simply not feasible. In that case, you'll have to be especially vigilant in watching for leaks or open windows.

The Multifamily Millionaire

Multifamily real estate has the power to turn you into a millionaire. We're living proof—and we want to see you use multifamily real estate to transform your life into an adventure that your children's children's children will still be talking about.

Buying any old multifamily property is not going to get you there. You must have the *right plan* to buy the *right property* in the *right place* to get the *right profit* using the *right financing*—and then manage the whole process *right*. That might sound overwhelming, but this book will make the mission a reality and turn you into a multifamily millionaire —all by using a simple method we call The Stack. It's time to see how this method can completely transform your financial life forever.

KEY TAKEAWAYS

- The difference between large and small multifamily investing lies in the approach. Small multifamily is much more hands-on and personal, while large multifamily is more corporate and professional. Understanding both is essential to becoming a real estate millionaire.
- Small multifamily real estate is powerful due to: the cash flow it can generate, the incredible financing options available, the commonplace nature of the investment, the reduced competition for deals, the speed at which you can grow your portfolio, the opportunities

to land great deals from burned-out landlords, the potential for house hacking, and the knowledge you'll gain that will get you to bigger deals.
- Multifamily isn't all rainbows and cupcakes—there are pitfalls. The guidelines laid out in this book will help you avoid them.

Chapter 2

FINANCIAL FREEDOM IN FIVE YEARS?

> *"The greatest shortcoming of the human race is our*
> *inability to understand the exponential function."*
>
> —ALBERT A. BARTLETT

The end of the universe may be closer than you think, thanks to artificial intelligence.

I'll explain. To do so, let's talk about *The Terminator* (yes, the indestructible Arnold Schwarzenegger fighting both good guys and bad across way too many movies).

In *The Terminator*, humanity is on the brink of collapse because machines have become too intelligent and decided that they don't need us any longer. Although clearly fictional, the problem the world faces in these films is based on a legitimate fear that terrifies many scientists and futurists: the singularity.

The singularity is the result of technology improving faster and faster until, at some point in the future, it becomes smarter and more capable than humans and is able to make the world into a utopia for humans or destroy every living thing in its quest for power.

How could this happen? Two words: exponential growth.

Exponential growth is growth that increases not by fixed numbers but by percentages.

Let me simplify. If you start saving with one penny and every day you add one more penny to your piggy bank, after a month you'll have around thirty cents. Makes sense, right? (Yes, pun intended!)

We call that linear growth because it happens in a straight line. It looks like this:

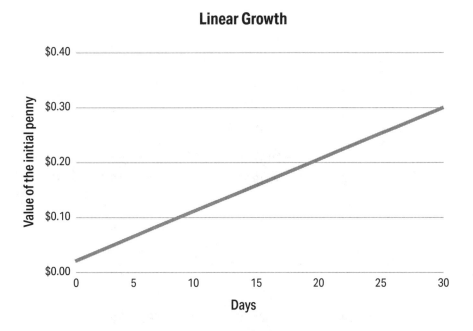

What if, starting with that same penny, you doubled your savings' value each day (100 percent growth daily) instead? The first day, you'd have $.01. The second day you'd have $.02. Then $.04. Then $.08. This might not sound like a big deal, but spread out over time, the results can be explosive. Check out the chart below to see the difference between that penny's linear growth ($.01 added each day) and its exponential growth (value doubled each day).

Day	Linear Growth	Exponential Growth
1	$0.01	$0.01
2	$0.02	$0.02
3	$0.03	$0.04
4	$0.04	$0.08
5	$0.05	$0.16
6	$0.06	$0.32
7	$0.07	$0.64
8	$0.08	$1.28
9	$0.09	$2.56
10	$0.10	$5.12
11	$0.11	$10.24
12	$0.12	$2048
13	$0.13	$40.96
14	$0.14	$81.92
15	$0.15	$163.84
16	$0.16	$327.68
17	$0.17	$655.36
18	$0.18	$1,310.72
19	$0.19	$2,621.44
20	$0.20	$5,242.88
21	$0.21	$10,485.76
22	$.022	$20,971.52
23	$0.23	$41,943.04
24	$0.24	$83,886.08
25	$0.25	$167,772.16
26	$0.26	$335,544.32
27	$0.27	$671,088.64
28	$0.28	$1,342,177.28
29	$0.29	$2,684,354.56
30	$0.30	$5,368,709.12

Amazing, isn't it? Exponential growth caused that initial one-penny investment to be worth more than $5 million in thirty days versus less than $1 for linear growth. You're going to need a really big piggy bank.

Notice in the above chart how dramatically the dollar amount climbed toward the end. I mean, by day twenty-four we hadn't even crossed the $100,000 mark; yet just six days later, we eclipsed $5 million. That's what exponential growth does: It moves along fairly slowly, then accelerates rapidly. Take a look at the following graph that illustrates this growth:

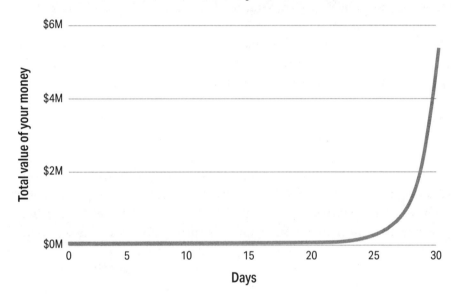

Effect of 100% Daily Growth on 1 Cent

That "hook" on the right side is often referred to as the hockey stick curve, and it can be an incredible answer to the question: How do I achieve financial freedom *quickly*? I'm guessing you don't want to wait until you're sixty-five to retire like the rest of the world. You have an amazing life waiting for you once you have the income to pursue your true passions. Let's get you there faster.

Consider this: You've purchased a house as an investment property. Let's say the property rents for $1,000 per month. You have a mortgage payment that comes to $500 each month, plus other required expenses (taxes, insurance, repairs) that add another $300 a month. You're left with around $200 in actual profit (cash flow) at the end of the month.

Many people read this and a sinking feeling starts developing in the pit of their stomach. Two hundred dollars? That's it? How could I go through *all* that work to find a great house, deal with the hassle of financing that purchase, fix up the property to get it ready to rent, and handle annoying tenants each month, only to make a measly $200 per month!? I could go sell cookies to my neighbors and make $200, and that's way easier! Plus, I could eat the leftovers.

True. Buying and managing a rental property is a lot of work for just $200 a month. No one is getting rich, quitting their job, moving to Hawaii, and driving a Tesla because of $200. And even if you did this every year (buying one home per year), after ten long years you'd have only $2,000 a month coming in (10 properties × $200 each per month). Of course, $2,000 a month is not a bad number, but let's be honest: After ten years of working this business, you'd like to be making more than $2,000 a month. If you need $10,000 per month to quit your job, that could take decades!

This is why we love multifamily properties: They allow us to scale our portfolios significantly faster than buying single-family houses. That's where The Stack comes in. The Stack will help you achieve your financial goals faster than you think.

In fact, we believe that the average individual (without existing wealth, experience, or knowledge) could achieve level-one financial freedom within five years by following The Stack model. Level one is when you are making enough passive income through investments to pay all your usual bills. You aren't buying a jet (level two) or the New York Jets (level three) yet, but if you want to quit your job and enjoy life more fully, level one is a great target to aim for.

The Stack

What is The Stack? It is exponential growth applied to real estate. Rather than adding one home to your rental portfolio each year (like adding one penny to your piggy bank each day), you will be exponentially increasing the number of units you purchase each year (like doubling the penny each day). For illustration purposes in this book, we're going to discuss the idea of "doubling" your unit purchase each year, but please don't get caught up in being exact. We're sharing a concept here, not a precise recipe. Let's review an example to make this clearer.

Year One

This year, you decide to get out there and take some action toward achieving your dream: financial independence. You pick up a couple of books on investing in multifamily real estate, written by two incredibly handsome and charming men. You read these books, listen to podcasts, begin networking, and put your plan into action. Good for you!

After months of learning, searching, saving, and hustling, you purchase a nice duplex in a decent part of town. This duplex happens to produce about $150 per unit in cash flow, after accounting for all bills (mortgage, repairs, reserves, and so on). That's a total of $300 per month in cash flow from your first investment. As with the earlier single-family home example, this isn't life-changing money. You aren't going to stick it to the man and quit your job tomorrow.

But something amazing *has* happened. Your identity has changed. You're no longer just a wannabe real estate investor. You *are* a multifamily real estate investor! And here's the best part: It's not the money, it's the momentum. It takes a tremendous amount of effort to get that locomotive moving on the tracks. At first it moves just an inch. Then two inches. Then a foot. So much energy and effort go into that train to get it going. So much power. Then it begins to pick up steam. And so do you.

You see, you may not be rich as a result of that first deal, but you gained an incredible amount of knowledge of how real estate works and especially how it works in that specific market. Additionally, you've got some money coming in now, so you can begin saving for future purchases. You've built some solid connections in the industry, from agents and lenders to contractors and property managers. Best of all, you've gained confidence. You're actually doing it. You've earned something, which will encourage you to continue.

Now, let's continue on your journey—because you're just getting warmed up. You've bought that duplex and learned all the ins and outs of managing those tenants (or perhaps you've outsourced that management to a local property management company). A whole year has passed, and you're ready to buy again.

Year Two

At this point, many investors simply grow linearly, buying another duplex or maybe a single-family house. They stay small because that's where they feel most comfortable. But you want financial freedom fast, so you're going to grow exponentially.

Instead of buying another duplex or single-family house, you double down and buy a fourplex. After all, you've gained a significant amount of knowledge, experience, connections, and confidence—and have owned and operated a duplex for a whole year. Landing a fourplex should be no problem at this point. (We'll discuss financing in detail later in this book.)

Here we are at the end of year two, and you now are the proud owner of six units, two from the first year and four from the second. Let's assume that each of these units (as with all units in subsequent years) continues to produce $150 per month in income. That means you are now clearing $900 per month in cash flow. Not life-changing, but nothing to sneeze at either.

Year Three

Another year has passed, and you're ready to buy again. You now have two full years of experience at your back. You've been running six units and have even more knowledge, more experience, more connections, and more confidence. You start your search for a new property. But this time, rather than a fourplex like last year, you buy an eight-unit small apartment building, taking your portfolio from six units to fourteen.

Are there some growing pains? Of course. Do you have to learn some new skills, like how financing differs on an eight-unit? Yep. Can you pull it off? You already own six units, so adding eight more isn't impossible for you. It's just growth. Best of all, your cash flow from your portfolio also more than doubled with this purchase, climbing to $2,100 per month (14 units × $150 per unit per month in cash flow).

Year Four

You're starting to get the picture here, aren't you? In year four you expand again. You purchase a sixteen-unit apartment complex. At this stage, you're starting to make the transition from small multifamily to large multifamily, adding new systems and learning how to run more of a business with less day-to-day tenant interaction. As with all previous purchases, each of these sixteen new units is bringing in an average of $150 per month in cash flow, adding $2,400 per month in cash flow to the existing $2,100 per month, for a total of $4,500 per month in income.

For the first time, you *feel* it: the momentum. The hard work is starting to pay off. Forty-five hundred dollars per month in extra income is a huge stress reliever; you could pay most of your vital bills using the cash flow if you had to. But it's not quite enough for you to "retire" on yet, so you're going to make one more purchase and see where that leaves you.

Year Five

You never would have imagined, five years earlier, that you'd be able to purchase a midsize apartment building with thirty-two units, but that's exactly what you do in year five of your journey. You've gained so much knowledge, experience, connections, and confidence that taking down the thirty-two-unit property actually feels *easier* than buying that first duplex. The thirty-two-unit adds $4,800 per month in income to your life, bringing your total monthly cash flow to $9,300 per month, or $111,600 per year. Congratulations! You've achieved level-one financial freedom in five years.

You're now earning six figures in annual rental income. Yes, tenants complain, pipes leak, appliances fail, turnover happens. But you have systems and people in place to handle everything. And remember, all that income ($150 per month, per unit, in this example) is your cash flow *after* setting aside money for those pipe leaks, appliance failures, and turnover costs—something we call "pure cash flow."

Your mini empire of small multifamily real estate, just sixty-two units, gives you the ability to enjoy life far more abundantly. Maybe you take a month off to travel to Europe, or buy that car you've always wanted, or pay off your house, or put your kids through college, or all of the above. Or maybe you quit that nine-to-five that's sapping all the joy from your life. The choice is yours when you're financially free. In the meantime, your systems keep your rentals on track and steadily spitting out cash like your own private ATM.

Free in five, indeed.

The Fivefold Beauty of The Stack

This story does not have to be fiction. This could be your life, and it could be your life sooner than you imagine. It works, if you work it. And so far we've discussed only cash flow; we haven't even mentioned the other great aspects of owning real estate. You'll also be *paying off* those properties over time, increasing your net worth each year. Plus, on average, the value of real estate increases each year, so your net worth will be climbing higher from that too.

Even better, the example we used to showcase the power of The Stack assumed that the rent was never increased, but rent *does* increase. In fact, according to the U.S. Bureau of Labor Statistics, over the past thirty years, the rent for a primary residence in U.S. cities has increased an average of 3.1 percent per year.[1] At the same time, your mortgage payment is probably locked in place at the exact same amount month after month, year after year. What happens when your income rises each year and most of your expenses stay the same? That's right: Cash flow increases.

Finally, when you own real estate, the government offers some pretty amazing tax benefits that allow real estate investors to keep more money. We'll talk much more about this in Chapter Twenty-One of this book, but let's look at a quick example: If John earns $100,000 gross from a W-2 job, and Sarah earns $100,000 in cash flow each year from owning rental properties, who gets to keep more?

I ran this scenario by my CPA, Amanda Han, owner of Keystone CPA (a firm that specializes in helping real estate investors with their taxes) and coauthor of *The Book on Tax Strategies for the Savvy Real Estate Investor* and *The Book on Advanced Tax Strategies*. Her response? John may be keeping only around $60,000 of his income, while Sarah could potentially keep the entire $100,000.

How is this possible? The government *loves* real estate investors because we provide housing for the masses. At the end of the day, earning $100,000 from the cash flow from real estate can be similar to earning $167,000 at a W-2 job, depending on your specific tax situation. Beautiful, huh?

The Stack FAQs

Is this a specific example I should strive to follow—one property every year and each unit needs to cash flow $150?
As we mentioned when we introduced The Stack, please don't get too caught up on the specifics. The buying timeline can vary depending on your market, skill set, energy, and just plain luck.

The $150 cash flow per unit was just an example, based on the metric we aim for with small multifamily properties. You can aim higher or

---

[1] "Consumer Price Index for All Urban Consumers: Rent of Primary Residence in U.S. City Average," U.S. Bureau of Labor Statistics, retrieved from FRED, Federal Reserve Bank of St. Louis, https://fred.stlouisfed.org/series/CUSR0000SEHA, December 14, 2020

lower. That's fine! Maybe your market will allow for only $100 per unit per month, or $75. Maybe you can earn $300 per unit per month. Just be careful here. We are talking pure cash flow, which is the profit after *all* expenses, even saving for future expenses, are taken out.

Do I have to stop at sixty-two units?

Of course not! The beauty of small multifamily properties is that they give you the ability to progress into larger multifamily. After acquiring fifty, sixty, or seventy units, maybe you'll decide that's enough and spend your time homeschooling your kids and volunteering at your local food pantry. Or maybe you'll decide that you're not generating quite enough cash flow, and you'll begin raising money to buy hundreds of units, creating millions of dollars in income and employing dozens of people. Or maybe you'll do both: build a massive business while also homeschooling your kids and volunteering—because you'll have the freedom to do so. The choice is yours, and The Stack prepares you for whatever you may choose.

Do I have to double my holdings each year?

Nope! Maybe you start with a triplex, then buy an eight-unit, then a twenty-two-unit. Or maybe you start with a single-family house and then buy a fourplex and a ten-unit. The point is *exponential growth* (as opposed to linear growth)! It means adding more units each time you buy, and investing outside your comfort zone but within your ability zone.

Between Comfort and Ability: Your Growth Zone

You might be thinking The Stack method sounds too good to be true. After all, if the only thing a person had to do to achieve financial freedom was grow exponentially, why wouldn't everyone do it? Because it's *uncomfortable*.

I don't want to gloss over this point. When I first got into real estate investing, I stayed small for *too long*. I bought some small multifamily, then some single-family, then some other small multifamily properties. I didn't venture into anything larger than a fourplex for several years. Why? Because I was *comfortable*. When we find ourselves in a position of comfort, we typically don't push ourselves to grow. This applies to business, relationships, and even fitness. As author Roy T. Bennett said,

"We have to be honest about what we want and take risks rather than lie to ourselves and make excuses to stay in our comfort zone." The same applies to real estate. The longer you invest within your comfort zone, the longer your portfolio will take to grow. At the same time, maybe you are wondering, "Why not just start by investing in a sixty-unit apartment building that makes $150 per month per unit, and I'm done!

Wrong. Like a weight lifter who develops strength, technique, and confidence by starting with light weights and slowly increasing them, you need to increase your real estate investments gradually. Weight lifters are not created overnight, and your real estate business shouldn't be either. You must invest within your ability! What can you reasonably do? If you own ten units, buying a twenty-unit would probably fall within your ability zone, but buying a ninety-unit would fall outside that zone.

That's why The Stack is such a powerful framework for thinking about real estate growth. It encourages you to focus outside your comfort zone but within your ability zone, as shown in the following image. You grow aggressively yet conservatively. You grow with caution yet with a degree of adventure. You grow quickly yet safely.

There's a reason exponential growth has been called the most powerful force in the universe. It can turn a penny into millions. It can turn a civilized world into a dystopian landscape where artificial intelligence seeks to destroy the human race. And it can help you build the kind of future that, up until now, you have only dreamed of.

If you want to achieve the freedom that comes from building a sizable real estate portfolio, use The Stack. Build outside your comfort zone. While you may not be able to travel back in time like *The Terminator* to help save the future, you can take action now to save your own *financial* future.

KEY TAKEAWAYS

- Exponential growth means growing by percentages, such as doubling each time, rather than linearly. If you want to achieve financial success fast, you must rely on exponential growth.
- The Stack is a framework for thinking about real estate growth exponentially. Buy a very small multifamily property, and then buy one with twice as many units each successive year. Within five years, you can have financial freedom.
- Don't fall for the trap of getting stuck operating only within your comfort zone. But don't risk going into your inability zone either. Instead, seek growth within your ability zone.

Chapter 3

GETTING CRYSTAL CLEAR ON YOUR CRITERIA

*"Good business leaders create a vision, articulate
the vision, passionately own the vision, and
relentlessly drive it to completion."*

—JACK WELCH, FORMER CHAIRMAN
AND CEO OF GENERAL ELECTRIC

As the story goes, it was the year 1212 when a 12-year-old boy named
Stephen of Cloyes began to raise an "army" to take back the Holy Land.
Despite his age, he attracted a following that some historians believe
numbered more than 30,000, many of them young people like himself.
However, he and his followers never made it to the Middle East. Due to
bad planning and bad luck, thousands died of hunger and other calami-
ties. Stephen also died attempting to cross the Mediterranean Sea when
his ship went down in a raging storm. No matter how strong Stephen's

passion was for this crusade, his lack of a clear plan led to a disastrous outcome. And while you might not be looking to raise an army and conquer a new land, the same principle applies to your multifamily millionaire journey: Bad planning leads to disaster.

When attempting to build a real estate portfolio, many treat their business with a lot of passion and excitement but not enough research. Passion is great and excitement is inspirational, but it's a solid plan that will get you victory. If only Stephen made a solid plan, his legend may have been remembered differently than a cautionary parable in a real estate book.

Developing Crystal-Clear Criteria

Before you begin searching for your next small multifamily property, it's important to develop what we call your crystal-clear criteria, or CCC. Your CCC are designed to help narrow your focus so you'll be better equipped on your journey.

Your CCC are five criteria you'll need to identify before you begin your search:

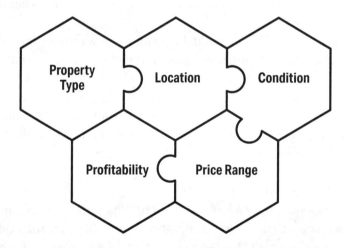

The five criteria above can be thought of as a puzzle, as each separate piece connects to the others to form a solid picture. When you know what each puzzle piece looks like, you can bring all the pieces together to form a beautiful display. Therefore, the next five chapters of this book are focused on this list, one chapter per puzzle piece. We'll make sure that by the time you finish the next five chapters, you'll know what type of multifamily you're going to buy, where you're going to buy it, what condition is ideal for your strategy, how profitable the property should be, and the exact price range you'll be considering. Then you'll know precisely what metrics make an investment a good deal. In short, you'll have a road map to victory. Your puzzle will be complete. But first, a brief introduction to the power behind the CCC.

We fully recognize some might be tempted to skip this section and simply want to move on to finding deals or running the numbers. Please don't! Establishing your CCC up front will give you the highest probability of success. How? Well, here are seven reasons why developing your CCC will help you accomplish more faster—and with less risk. Having a clear approach:

1. Guides You

When you have clarity about what you want to invest in, you'll more easily recognize the right purchase when you see it. For example, when shopping for a new car, knowing what you want will make the experience easier, faster, and more fun. No sense looking at a Hummer when all you wanted was a Prius.

Furthermore, having CCC will help you avoid wasting time on duds, allowing you to scale your business faster. You'll also increase your ability to attract the deals that are for your business. How would your approach change if you were fishing for a specific fish versus fishing for anything you could catch? Would you use different bait? Different lures? Pick a different location? Of course! The same is true for finding deals. Clarity will help you reel in exactly what you want most.

2. Helps You Become an Expert

Real estate investing can have a lot of moving parts, so becoming an expert on one particular type of investing will help you minimize risks and land better deals. Not to mention, if others in your real estate network start to view you as an expert for your area, guess who they'll bring their best deals and opportunities to first?

Perhaps the most important aspect of becoming a subject-matter expert is developing your ability to accurately analyze a potential property. Deal analysis, which we'll cover in detail in Chapter Eight, is one of the most important skills an investor can have, and each type of property has unique considerations that can affect the financial analysis. Being a subject-matter expert ensures your analysis is spot-on.

3. Gets Your Subconscious/RAS Working on the Problem

Have you ever heard a song on the radio for the first time and then heard the same song over and over wherever you go? Or perhaps you've gained interest in a new type of car and suddenly you see that car everywhere? That's your reticular activating system (RAS)—a small part of your brain that plays a big role in getting you what you need—at work.

Your RAS is responsible for taking in all the tiny bits of information that your five senses observe—from the sound of the kitchen faucet dripping, to the color of the shirt you put on, to the smell of the coffee brewing, to how the hardwood floor feels on your feet. If your mind had to consciously process all this information—thousands of stimuli coming in at every single moment—you'd go insane. Your RAS is the part of your brain that decides what moves from unimportant to important. Put another way, the RAS is the gatekeeper that holds back everything but the necessary.

How does your RAS determine what's important? It knows based on what you've told yourself is important. Need a new car? Your RAS is going to let in information that it thinks, subconsciously, will help you get closer to that new car. Need a real estate deal? Your RAS can help with that too, but it's not enough to want just "a real estate deal." The RAS needs specific instructions. What kind of real estate deal do you want? Identify it, using the CCC, and get your subconscious mind working for you—even while you sleep.

4. Helps You Establish Clear Goals

Identifying your CCC will also help you set clear, achievable goals. In other words, you'll know exactly what the target is, and you'll know whether you're getting closer or farther away. From there, you can establish smaller benchmarks and track other metrics that will get you closer to the goal. And of course, the more focused you are on your criteria, the faster you'll reach your destination.

An ancient proverb says, "If you chase two rabbits, you'll catch neither." The same is true for chasing too many goals. Although you might think by casting a wider net (that is, being open to all types of real estate investments), you'll catch more deals, the reality is your lack of focus will only slow you down. You won't gain the skills, knowledge, confidence, or experience in any one area that will enable you to progress quickly.

5. Helps You Focus and Motivate Your Team

Have you ever had a boss who wouldn't lay out clear goals for you and your coworkers? The results are often disastrous. One of the truest signs of a good leader is their ability to align all the members of their team and inspire them toward a common mission. When you have clear goals and you communicate them effectively, your team can work together effectively to achieve them. (When we say "team" we don't necessarily mean "employees." They could also be those you network with, real estate agents, lenders, other real estate investors, and so on.)

6. Elicits Help From Others

The clearer your goals are, the more others around you will want to help you reach them. For example, imagine two friends are out of work and both ask you for assistance. The first says, "I'm looking for a job. Any job at all. I don't really care what it is." The second says, "I'm looking for a job, preferably an HR admin role at a hospital in town. Know anything?" Even though the first friend cast a much larger net (no CCC), you're much more likely to be able to help the second friend because their request is so specific that it focuses your brain's efforts and makes you think, "Hm... Who do I know that works in the hospital?" This second friend actually made your job of helping *easier* by being more *specific*.

The same is true for real estate. Imagine telling a real estate agent that you are looking for a good deal. Although that agent will smile and tell you how willing they are to help, the truth is they are probably thinking, "Aren't we all!? Another newbie here to waste my time." But if you go to an agent with a request that sounds more like, "I'm looking for a duplex or triplex, something I can fix up and buy for less than $200,000 within city limits," that agent will get excited. Now they can get on their computer, show you exactly what you want to see, and even set you up with automatic emails for potential deals that match your criteria. Developing a CCC makes it easier for others to help you.

7. Prepares You to Handle Problems More Easily

Similar investments have similar problems. By narrowing your focus to particular types of investments, your CCC will give you the opportunity to learn the pitfalls associated with those investments and how to avoid them in the future. No sense in making brand-new mistakes in several different niches. Make your mistakes once and learn from them.

What if You're Not Sure What Criteria to Choose?

Decisions, decisions, decisions.

At this point, you're probably wondering, "How do I establish my CCC if I haven't invested before? It's not like this thing comes with a map!"

True. No map included. But that's the great news: You get to create your own! Most likely, this is one of the features that drove you to want to invest in real estate in the first place: You wanted the freedom to do it your way. Now it's time to make some decisions and do it your way. The perfect CCC for you can't be dictated by someone else, because what works for one person might not work for another. The path you take is found at the convergence of several unique-to-you circumstances, including:

- **Your location:** Some of your CCC will work in certain areas but not in others.
- **Your ability:** You were born with certain talents and have developed others along the way. How can you best use these skills? For example, are you good at construction? Math? Relationship building? Advertising? Project management?
- **Your interest:** No one wants to work for years on a project that doesn't interest them, so try many things and find out what interests you.
- **Your financial position:** Your net worth, income, and savings balance will affect the kind of loans you can obtain, as well as determine the level of risk you should be taking.
- **Your goals:** No sense in climbing the ladder for years only to find it leaning against the wrong wall!
- **Your network:** Who do you know that can help you? Are you going solo or partnering? Do you have good relationships with local lenders, Realtors, and contractors?

The perfect criteria lie at the intersection of these unique circumstances, as illustrated in the following image.

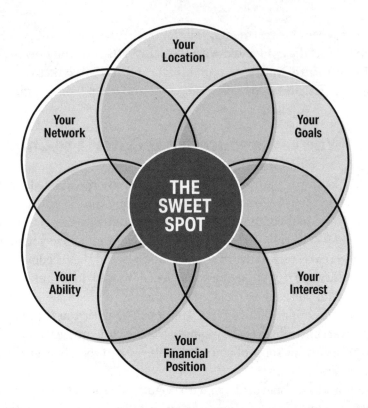

For example, you shouldn't focus your efforts on old, dilapidated small multifamily properties that require massive rehab if that strategy doesn't align with your interest and ability and gets you no closer to your goals. Maybe the idea of dealing with contractors makes you want to hide under the bed and cry. Maybe your job has you working eighty hours a week, so you need to focus on efforts that require less time for now.

If you're still struggling with what criteria to set, here are five quick suggestions to help you out:

1. Know Thyself

The first step in deciding what your CCC should be is to take careful inventory of *yourself*. What fires you up? What energizes you, makes you want to wake up early and stay up late? What are you good at? Alternatively, what makes you dread getting up in the morning (maybe your current nine-to-five)? What makes you want to run and hide? In other words, get to know yourself and trust your gut.

2. Read General-Knowledge Real Estate Books

Read a few *general* real estate books, as opposed to those that focus on a specific niche. Find a book or two that can help you see the broad picture of real estate investing. For example, my previous book, *How to Invest in Real Estate* (cowritten with Joshua Dorkin, founder of BiggerPockets.com), will give you an overview of many different options. You'll inevitably find yourself attracted to certain tactics and strategies, which will help you establish your CCC.

3. Listen to Interview-Style Podcasts

Real estate podcasts, especially interview-based episodes, are exceptionally helpful for guiding you toward your CCC because you'll be able to hear what many other investors are doing in their respective markets and niches. When you listen to story after story, you'll naturally feel yourself drawn toward certain areas of real estate investing. For example, after interviewing several podcast guests who focused on investing in mobile home parks, we found ourselves more and more drawn to the niche, which led us to begin working together to acquire parks. We now have well more than 2,000 pads and counting, and it all began with a podcast.

4. Talk with Local Investors

If you plan to invest locally, begin having conversations with others who are investing in your area. Find out what works for them because it will likely work for you too. No sense in reinventing the wheel! By talking with local investors, you'll find out which criteria are reasonable and which are simply impossible.

Let's say you live in an expensive market like New York City. After attending a local real estate meetup, you learn that you can't find multi-family properties for less than $400,000 in that market. This data helps you narrow down your CCC because now you know that if you plan to invest locally, your price range will need to be above $400,000. Otherwise, you'll have to focus on a different location and invest long-distance.

5. Make a Decision

Finally, understand that, as author Gino Wickman writes in *Traction*, "It's more important *that* you decide than it is *what* you decide." By not making a decision, many wannabe real estate investors fall off the path entirely—never to return to their quest for financial greatness.

Understand this: There is no perfect path for each person. You are not uncovering a hidden message. Think of yourself as a painter with a blank canvas before you. Weigh your options, examine yourself, and make a choice. After all, you can always change course later.

Fear Not

Now, a brief word of caution in establishing your CCC. Just because something scares you, that doesn't mean you shouldn't do it. If fear were a strong indicator of whether a course of action should be taken, humans would still be stuck in the Stone Age, clinging to their comfort zones in dark caves, avoiding all the great sparks and fires that have led humankind to where we are today. Remember: Focus on investing outside your comfort zone.

When reflecting on our own respective real estate paths, we can honestly say there is a direct correlation between the fear associated with projects we each took on and the progress we made toward financial freedom. Our only regret is not having tried to do more things that seemed too intimidating at the time. By finally embracing fear, we accelerated our growth, both personally and professionally.

How can you avoid having the same regret? To start, honestly acknowledge your fear, then look at it with a critical eye and ask yourself: Is this fear rational? Am I justified in feeling this way? Can it be reduced or outsourced? If so, how? What is the worst-case scenario? Is it really that bad?

Furthermore, it's important to understand that even if a real estate strategy doesn't necessarily fit within the center of that CCC Venn diagram, there may still be ways of making it work by asking the right question. Think in terms of "how/despite," such as "*How* can I accomplish this *despite* my situation?"

Perhaps you don't have the financial resources to purchase a million-dollar fourplex—does that mean you shouldn't pursue it? Maybe... but first we would encourage you to ask that powerful question, "*How* can I pursue this *despite* my current financial situation?" Simply switching from a "yes/no" to "how/despite" opens up your mind to the world of lateral thinking and problem solving, which finds solutions through creativity rather than simple logic. Let's say you have only $19 in your bank account. If the question is *can* you buy a $1 million investment property, logical thinking would lead you to answer no. But if the question is *how* to do so, lateral thinking might lead you to yes by way of a creative solution, such as bringing in a financial partner to carry the burden of the debt.

The next five chapters will address each of the five areas that make up your crystal-clear criteria (CCC), starting with the exact type of small multifamily property you've decided to pursue.

KEY TAKEAWAYS

- Before you begin investing in multifamily property, it's important to develop a set of criteria for deciding precisely what type of deals you want to pursue. We call these your crystal-clear criteria, or CCC.
- Developing your own personal CCC will help improve your expertise, your ability to land deals, your ability to attract others to work with you, and more.
- If you're unsure what to pursue, get some general real estate knowledge and then ask yourself, "What fires me up?" And remember, it's more important *that* you decide than *what* you decide.
- Fear is normal and valid, but it doesn't have to stop you. Instead of saying you *can't* do something, ask yourself *how* you can do something *despite* your obstacle(s).

Chapter 4
PROPERTY TYPE (CCC NO. 1)

"It is our choices, Harry, that show what we truly are, far more than our abilities."

—J.K. ROWLING, *HARRY POTTER AND THE CHAMBER OF SECRETS*

Staring down at hundreds of shiny stones, I was panicked: "There are so many options. How is someone supposed to choose the right one?!" As a struggling-to-survive 21-year-old, I didn't want to pick one that was too expensive. But I also didn't want to pick one that was too cheap, out of fear that for the next hundred years, my chintzy choice would haunt the left hand of my soon-to-be fiancée.

"Let's try to narrow it down," the sharply dressed salesperson said. Clearly, he had seen this overwhelmed face a thousand times before. "Do you think the special lady would like yellow gold or white gold?"

Finally, a question I could answer. "Yellow gold!" I shouted, perhaps a bit too enthusiastically. I knew Heather had other rings and jewelry that were yellow, so I felt confident in my choice.

"And is she someone who typically wears large, showy jewelry or more subtle designs?"

"Subtle!" I exclaimed, excited to be two-for-two in this expensive game of twenty questions.

"Wonderful," the salesperson sighed. "In that case, let me take you to this cabinet here, which features our Majestic Line of engagement rings."

After answering a few more simple questions, I had chosen a ring, maxed out my only credit card, and was on to the next phase in my secret mission: Catch my flight across the country to surprise my girl on the beach with that very ring, an acoustic guitar, and a sappy song to ask her to be my wife. But that's a story for another day.

Real estate investors experience a similar agony. They worry themselves into exhaustion over picking the right type of property because, like shopping for a ring, there are a *lot* of options out there. Let's use the same technique a ring salesperson uses to narrow them down to a more manageable set of choices. We'll start with the first puzzle piece of the five-point crystal-clear criteria.

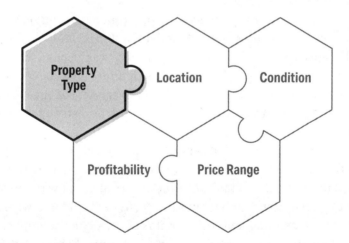

Narrowing Down

Chances are you've decided on a particular property type already: small multifamily. After all, that's what this book is about. But let's get a bit more specific. Do you plan to buy a duplex or triplex, or are you aiming for something a little larger, such as a twelve-unit apartment building? Perhaps you know you want to house hack this property (live in one unit while renting out the other unit[s]); this will help you narrow down your choices.

As you read through the many different multifamily property types available, focus is important, but we caution you not to get *too* specific. For example, you might miss a great deal on a triplex because you said you wanted only a duplex, or you might miss a great six-unit because you said you wanted a ten-unit.

Here's an overview of seven of the most common types of multifamily properties to help you recognize what you may encounter, as well as the pros and cons of each.

1. Single-Story Side-by-Side

A single-story side-by-side multifamily property is exactly what it sounds like: several units sitting side by side, usually with just one wall shared between units. Typically these are duplexes and triplexes, although some larger properties fall into this category too. One example would be converted motels. Brian partnered with his daughter, Alexa, to invest in a twenty-unit single-story side-by-side property that's made up entirely of small studio apartments.

The key marker of a side-by-side property is that no tenant's floor or ceiling is shared by another tenant. Both tenants and landlords love this feature because it eliminates the noise complaints associated with having neighbors above or below. Most side-by-side units also enjoy their own private entrance, which tenants tend to appreciate. For these reasons, many tenants prefer to rent a side-by-side unit, and strong demand for this style can sometimes support slightly higher rents.

Finally, an often underused benefit to side-by-side multifamily properties is the ease with which water can sometimes be separately metered and billed to each unit. You'll learn much more about how to implement this strategy in a later chapter, but for now, understand that when units are not stacked on top of one another, it is generally less complicated to separate each unit onto their own water meter, thus shifting some utility responsibility onto the tenant.

2. Up-and-Down

An up-and-down multifamily property is also just what it sounds like: a unit upstairs and a unit downstairs, usually with some sort of stairway on the outside that leads to the upstairs unit. This property type is most common among duplexes. But it's not uncommon to find three or four units stacked on top of one another, with one unit per floor.

You may also find an up-and-down multifamily property that is essentially two stacked single-story side-by-side duplexes, for a total of four units. Up-and-down properties may not be as ideal as single-story side-by-sides, as the downstairs tenant must put up with the noise from above, but they can be solid cash-flow generators that attract good tenants.

3. Cottages

It was, hands down, the most disgusting house I had ever been in—and it was all mine. I also owned the four other almost-identical houses on the street, lined up like prisoners facing a firing squad. Each was unique in its level of vileness, but the one I stood in on that warm Tuesday afternoon had my skin crawling and me asking myself, "What did I get myself into?"

I had found the property by sending out letters to landlords in my area (a strategy known as direct-mail marketing, which we'll explore in Chapter Twelve) and making offers, hoping something would stick. Well, something stuck all right... all over my feet as I walked through my brand-new investment. The tenants apparently had been garbage hoarders, and it looked like they hadn't taken their trash out in a decade.

Every inch of the small home had garbage bags, old food, furniture, roaches, magazines, and other items I've willed myself to forget piled as high as the ceiling. I walked the narrow path through the trash, treading carefully to avoid the rodents that scurried by my feet. As I entered the bathroom, the worst room in the house, I uttered seven simple words, the understatement of the century: "This is going to need some help."[2]

This story is not meant to scare you. Although hoarder houses *are* real, we don't recommend this type of rehab for a new investor. The point of this story is that it has a happy ending: Today the former hoarder house is part of one of my best-performing properties. Last year I averaged more than $1,500 *per month* in pure cash flow. The four small houses on that street have all been 100 percent remodeled and, in fact, stand out on their street because of how nice they look. Neighbors thanked me, the

---

2   Check out the video of my walk-through at www.biggerpockets.com/brandonshoarderhouse

city thanked me, and my bank account thanks me each and every month.

But the best part about this investment? My wife, Heather, and I have it set up on a mortgage that will be paid down to zero by the time my daughter, Rosie, is ready to go to college. At that point, the property should be worth more than $300,000, with nothing owed on it. In other words, that property is going to give Rosie a free ride to college, in addition to the cash flow I make each month. That's the power of small multifamily properties, and a great example of why I like cottages as an investment opportunity.

Cottages, for the purpose of real estate investing, are small groupings of little homes in one location. There could be up to ten homes (or more) in one spot. Often originally built by titans of various industries to house their workers together, today these quaint homes can be a terrific investment for the savvy real estate investor. Cottages are generally small, often with just one or two bedrooms, thus attracting young adults and the elderly (tenants without kids and often with limited income).

I love this style of property for many of the same reasons I love side-by-sides: Each home is a stand-alone house not sharing any walls with its neighbor, so it feels much more like renting a single-family home and much less like renting an apartment. This will support higher rent and attract a higher-caliber tenant. Additionally, because each home is separate, as with side-by-sides, utilities are much easier to separate and tenants rarely object to paying their own utilities. (After all, the tenant feels like they're living in a single-family house, and tenants usually pay all the utilities in a single-family house.) This can lead to more stabilized cash flow—something we always want to see in our investments.

Keep in mind that cottages are almost always old. It's rare for someone to have built this kind of property in the past fifty years. Thus, the property may have higher ongoing maintenance costs and may need some additional rehab upon purchase—just hopefully not as much as mine did!

4. Monster House

It's big! It's ugly! It's got unnatural appendages jutting out from all sides of its body! It's... it's... a monster house?! Yep, right up there with Bigfoot, the Creature from the Black Lagoon, and Frankenstein's creation, are the monsters of the real estate world. Some of these malevolent demons can destroy your soul if you're not careful. But the right monster house can also be tamed and transformed from a vicious villain into a cash cow.

A monster house is a single-family home that has been renovated to include multiple unique dwelling units within the structure. The primary characteristic of a monster house is that it was not meant to be a multifamily property but is now being used that way. Many "enterprising" landlords have remodeled these homes to turn the basement into a unit, the attic into a unit, the garage into a unit. Some have even thrown up a bit of plywood to make an extra unit in the backyard. Maybe they split a four-bedroom home down the middle, adding a cheap kitchen to the kitchenless side, and suddenly it's a duplex. You get the idea.

Monster houses are not necessarily bad. In fact, I own several and they provide great cash flow. For example, one of my properties clearly had been a very large single-family home with approximately 4,000 square feet, plus a detached garage. But then, seventy years ago, the owner took the basement of this house and created a one-bedroom apartment, complete with kitchen, bedroom, bathroom, and living room (it's actually a very nice basement unit).

In addition, someone decided to add another one-bedroom unit above the garage. Now this once huge single-family home (that, in today's market, would rent for around $1,400 per month total) is bringing in $1,200 for the main house, $600 for the basement, and another $600 for the above-garage unit. In total we are receiving $2,400 per month in rent from this property, and clearing more than $1,000 per month in cash flow after all the bills have been paid.

Sounds like a dream property, doesn't it? Then what's the problem with monster houses? Let's look at five separate but interconnected concerns and how they apply to monster houses: zoning, permits, lending, legal, and management.

Zoning

Zoning is a process by which the local government (usually at the city level but sometimes at the county level) decides what types of properties to allow in certain areas. For example, some areas are designated for single-family homes only, others allow only commercial properties, and still others are restricted to industrial properties. And some areas are designated for multifamily properties.

What if you have a property that exists inside an area where zoning does *not* allow for that type of property? This is known as a non-conforming property. The fact is, many monster houses do not conform to the zoning laws in their particular area. This begs the question: If you buy a small multifamily property in an area that is only zoned for single-family houses (as is common), what can you do? It depends.

If the multifamily property was, at one point, considered legal and the zoning changed, your property will most likely be "grandfathered" in. In other words, the government wouldn't make you change it back to a single-family home. Of course, every state and county has different laws and zoning regulations, so be sure to check with yours. This is known as legal, nonconforming use and is usually due to changes in the zoning laws since the property was built. The triplex just mentioned falls into this category. It's allowed by the government, but only because the conversion into a multifamily was done before the current zoning policies were enacted.

However, if the property had been *illegally* converted to a multifamily property in violation of zoning laws and the government were to find out and care, they could force you to make this property conform to the modern zoning requirements or shut down the rental entirely. This is known as an illegal, non-conforming property and is the worst kind of property for a landlord to own as a rental. Don't buy one unless you have a solid plan to make it legal and conforming, which is a challenge we do not recommend for new investors.

Some municipalities are extremely strict when it comes to zoning and can even force you to completely demolish your property if certain zoning laws were ignored. Other areas, however, seem to operate on a "don't ask, don't tell" policy (for example, much of Hawaii), and as a result, monster houses are rampant. Regardless of whether the zoning laws are strictly enforced, we never recommend violating those laws with your rentals.

Permits

Turning a single-family house into a multifamily is not as simple as paint and carpet. Typically, you'll need to add or tear down walls. You'll also have to run new electrical and plumbing lines, and the entire floor plan may need to change. These are not insignificant changes and probably require permits.

But on many monster house rehabs, the owners never obtained permits or had the property inspected afterward. Perhaps this is because the area where the property is located would not approve the permits due to zoning, or perhaps the owner simply did not want to deal with the hassle or cost of obtaining them. Regardless, as a real estate investor, you'll probably encounter many properties that have been remodeled without proper permits. Consequently, there is no good way to verify that the work on the rehab was done correctly, safely, or up to code.

In instances such as the above, you can can hope the water lines were installed correctly, but you could discover otherwise when a thousand gallons of water pour through the ceiling of your property. You might assume that because the electricity works in the kitchen, the work is up to code, only to realize differently when you're standing in front of the burning carcass of your rental. Or maybe the work was done in an outstanding manner and will hold up for the next one hundred years. The problem is that you just don't know. Even a home inspection might not reveal what's behind the walls, and if the work was done without the local government's approval, you're opening yourself up to unnecessary risk.

Must everything you buy have a perfect permit record going back to the day the property was built? No, and if you're buying older properties, good luck finding any that have a perfect remodel-to-permit history. That's part of the risk of owning real estate, and one of the reasons we recommend having financial reserves before jumping into an investment (more on that in Chapter Eight). But there's no reason to increase your chances of getting a fundamentally flawed property by purchasing a monster house with a massive unpermitted remodel.

Even worse, when you go to pull a permit on future work (which you will undoubtedly do at some point), the local government may refuse to give you one without first making you turn the unit into a conforming property. And, of course, if the property you buy lacks permits on the additions or remodeling that was already done, it may also be harder to sell the property to a new owner someday. Permits are not (just) a way for the government to take more of your money. They truly do serve a valuable purpose, and we recommend always making sure any large remodel (like additional units) has the proper permits pulled either when you purchase the property or if you do the remodeling yourself.

Lending

Although some investors choose to pay all cash for their properties, most get a loan from a bank, credit union, or other lending institution to finance their property (which we'll talk about in depth in Chapter Fourteen). One major drawback to purchasing a monster house (specifically, an illegal or nonconforming monster house) is the inability to obtain traditional (bank) financing due to the zoning issues we just mentioned. Simply put, most lenders will only loan on a property that is conforming—in other words, no illegal multifamily properties! Even if the property has been fully remodeled and you're getting a screaming-good deal on it, if the property is illegal, you probably won't be able to obtain a loan, so you'll have to buy the property with cash or turn to creative financing.

Legal

If your monster house is operating as an illegal rental unit, you may also expose yourself to potentially drastic legal liability should, God forbid, a catastrophic event occur in the property. A Washington, DC, landlord was charged with second-degree murder because of a fire that killed two people, including a 9-year-old boy. According to news reports,[3] the landlord had been operating this twelve-unit property (twelve one-bedroom row homes with shared bathrooms and two shared kitchens) illegally when the fire started. The building was not licensed for residential use, and the landlord did not apply for the necessary business license. Avoid the legal issues, and potential jail time, by doing your due diligence and avoiding illegal monster houses.

Management

Finally, let's talk about one of the drawbacks to monster houses that has nothing to do with the legality of the property: the tenants. With their usually odd layouts, thin walls, and close-quarters neighbors, monster houses lend themselves to issues among residents. As such, these units tend to rent for lower rates than other multifamily properties, and you may experience significantly more wear and tear, plus higher turnover and more time when units sit empty (known as vacancy).

This gets even more complicated if you are renting an illegal property and things do go poorly with a tenant. BiggerPockets' forum moderator and real estate investor Russell Brazil says that in his Maryland-DC area, you'll likely have tremendous difficulty evicting a tenant if you don't have the right license to rent out a property (which, of course, an illegal, nonconforming property would not have). Why? Because you weren't supposed to be renting to them in your illegal property anyway! That's

---

[3] WJLA news staff, "DC Landlord Charged with 2nd-Degree Murder in Fire That Killed Two, Including 9-Year-Old," WJLA website, January 15, 2020, https://wjla.com/news/local/dc-landlord-charged-murder-fire-killed-two

just one more strike against investing in illegal small multifamily properties. It's just not worth it.

One final note concerning the way monster houses operate: The utilities in these properties, including electricity, are generally not separated. This means you, as the landlord, may end up paying for all utility bills on the property, so when a tenant takes ninety-minute showers twice a day, it's coming out of your pocket—not necessarily a deal breaker if you work those numbers into your analysis, but something to be aware of before proceeding.

So, should you buy a monster house? I think the answer is clear. If it's legal, consider it. If not, can you make it legal? Then consider it. If you can't operate it legally, though, just don't. Given the number of completely legal real estate investment opportunities out there, it's just not worth the risk. Review your options briefly below:

1. **Legal, Conforming:** This means the property is legally allowed to exist in its current form, and the specific type of property is legally allowed in the area. The right permits were pulled, the right processes were gone through, and everything is great. These can be excellent investment properties to own, and in terms of monster houses, have the least amount of risk associated with them.

2. **Legal, Non-Conforming:** This means the property is legally allowed to exist, but the specific type of property is no longer allowed in the area. This is usually due to changes in the laws since the property was built. The triplex discussed earlier falls into this category: It's allowed by the government, but only because the conversion into a multifamily was done before the current zoning policies were enacted. This type of property can be a gold mine—and legal to boot. Of course, every state and county has different laws and zoning regulations, so make sure to check with yours.

3. **Illegal, Conforming:** This means that the property would technically be allowed to exist in the given area, but the property did not go through the proper channels to become legal (for example, the property was converted from a duplex to a triplex without permits). The best-case scenario in this situation is for the property owner to go through the proper channels to make the property legal. Get the permits and get the sign-off from the local government inspectors, and you'll have a legal, conforming investment property and won't have to worry about breaking any laws.

4. **Illegal, Non-Conforming:** This means, of course, that the property is not legally allowed to be a multifamily and the area's laws also don't allow for the property to exist there.

5. Starter Apartment Building

For the purposes of this book, a starter apartment building is a multifamily property that contains several small units (usually between four and ten) inside a single building. I call them starter apartments because of their size and relatively low rent, which makes them perfect for tenants living on their own for the first time. The buildings are often older, simple, and rectangular (boxy) in shape, and commonly have a hallway down the center with units on each side. Although each unit typically has its own kitchen and bathroom, there's usually only one bedroom—or none, in the case of studio apartments. A number of these properties were once used as official boardinghouses, but many were built exactly as they are and simply resemble the boardinghouses of old. If you live in a fairly urban area with extremely old real estate (think pre–World War II), you likely drive by these properties every day—and there's a good chance you've never even noticed.

These small apartments can provide good cash flow, as the price per unit tends to be much lower than for more modern multifamily real estate. But be warned: The age of these properties often means higher repair and maintenance costs while you own and operate the rental. Because many of these properties were built before World War II, don't be surprised to find outdated wiring with ancient electrical panels, cast-iron plumbing (prone to leaks), lathe and plaster walls (as opposed to the modern use of drywall), and paper-thin walls. (Not actually paper thin... but it's not uncommon to hear your neighbor chewing their oatmeal!)

Of course, it is entirely possible to find one that has been well-maintained and continually modernized over time, and you may experience very few ongoing maintenance headaches. Additionally, because starter apartments are usually very small, your tenant base may be significantly more transient in nature, leading to higher turnover costs. On the other hand, if the property is located in a high-rent area or near a college or hospital, you may find a great tenant base in love with the lower price tag. This further speaks to the importance of understanding your local market, which we'll address at length in the next chapter.

6. Garden Apartment Building

Travel to nearly any suburb in America and you'll find garden apartments everywhere. Although the exact definition varies, the basics of a garden apartment building are the following:

- Two stories tall (though some could have three stories)
- Usually contains greenery around the property (trees, grass, bushes)
- Units often have a patio or balcony
- Each unit has its own exterior entrance
- Units contain two or more bedrooms
- Property has a more modern design with modern building materials

Essentially, these are just nice, modern, multifamily buildings in a suburban setting. Garden apartments can make for great rental properties, as they tend to be newer than many of the other styles we've talked about in this chapter, and as a result, they also tend to attract higher-quality tenants and command higher rents.

7. ADU

When you think about the coolest character in television history, one name tends to stand above the rest: the Fonz. Arthur Herbert Fonzarelli, played by Henry Winkler on the 1970s and '80s sitcom *Happy Days*, had it all: a killer hairdo, a thundering motorcycle, a leather jacket, and he lived his wild and cool life out of a small apartment above the garage of the Cunninghams. See? Real estate *can* be cool. There is hope for us all!

The apartment the Fonz inhabited is known as an ADU, which is short for accessory dwelling unit. But these apartments go by many names. In Hawaii, they are called *ohanas*. They are also known as *mother-in-law apartments*, *granny flats*, *garage apartments*, *carriage houses*, *secondary suites*, *English basements*, and *accessory apartments*—you get the picture. While the names differ, the concept remains pretty much the same.

The ADU is a secondary home, usually with one or two bedrooms, built in addition to a single-family residence on a single lot. Some ADUs are separate, stand-alone structures, while others are converted areas of the main home (such as a basement or an attic). Perhaps this sounds a bit like the monster houses we discussed earlier, and they do have a few things in common. However, for this book's purposes, when we refer to an ADU, we are discussing a much more standard conversion or addition of that extra unit rather than the often poorly executed conversions found in monster houses. ADUs are usually higher-quality units that were designed from the start to be separate rental units. However, unpermitted and badly built ADUs definitely exist.

For example, my home in Hawaii has an ADU in the backyard—a separate, one-bedroom home with its own foundation, roof, electric service, water heater, and balcony. I am able to rent out this unit, which helps to cover a sizable chunk of my mortgage payment. In fact, in both Hawaii and California (two highly expensive markets), the state government is finding ways to encourage the addition of ADUs (through changes in the law, loan subsidies, and more) because the ADU is seen as a partial solution to the problem of affordable housing.

Think about it: The government knows that housing prices are soaring, yet much of the population's wages are still low. Where are all the baristas, bank tellers, mechanics, and cleaners going to live if they can't afford to rent a house? By allowing ADUs, the government kills two birds with one stone. Renters can lease these smaller homes for less than the cost of renting a large one, and owners can offset a large chunk of their mortgage payment with the rent they generate. The government then collects tax revenue on the entire operation. It's a win-win-win.

ADUs are incredibly common (according to some estimates, there may be as many as 13 million ADUs in the United States), and they can be a fantastic investment for real estate entrepreneurs looking to start off in the world of multifamily properties.

First, if you own your own home and your local jurisdiction allows it, you could add an ADU to your property and turn your single-family house into a multifamily just like that. As we've discussed, this is called house hacking, and it's exactly what I and perhaps tens of thousands of others are doing across the country. You could also add an ADU to an existing single-family home that you own, turning that into a multifamily. Or, of course, you could purchase an investment property that already has an ADU.

If you choose to purchase a property with an ADU or plan to add an ADU to your home, consider the implications for your utility bills. With many ADUs (especially detached ones), the water and electricity can be separated from the primary house, meaning you can shift the responsibility for those bills to the tenant and remove those expenses from your bottom line.

Moving On

Now that you've read this overview of small multifamily property types, along with the pluses and minuses of each, we hope you've found one that's especially appealing to you. For example, I've identified the side-by-side duplex as a personal favorite. Whenever I search online for properties for sale, I will almost always click to learn more if I see a property of this type. You should be getting ready to do the same.

Remember: Shopping for investment real estate is like shopping for an engagement ring. By narrowing down your choices to the exact type you want, you'll make the best decision possible.

KEY TAKEAWAYS

- There are many different styles of small multifamily properties, and it's important to be familiar with each kind to learn which might be a good fit for you.
  - **Single-Story Side-by-Side:** A property consisting of several units sitting side by side, usually with just one wall shared between units; most common in duplexes, triplexes, and some fourplexes.
  - **Up-and-Down:** A property that consists of several units, usually two to four, stacked on top of one another.
  - **Cottages:** Several small single-family houses located on one lot.
  - **Monster House:** A large single-family home that has been turned into a small multifamily property, sometimes legally, sometimes not.
  - **Starter Apartment Building:** A property that contains several small apartment units (usually between four and ten) inside a single building.
  - **Garden Apartment Building:** Modern buildings located in greenery-laden locations, usually with two to four units, each with an outside entrance and often a balcony or patio.
  - **ADU:** A secondary home, usually with one or two bedrooms, built in addition to a single-family residence on a single lot.

Chapter 5
CHOOSING YOUR LOCATION (CCC NO. 2)

"Travel isn't always pretty. It isn't always comfortable. Sometimes it hurts, it even breaks your heart. But that's okay. The journey changes you; it should change you. It leaves marks on your memory, on your consciousness, on your heart, and on your body. You take something with you. Hopefully, you leave something good behind."

—ANTHONY BOURDAIN

In the United States alone, there are nearly 42,000 zip codes and almost 20,000 cities. Within them, you'll find approximately 139 million housing units.[4] All that choice can be overwhelming and dangerous to an investor who's looking "anywhere" for a good deal. Without focus, you'll never build the expert-level knowledge of a real estate market needed to make informed decisions. Therefore, it's time to narrow down your choice of location, the second piece to the CCC puzzle. And when it comes to location, the first question to consider is this: Local or long-distance?

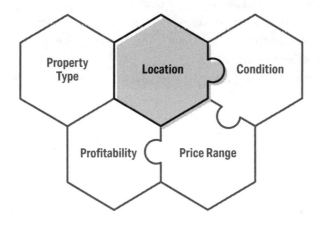

Local or Long-Distance

It was nighttime and I noticed a man with a sad but determined look on his face on my street. He bent alongside parked car after parked car. Before moving on to the next car, he'd stand and look around his feet. I approached the man and asked if I could help him find what he had lost. He explained that he was looking for his wedding ring. Naturally, I began to help, even recruiting other neighbors to comb the area with us. We examined the edges of the road, dug through individual blades of grass, scoured the sidewalk cracks.

After nearly thirty minutes of searching, I exclaimed in frustration to the elderly man, "I'm sorry we can't find it. Are you sure you lost it here?" The man replied, "Oh, goodness no! I lost it six blocks up that hill over there. But the only streetlight was here, so that's why I chose this spot."

---

4 "December, 2020 Facts & Stats," Zip-codes.com, https://www.zip-codes.com/zip-code-statistics.asp; "How Many Cities Are in the US," World Population Review, https://worldpopulationreview.com/us-cities/how-many-cities-are-in-the-us/; "Number of Housing Units in the United States from 1975 to 2019," Statista, May 13, 2020, https://www.statista.com/statistics/240267/number-of-housing-units-in-the-united-states/

A silly joke, of course! (And one I've probably already used in another book or two. But great jokes, like exaggerated fishing tales, are meant to be told again and again.) I really had you going, didn't I? The truth is that this is exactly what many new real estate investors do. Rather than searching in the right area for their prize, they search where it's most convenient. Specifically, we're talking about investors who choose to invest in their local area simply because they live there, not because it provides them the best options. Perhaps local investment *is* best. But perhaps long-distance investment is the way to go. Let's review some of the pros and cons of each.

When you invest locally, you may already have a pretty good understanding of the market. This means having a solid grip on what areas are hot, what areas are cooling, what areas are full of crime, what areas are wealthy, where the best schools are, and where the path of progress seems to be headed. This home field advantage helps you make more informed decisions about what properties to pursue. That said, many local investors are often less aware of the true condition of their market because they've been blinded by living there and haven't done the work needed to learn about their market. It's hard to see the entire forest when you're living among the trees. The bottom line: Both local and long-distance investors must have intimate knowledge of the markets they choose to invest in. More on that soon, but first, let's look at a few essential considerations when deciding between local and long-distance investing.

When you invest locally, you are *there*. When shopping for a property, it's no big deal to hop into your car and check out a property anytime you want. When you hire a contractor to paint a building, you can check their work when it's finished to make sure it's been completed correctly. When you need a plumber to clear a clogged sink, you probably know a half dozen and, if not, you can ask nearby family or friends for recommendations. You might even take care of many or all repairs and ongoing maintenance concerns yourself.

But here's a funny thing about the paragraph you just read. While it seems to list the advantages of local investing, you could also read that entire paragraph as being about the *disadvantages* of investing locally. After all, when you're local, it's easy to just jump in the car and check out a property, but is that what you want to do? Or would you rather have *someone else* do that for you?

Do you want to have to check up on your contractor to make sure the work was done correctly, or would you rather have others handle that? Are you sure you want to deal with contractors at all? And when you're local, doing your own maintenance work might seem like a good idea to save money, but are you doing $50-per-hour tasks (like fixing a leak) when you could be doing much more valuable work (like finding your next deal)? Depending on your outlook and investing strategy, many of the advantages of being local can also be disadvantages!

More importantly, local investors tend to ignore creating the systems needed to make their business run smoothly. They pick up rent in person because it's easy. They fix toilets because they can. They deal with contractor headaches because they hired the guy they met in the Home Depot parking lot rather than screening and vetting several contractors to find the best. In other words, most local investors spend too much time *putting out fires* and not enough time *making their properties fireproof.*

That's not to say long-distance investors always do their homework and perfect their systems. Many don't, and many fail. But when you invest at a distance, those systems are immediately put to the test. It's trial by fire, and your investment will quickly fail if you don't have the right systems in place. Necessity will compel you to create systems that work without you being there.

There's one more benefit to long-distance investing that's greater than everything we've talked about so far: *limitless* opportunity versus *limited* opportunity. When you invest locally, you have one market and a finite number of properties to choose from. Maybe that's not a bad thing. Perhaps your market has an abundance of properties that perfectly meet your CCC and you can invest forever in your own backyard.

On the other hand, your local market might have limited options for the strategy you want to pursue. Like the man searching for his wedding ring on the wrong block, you could wind up searching for a deal that simply doesn't exist in your location. Not every area is right for every strategy—just like every strategy is not right for every investor. Some areas are better for certain strategies while some areas are better for others. Therefore, it's vital that you choose a location that fits your needs and aligns with your goals.

In his book *Long-Distance Real Estate Investing*, David Greene writes:

I started investing in out-of-state properties because I had no choice. Properties in my own backyard had appreciated to the point that they no longer cash-flowed positively. What began as something I thought was a necessity became something I've become extremely excited about. It ended up making me a millionaire by the age of 30, without my realizing it was happening! The potential to buy in different markets and enjoy the fruits of those market strengths opened up doors for me I never thought were possible. With that came exciting opportunities! Once you understand the fundamentals of real estate investing, you will learn to apply them anywhere.[5]

David discovered that by investing long-distance, he wasn't restricted to strategies that worked only locally. He wasn't slowed down by the limited inventory in his local market. Instead, he could focus on buying *wherever* the best deals were. Some markets just provide more cash flow than others. Some markets have better job growth than others. Some markets have fewer expenses associated with owning there. And as David says in the above quote, once you understand the fundamentals, you can apply them anywhere.

At the end of the day, long-distance investing works—when you work it correctly. But local investing works too, if you work it correctly. When you use the right systems and processes and have the right people doing the right jobs, real estate investing works. *It's that simple.* But it's your job to choose the path that's right for you and your financial goals.

I spent the first ten years of my investing career investing only in my local market (at the time, Grays Harbor, Washington). Grays Harbor was a decent rental market with cheap properties, which fit my investing plan. However, because I was local, I spent the first half of that decade doing 100 percent of my own management and maintenance work. At the time it was easier for me to do it than to think at a higher level and create the systems for someone else to do it. As a result, instead of scaling quickly, I was merely surviving.

I'm not saying I *shouldn't* have done what I did. After all, it got me to where I am today. And I did begin scaling as I began to perfect my systems. In the meantime, I gained a tremendous amount of knowledge and experience, as well as a solid reputation, by being hands-on. Most importantly, because I had very limited cash resources (in other words, I

---

5 David Greene, *Long-Distance Real Estate Investing*. Denver: BiggerPockets, 2017, p. 23

was broke most of the time), I had to rely on hustle and local connections to get deals done. That would have been tremendously difficult had I invested in a long-distance market. Now let's fast-forward a few years.

A Tale of Two Long-Distance Investments

I wanted to purchase some larger multifamily properties and I couldn't find anything local, so I made the decision to invest long-distance. I had about $100,000 saved to invest as a down payment, so after a lengthy search, I bought two properties: a twenty-four-unit apartment complex outside Cincinnati, Ohio and a fifty-lot mobile home park outside Bangor, Maine.

Immediately, I began to have problems with the apartment complex in Ohio. My property manager refused to return most phone calls in a timely manner. Contractor after contractor refused to call me back for bids to improve the exterior of the property. Units sat empty for months while, supposedly, work was being done on them. (You guessed it: Work was *not* being done on them.) When I bought the property, all twenty-four units were filled. Within six months, only eighteen were filled. After fighting with various different managers and clawing back from despair, I filled the property and sold it for just a tad more than I'd paid. Two years of stress and nothing to show for it.

However, while the Ohio property was falling apart, the mobile home park underwent a fantastic transformation. Occupancy increased from 60 to 100 percent over the first year, driving cash flow through the roof. Units were rehabbed on a timely basis, and tenants paid rent on time or were swiftly removed and replaced with responsible tenants. This mobile home park had turned into an ATM!

Why did the apartment complex fail so badly while the mobile home park succeeded? Is it because mobile home parks attract better tenants? Hardly! The truth comes down to two failures on my part.

1. **Team:** In Ohio I didn't have the people in place needed to control the investment. In Maine I brought in a local partner who understood the market and had connections with all the best local vendors, including a rock-star property manager. My partner's local knowledge, combined with the property manager and his team of contractors, made that project a success.

2. **Time:** I fully admit that the Ohio apartment failed because I didn't give it the time and attention it needed and deserved. Rather than

interviewing and vetting multiple property managers, I went with the first one I spoke with. When things started to go bad, I was preoccupied with a dozen other projects and simply hoped things would work themselves out. They didn't. Instead, the situation just kept getting worse. It wasn't until I stepped in and took "ownership" of the project that things turned around in time for me to sell. Real estate investing, especially multifamily, *can* be passive. But thinking that just because you hired a property manager you can let go of the reins is a mistake. Passive income is earned, not bought. Read that again.

The goal of this case study is not to scare you away from long-distance investing. In fact, the same lessons apply to all forms of landlording: You must give your investments the time and the team they need in order to succeed.

Appreciation versus Cash-Flow Markets

Let's carefully define two things to make sure we're all on the same page:
- When you make extra money each month on your rental property, you are creating profit through *cash flow.*
- When that property increases in value from $200,000 to $300,000, you are creating wealth through *appreciation.*

Of course, the two are not mutually exclusive, and when you buy a small multifamily property, we hope you get both. However, it's important to recognize that in some real estate markets, cash flow may be high and appreciation low, whereas in other markets the opposite may be true. For example, many coastal markets (Seattle, Los Angeles, New York) experience tremendous growth through appreciation. Seattle has seen an average increase of 9.2 percent per year[6] (median home price from 1998 to 2018), whereas Cleveland saw an increase of just 1.52 percent per year over the same time period.[7] But trying to find a solid cash-flowing rental property in Seattle will be significantly more difficult than finding

---

6 "All-Transactions House Price Index for Seattle-Bellevue-Kent, WA," Economic Research, Federal Reserve Bank of St. Louis, https://fred.stlouisfed.org/series/ATNHPIUS42644Q#0

7 "S&P/Case-Shiller OH-Cleveland Home Price Index," Economic Research, Federal Reserve Bank of St. Louis. https://fred.stlouisfed.org/series/CEXRSA

a cash-flowing rental property in Cleveland.

That said, don't write off appreciation-friendly markets just yet. Although your cash flow may not be significant compared to that in a cash-flow heavy market at the start, that could change because over time rents change. In fact, let's compare Seattle and Cleveland again. Between those same years, 1998–2018, Seattle saw an average rent growth of 3.6 percent per year (meaning if you obtained rent of $1,000 in 1998, your rent probably would have climbed to $2,029 by 2018). On the other hand, Cleveland saw an average rent growth of just 1.6 percent per year between 1998 and 2018, so your $1,000 rent in 1998 probably would have climbed to $1,374 by 2018.

In both cases, if you had obtained a fixed-rate mortgage (one in which the monthly payment stays the same for the entire length of the loan), then your largest expense (the loan payment) would not have increased at all on either property! This means that although your cash flow might be limited in the beginning, your Seattle property, over time, would increase at a much faster rate, potentially giving you a great cash-flowing property several years down the road.

Of course, purchasing an expensive property requires significantly more capital than purchasing a cheaper one. After all, 20 percent down on $200,000 is much less than 20 percent down on $1 million! Therefore, the amount of cash you're able to invest could also dictate whether you pursue investments in a cash-flow-heavy market or an appreciation-heavy market. Furthermore, if your goal is to generate maximum cash flow now so you can quit your job sooner, you should choose a cash-flow-friendly market. But if accumulating long-term wealth is more your style, you'll want to aim for a more appreciation-friendly market.

Finally, keep in mind three facts about cash-flow-heavy versus appreciation-heavy markets:

1. Just because a market has historically been more conducive to cash flow than appreciation does not mean it will always be that way. Economies change, and who knows? Maybe Seattle will stop appreciating and prices in Cleveland will skyrocket in coming years. The past is not always a good predictor of the future.
2. Large markets contain many submarkets. There are probably several submarkets within Cleveland that act more like Seattle and several submarkets in Seattle that operate more like Cleveland.

This is one reason why it's critical to know your market all the way down to the neighborhood level. When evaluating markets, be sure to focus in on their submarkets.

3. Just because a market is appreciation-friendly does not mean you should accept negative cash flow. Cash flow helps ensure that you can hang in long enough for your property value to increase and your loan to be paid down. As David Greene noted on an episode of *The BiggerPockets Podcast*, "Cash flow is a defensive metric."

Buying a property that loses money with the hope that appreciation will help you win over time is a gamble, because you can't predict the housing market. Unless you have the financial resources to take on that kind of risk, we don't recommend it. Cash flow is still king, even in an appreciating market. The question is, how little cash flow are you willing to accept?

We encourage you to strike a balance and position yourself to reap the rewards of both cash flow and appreciation. Buy in markets where appreciation is likely, but also make sure your property provides good cash flow now and in the future. Yes, you can have your cake and eat it too, depending on the market and submarket you choose—so choose wisely. Do your homework. Dig into the numbers on your market and submarkets. And pick a location that best serves you and your goals.

Spotting the Difference

When it comes to the likelihood of appreciation, we have a few indicators. First, there's the simple truth that expensive markets tend to be appreciation-friendly and cheaper markets tend to be cash-flow-friendly. Cities like Cleveland, Orlando, and St. Louis have historically been considered cash-flow-friendly. Cities like Los Angeles, New York, Boston, Honolulu, Denver, Austin, and Nashville have historically been considered appreciation-friendly. Again, this can change at any time and past performance doesn't guarantee future growth, so be sure to check out BiggerPockets Insights at www.biggerpockets.com/insights to keep tabs on market trends.

You also want to consider current trends when trying to predict future appreciation for a market. For example, property values are largely dictated by supply and demand: If there isn't enough housing, prices go up. So where are people moving to? High population growth can be a good indicator of future appreciation. To research population growth trends, check out www.worldpopulationreview.com.

To determine whether a market is more cash-flow or appreciation-friendly, it's also wise to listen to what others are doing or saying. (If Landlord Larry is getting great cash flow in XYZ market, you probably could too.) This is another reason why listening to interview-style real estate podcasts can be helpful. You should also speak with a knowledgeable real estate agent, someone with years of experience in a given market. They will have both the factual data and the insider knowledge to spot hot up-and-coming markets.

Most importantly, especially when it comes to determining cash flow, you'll have to learn to run the numbers and do the math. That's why we've dedicated Chapter Eight to the process of analyzing a deal. Due to the vast number of other factors at play, the value of a property doesn't tell you much about its potential cash flow. For example, one market may have exceptionally low property values but monthly tax bills that are more expensive than the mortgage payments! Another market may have incredibly low taxes but high property values. At the end of the day, both scenarios may produce the same—or drastically different—cash flow. You won't know until you do the math.

Spotting an appreciation-friendly market or a cash flow-friendly market is not an exact science. We can't know the future, no matter how hard we try to predict it. What we can do, as real estate investors, is conduct our research and plan carefully in order to mitigate our risks while putting ourselves in the best possible position for success. That's what being a real estate investor is all about.

Neighborhood Classification

Take a moment to think about your town. Think of a spot that has really nice recently built houses. A place with nice curbs, new roads, kids out playing hopscotch on the sidewalk, perfectly manicured lawns—you get the picture.

Now think of a spot where the houses could all use some paint. Sidewalks, if they exist at all, are cracked and threatening to break an ankle. Cars that haven't been moved in a decade sit idly atop cinder blocks in the driveways. A police car rolls slowly through the streets. Chances are you know exactly the type of neighborhood I'm talking about, because no matter how nice a market you live in, there are always these neighborhoods.

What you've just done is identified a Class A neighborhood and a Class C or D neighborhood. In the world of real estate investing, investors often classify neighborhoods by a certain letter (A, B, C, or D) based largely on subjective criteria. Class As are the nicest neighborhoods with the best homes and businesses. Class Bs have more working-class residents, slightly older homes that are still quality properties, and low crime. Class Cs are much more working-class, with lower-income residents calling the neighborhood home. Finally, Class Ds are the worst locations, places where crime and unemployment are high while property values and conditions are low.

These class designations aren't official, but most investors understand A, B, C, and D based on the above descriptions. In addition, as with letter grades, a plus or minus can be added to the class to further clarify. For example, you might have an A– location (not quite as good as A but only barely less so) or a C+ (better than what someone might consider C but not worthy of B). As we said, it's relatively subjective and open to interpretation, but most investors understand the general feel of Class B versus Class D. The neighborhood class system is really nothing more than a simple framework for you to compare submarkets and discuss those locations with other investors.

At this point you might be wondering, "Why would anyone choose anything but a Class A area?" And you're right—Class A neighborhoods can be fantastic areas, someplace you would love to raise your family. The problem lies in the *profitability* of investments in those neighborhoods. Both Class A and Class B properties are often too expensive to provide good cash flow, so they're generally considered more of an appreciation play. If your goal is to generate enough cash flow to quit your job, Class A might not get you there. At the same time, although properties in a Class D area tend to go for exceptionally low prices and, on paper, would seem to provide massive levels of cash flow, the challenges associated with such neighborhoods might negatively impact your goals.

In addition to understanding what class a neighborhood is, you must also be aware of any trends affecting it. Is the neighborhood falling into further decline or showing signs of revitalization? Look for evidence of investment and construction activity. Are new businesses opening? Are renovation projects under way? If you are able to invest in a neighborhood that is showing signs of turning a corner, it could be a great opportunity to achieve strong rent growth.

Choosing a neighborhood on which to focus your investing efforts will help you narrow down the potential deals in your market. Once you've decided you won't invest in a certain area, you won't waste time looking at deals there. After some investigation, you should be able to identify a neighborhood that meets your comfort level as well as your goals for profitability.

Crime

Closely related to neighborhood class is the level of criminal activity in a particular area, though the two are not always 100 percent correlated. Of course, avoiding all crime is impossible. Nonetheless, you'll likely want to steer clear of areas that have consistently high levels of crime or are trending in the wrong direction. Thankfully, the internet makes researching crime a fairly quick and painless process. Check out www.cityprotect.com to search for recent criminal activity and see any registered sex offenders in an area. Speaking with local law enforcement can also be helpful.

Schools

School districts are a big deal to a lot of people, so property in a desirable school district can be worth substantially more than a similar property in an undesirable school district. However, because most school districts are based upon lines drawn on a map, homes that are located across the street from each other can be in different school districts. In our experience, the higher the neighborhood class, the more the residents will care about the school district. If you plan to invest in Class C neighborhoods, school districts will play a less vital role than if you are buying in a Class A location. Additionally, if you plan to invest only in smaller units that wouldn't attract tenants with children anyway, the quality of the school district will be less important to you.

Like neighborhood class designations, the ranking of school districts is largely subjective. Nonetheless, most parents of small children will quickly be able to tell you where the good and the bad ones are. To access a more objective system for identifying the best school districts, check out www.greatschools.org.

Population Trends

As mentioned previously, the price of real estate and the rents that can be charged to tenants are based largely on supply and demand. The more people who want to live somewhere and the less housing available, the higher the cost of rent. That's why places like California, Hawaii, and New York City are known for exceptionally high rents and property values.

Therefore, one important factor in determining which real estate market to enter is the general trend of population growth (or decline) in an area. After all, if a population is decreasing over time, supply and demand may force rents and values *down* in that area—not something a landlord wants. Keep in mind that a slightly declining population doesn't necessarily mean you should not invest in that location. Population trends may reverse and change in any area, and even if they continue downward, the current population still needs a place to live. However, given a choice, we would much rather focus on locations where the population trend is upward. To learn about a location's population trends, go to www.opendatanetwork.com or www.worldpopulationreview.com.

Job Diversity

When it comes to buying multifamily real estate, you need to make sure your tenants can pay the rent. If you're considering a location where only a small number of employers or industries support most of the tenants, you may want to think twice about investing there. If that company or industry decides to relocate or goes bankrupt, most tenants could be unable to pay their rent. An economy with a diverse workforce will help reduce the risk of all your tenants losing their jobs at once.

KEY TAKEAWAYS

- Investing in real estate can be done locally or long-distance, depending on your goals. Don't assume you're limited to one or the other, because there are pros and cons to both. Weigh the options and make a decision—but be sure to start by focusing on getting to know just one market really well.
- Taking the time now to decide on the right location/market for you will help you narrow your search and avoid wasting time later looking in areas that don't fit your goals.

- Some markets produce great cash flow but have very little property value growth (appreciation). Other markets offer the opposite, and some markets offer both. Find a market that supports your goals.
- When focusing on a neighborhood, determine its class level and research crime statistics, school ratings, and job diversity in that area.

Chapter 6

PROPERTY CONDITION (CCC NO. 3)

"I always thought that the 'thriving' would come when everything was perfect, and what I learned is that it's actually down in the mess that things get good."

—JOANNA GAINES, THE MAGNOLIA STORY

When Brian saw that the nine-unit monster house at 201 Sterling Street had gone up for sale, he was astonished by how low the price was, even considering the fact that it was an absolute dump. Resting amid a wildly overgrown, trash-strewn yard, 201 Sterling was the scourge of the neighborhood and a veritable beehive of unsavory activities.

Brian knew that this blighted, scary apartment building represented the last bastion of depravity on the block. It was surrounded by much more innocuous and stable properties, which made it more appealing.

In fact, he already owned the property next door, and across the street from 201 Sterling was the municipal building, which housed the city's administrative offices and the city court. Unfortunately, the close proximity to the municipal building didn't seem to matter to the occupants of 201 Sterling or their perpetual parade of guests, who would lounge on and around the porches, leering at passersby.

When the "For Sale" sign popped up in the yard at 201 Sterling, Brian contacted the broker and was surprised to learn that all nine units were full, and the rents were far higher than he'd expected. The financials were encouraging, and given his experience with turnarounds, he decided to extend an offer. After some back-and-forth, he put the property under contract for only $135,000, which left a hefty cushion to make the vast, necessary improvements.

The inspection was an adventure, and Brian uncovered enough problems to fill a book, but nothing he couldn't handle. For the most part, the tenants put on quite a show, screaming at Brian's team and the broker. Two of the tenants had changed their locks and refused to allow entry into their units. Somebody else had dumped borax all over the hallway floors upstairs in a desperate attempt to rid the building of its bedbug infestation.

It turns out the rents were so high because you can charge a lot more if you're willing to accept people that nobody else is willing to rent to. After inspecting the property and weighing all of his options, Brian decided to evict everyone from the building and do a full restoration, including a new roof, new siding, and a complete renovation of all nine units.

The plan seemed sound, but the six months following closing were a disaster. Once the tenants were out, one of them kept breaking back in and squatting. Several tenants did physical damage, while many others left their units trashed and filthy. One kept calling and leaving nasty messages. Another earned bonus points for creativity by applying a thick layer of grease to the entire stairwell and second-floor hallway.

Once everyone was out, Brian hired an abatement company to clean up all the filth; they sent out two workers in Tyvek suits. The pest control company said that in addition to clearing out all the trash, the paneling, carpet, and ceiling tiles would all need to be removed in order to properly treat the rampant roach and bedbug infestations. The seasoned pest control technician was in awe—the property boasted the worst bedbug infestation he had ever seen. In one of the units swarms of them were actually visible on the walls and ceiling. Ugh!

The worst news came when it was time to get access to the attic for the roof repairs, which posed a dilemma. During the inspection nobody had been able to locate any way to get up there, but now that the building was empty, they cut a hole through the ceiling in one of the units to gain access. The contractor climbed up into the attic to discover an old metal cable running across the width of the building. From prior experience, he immediately suspected what its purpose was. To be sure, he went downstairs and examined the building from the exterior, which confirmed his fear: The building was splitting down the middle. That rusty old cable was literally the only thing keeping it from collapsing. After hearing this, Brian walked in disbelief to the front of the property and saw that the contractor was right. If you looked close enough from straight ahead, the sides of the building were leaning slightly outward. Ugh! He couldn't believe no one had noticed this before, including himself.

The building was structurally unsound. This had been completely missed during the property inspection, and the cost to fix this problem was not in the budget. Factoring in the work necessary to stabilize the building, the total project cost now far exceeded his projections, even though he had included a generous contingency. Financially, the deal didn't make sense anymore. In the end, Brian made the difficult decision to cut his losses and walk away. Fortunately, he would later reach an agreement with the local municipality to demolish the building and sell them the land for parking, which allowed him to recoup much of his costs.

The 201 Sterling Street project was a failure. It was a humbling experience, and Brian learned several painful lessons. One was that prices are usually low for a good reason, and some properties should be avoided even if they're free. But the biggest lesson learned was that every property is unique, and while most of his turnaround projects had yielded great returns, they had also come with higher risk—and things don't always go as planned. When hunting for fixer-uppers, you must always exercise caution. As the third puzzle piece of establishing your CCC, you'll need to determine what condition the properties you are willing to pursue should be in.

In a perfect world, most real estate investors would love to avoid challenging properties altogether and buy a property that is brand-new, ready-to-rent, and in great condition. But this is not a perfect world, and although you can certainly find nice multifamily properties that don't need any work, they often result in poor or nonexistent cash flow. Perfect properties also attract the highest number of potential investors, driving up competition and lowering your chance of getting the property before others do.

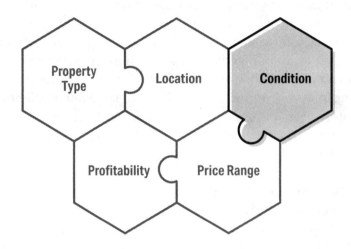

Of course, that doesn't mean you have to buy a nasty, dilapidated property with urine-soaked shag carpet just to make a buck. In reality, the truth lies somewhere in between. The type of condition you choose to focus on will largely depend on how aggressive you want to be on your investment's returns. Properties that are more run-down carry more risk but can offer higher rewards for the investor willing to tackle those rehabilitations. To help you decide whether such properties are right for you, let's look at a few of the pros and cons of investing in fixer-uppers.

Four Advantages of Investing in Fixer-Uppers

1. Better Potential for Getting a Good Deal

One of the primary reasons to purchase a fixer-upper is that very few people want them. The average home buyer wants to close on a property and move in the same day. The average investor wants to close on a property and start collecting rent the same day. Most people don't want to go through the hassle of rehabbing a property. Therefore, thanks to supply and demand, you can get significant discounts by purchasing a fixer-upper. This can help you get more equity and cash flow on your investment versus buying an already fixed-up property.

2. Opportunity to Reduce Repair and Maintenance Expenses

One reason I love to buy properties in poor condition is because I'm able to do a large amount of work to fix items that would likely break at some point in the near future. In other words, I'm able to proactively address concerns rather than reactively repair things. In 2016 I purchased a four-unit property in Aberdeen, Washington. I spent more than $120,000 rehabbing this property, including new siding, landscaping, all-new interiors and fixtures, and even mostly new plumbing. Since that time, I've had no more than a dozen maintenance calls on broken items—because everything is new!

3. Potential to Build Equity Quickly

Nasty properties tend to be significantly cheaper than nice properties, of course. But the beauty of buying these fixer-uppers is that once they've been rehabbed, their value can increase dramatically, giving you a fair amount of equity in the property.

For example, let's say you purchase a triplex for $300,000, but it needs a serious facelift, including a new roof, new cabinets and counters in all three units, new paint and flooring, and an exterior paint job. In total, this rehab might cost you $50,000. But as soon as it's finished, the property might be worth, let's say, $425,000 due to the higher rents you can command. Although you have only $350,000 invested in this deal, its new value is $75,000 more than that, giving you increased equity and thus a higher net worth.

This can be a great way to build massive equity up front and protect yourself should the market drop in price, since the equity provides a cushion between what you owe and what the property is worth. If your property is worth $425,000 after repairs and the value of real estate in your market drops 10 percent, causing the value to temporarily dip to $382,000, you still have only $350,000 total invested in the deal. In other words, adding value is a good way to prevent going "underwater" (when the value is less than the money you've invested). This added value is also the basis of the BRRRR real estate strategy, which we'll cover further in Chapter Seventeen. Stay tuned for that; it's pretty awesome.

That's not to say all rehabs suddenly make a property worth more money. By rehabbing a property, you aren't really adding value so much as you are bringing the value back to where it *should* be. This might be hard to understand, so I'll try to clarify. Real estate doesn't instantly become worth more because you spend money on making it nicer. A property is worth what it's worth based on what other recent sales of similar properties have been or on how much profit it generates. You can spend $5 million to rehab a nasty property, but that doesn't mean the property is automatically worth $5 million more—unless the comps (recent sales of similar properties) and profit support the higher value. There is a limit to how much a property is going to be worth no matter how nicely you fix it up.

Let's revisit the example of the triplex, the one that needed $50,000 of rehab work done. Earlier we mentioned buying that property for $300,000 and putting $50,000 of work into it, resulting in its now being worth $425,000. That would be great. But what if you had paid $400,000 instead? You'd have invested $450,000 (purchase plus rehab costs), but the property would still be worth only that same $425,000.

A property is only worth what it's worth, no matter how much you paid. The market doesn't care what you bought it for. The market doesn't care how much you spent fixing it up. The market doesn't care about you at all. The market defines what that property is worth based on comparable sales (or in the case of larger multifamily, based on how profitable the investment is, which we'll speak to in a later chapter). It's not about you; it's about the property. Don't assume that a fixer-upper is automatically a great deal. If you don't know your numbers well enough, you might have just the opposite. That's why it's so important to:

- Get the property for a low enough price to make it profitable
- Have confidence in your rehab's after-repair value (ARV)
- Keep your rehab from going over budget

4. Opportunity to Command Higher Rents

I recently started selling my own blend of coffee, BeardyBrew (www.beardybrew.com). It's good. Really good. But it's not cheap like the mass-marketed stuff you'd buy in the grocery store. Why would someone pay around $25 a pound for my coffee, when you can probably find cheap coffee for half the price? Because people pay for quality. Most everyone would agree that BeardyBrew coffee is significantly better quality—in terms of flavor and overall experience—than the cheap stuff. Quality is simply worth more.

Therefore, when you rehab a property, you can often get slightly-higher-than-average rental rates. After all, tenants prefer a nice, clean, newer unit to something older and uglier. This is especially true if you're buying in an area that has many awful properties (which is common in Class C neighborhoods). However, in a Class A neighborhood, tenants expect a Class A product, so don't plan on getting above-average rent.

Also keep in mind that just because your product is nicer than average, that doesn't mean you can charge whatever you want for rent. People will be willing to pay more for higher quality, but only within limits. If the average rent is $1,200 for a unit in your area but you do a better-than-average rehab, you might be able to get $1,300 or even $1,500 for the space per month. Don't expect to suddenly get $2,500. Chances are those who can afford to pay $2,500 per month are going to be looking in an area where $2,500 is the average, not in an area where it's $1,200. Like property values, rents are largely determined by what's considered normal for the location, although you can definitely push them to the upper end of the spectrum when you have the best product on the market.

Four Disadvantages of Investing in Fixer-Uppers

Of course, not everything is sunshine and rainbows when it comes to buying a fixer-upper. Sometimes rehabs are not good. Sometimes they can be downright awful. Let's look at a few of the negative aspects of buying a fixer-upper multifamily property.

1. Harder to Finance

A bank's number one job is to make a profit. Shocking, right? They are a business, after all. Even credit unions and nonprofit lenders don't exist to *lose* money. And since nearly all a bank's profit comes from loans, every bank makes decisions to fund those loans based upon one thing: risk. In other words, is the bank likely to get paid back or not? From most banks' point of view, a rehab is risky. They don't know your ability to fix up a property, and should the worst happen, they don't want to end up foreclosing on you and having to take control of a nasty, broken-down building. That's why when it comes to fixer-uppers, most banks just say no.

Of course, not all banks refuse to fund rehabs. The truth is, many banks have loan programs built specifically for this purpose, but these "rehab loans" are often difficult to qualify for, have higher down-payment requirements, may have significantly higher interest rates and fees, and are much shorter in term, giving you less than a year or two to pay them back. For these reasons, many investors bypass banks when seeking financing and resort to using their own cash or borrowing from hard-money lenders to fund their rehab deals. Then, after the property has been fully repaired and rented out, they go to a traditional lender and get a new loan on the property, fully paying off the old lender and locking in a long-term, low-interest fixed-rate mortgage from that traditional lender. (If this sounds familiar, this is the BRRRR strategy we mentioned earlier and will spend more time talking about in Chapter Seventeen.)

Although this strategy works and it's one investors often use, it can add significant expense to your project. Also, you must be confident that you can obtain refinancing once the work has been completed. Otherwise, you may end up with a short-term hard-money loan and no way to pay it back.

2. Rehab Headaches

Rehabs are a messy business—and not just for the one covered in dry-wall dust. Managing a crew of contractors or trying to learn and do all the tasks yourself can quickly consume the better part of many days. Someone doesn't show up on time, the wrong material is ordered, there's damage to the floor that was just installed the day before, the contractor takes your money and runs without finishing the project—it's all possible when overseeing a rehab. Of course, managing a rehab is a skill, which means you can master it if you're willing to learn. Although you'll never be able to avoid all problems with a rehab, you can create the right systems and processes and find the right people to minimize the damage and your stress.

3. Cost Overruns

Unless your crystal ball works better than ours, accurately assessing the cost of a rehab project is incredibly difficult before the project has begun. While it's possible to know the cost of a new toilet and even possible to get an accurate estimate from a local plumber on how much that toilet will cost to install, you can't predict, for example , whether when the old toilet is removed rot will be found, which can cost an extra $$500 or more in labor to repair.

You see, it's the unknowns that cause cost overruns. Of course, the more rehabs you manage, the less likely there will be unknowns. Getting a thorough property inspection ahead of time is always a great idea to minimize the risk of finding the unknown, but even inspectors don't have X-ray vision to see inside walls. Additionally, it's rarely one item in a rehab that goes over budget; instead, everything tends to go over by a little bit. The total cost of the toilet was $250 not $225. The tile work on the shower was $1,200, but you forgot to account for the cost to dump the old tile, pushing that part of your budget over by $80. This death-by-a-thousand-paper-cuts is a real phenomenon when rehabbing properties.

Estimating the cost of a rehab is another skill that can be learned and improved upon. Resources like *The Book on Estimating Rehab Costs* by J Scott can simplify the process. Smart investors always estimate rehab costs with two financial cushions: They add a bit more to each line item for the paper cuts, and they add a larger "overage" or "contingency" budget to the total just to make absolutely sure they have the finances needed to tackle the full rehab.

4. Carrying Costs

Empty rental units generate no rent. Obviously. Therefore, if you purchase a small multifamily property that needs to be rehabbed, the units you are rehabbing will not produce any income until they are leased. Meanwhile, you continue to incur expenses such as insurance, property taxes, and utilities. For this reason, it's important to factor both lost rent and carrying costs into your budget as real expenses. And remember: Rehabs always seem to take longer than you anticipated (just as they always seem to cost more money), so plan accordingly and budget conservatively.

While not receiving rent is never fun, one advantage multifamily has over single-family real estate is that units can be repaired sequentially rather than simultaneously, giving you fewer vacant units at the same time and spreading out the damage. For example, you purchase a fourplex that is currently fully leased out but in bad condition. Old carpet covers the floor, appliances are stained with grease and rust, and the exterior hasn't been painted in at least a decade. You immediately get to work fixing up the outside of the fourplex with new paint, new landscaping, and even a cute decorative fence. You start with the outside because you want to change the neighborhood's opinion of the property, knowing that the outside plays a large role in the type of tenant you'll be able to attract in the future.

Soon one of the four tenants gives their notice to move, and the day they vacate, you're in that unit painting walls, replacing flooring, and updating appliances. Thankfully, the other three units in that fourplex are still paying rent while you work on this unit. Within a month, you've finished rehabbing the apartment and rented it out for $300 more per month than the other units. Now you simply wait for the next tenant to move out so you can remodel another unit. After a year of this, you've fully remodeled the interior and exterior of all four units, having never lost more than one unit's rent in any given month. Best of all, your improvements are bringing in an extra $1,200 per month in cash flow.

The Baby Bear Rehab

We all remember the story of Goldilocks, the sweet young girl who decides not only to engage in breaking and entering into the home of carnivorous bears but also goes so far as to eat their porridge, sit in their chairs, and fall asleep in their beds. Silly, of course, but the story does teach a valuable lesson. Recall that the first porridge Goldilocks samples (Daddy Bear's) is far too hot and the second (Mama Bear's) is far too cold, but with the third bowl (Baby Bear's) she discovers a happy middle ground.

Just as in this children's story, the middle ground is possible when contemplating a rehab. Your choices for what type of condition you want your ideal investment to be in aren't simply "perfection" versus "OMG, I can't believe people live here! Is that blood on that wall?!" Instead, the amount rehab properties require encompasses the full spectrum between those extremes. Some rehabs require $1,000 per unit (say, a thorough cleaning and painting just a bedroom). Others require $15,000 per unit (new paint, flooring, and counters). Still others need a complete $50,000-per-unit overhaul, including windows, drywall, cabinets, and exterior. If the idea of a $50,000-per-unit rehab is intimidating, we don't blame you. That's an awful lot of work! Therefore, it's important that you have a firm idea of how big a rehab you're willing to tackle.

For most investors, the "baby bear" rehab is known as a cosmetic fixer. This means the bones of the property are good and it needs only a facelift. Such properties can prove exceptionally lucrative because although they don't require much effort to rehab (several days and several thousand dollars), the "cosmetic" challenges scare away anyone who's looking for a perfect passive investment property. As an added benefit, properties that need just a light cosmetic rehab can often meet the minimum standards for traditional bank financing.

Rehabs should not be looked at as scary or something to be avoided, but you must decide at what level that rehab becomes too risky, time-consuming, or expensive for you to take on. Fixing up a nasty property can be an excellent way to supercharge your wealth creation, giving you instant equity and a higher-quality property. However, the time, effort, cost, and difficulty involved can quickly turn a great deal into a money pit if not tackled correctly. Decide what level of rehab you feel comfortable performing, and begin your search for that ideal property.

KEY TAKEAWAYS

- Investing in fixer-uppers can help you land good deals in competitive markets and offer several other key benefits. However, there are certain challenges that make taking on a rehab project something you should definitely think long and hard about.
- If choosing to invest in a fixer-upper, you will probably need to find alternative financing options, as most banks will not lend on a property that's in rough shape. You'll also need to work to improve your contractor management skills, as cost and time overruns can turn a good deal bad.
- Sometimes the best deals to pursue are properties that, while short of perfect, don't need too much work. We call these cosmetic fixers "baby bear rehabs," because these just-right properties can allow you to land a good deal without an overly complicated rehab project.

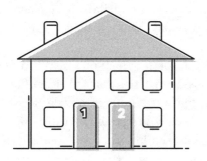

Chapter 7

PRICE RANGE
(CCC NO. 4)

"I'm like an expensive menu... you can look but you can't afford!"

—ANNA KOURNIKOVA, FORMER
PROFESSIONAL TENNIS PLAYER

My wife and I occasionally sit down to watch those "house-hunting" shows on television, where the cute couple tours house after house, searching for their forever home. (We were even scheduled to appear on one of those shows while purchasing our latest home in Hawaii, but we backed out at the last minute due to the overwhelming stress of moving across the ocean with a baby, a dog, and a shipping container that held everything we owned!) But what always makes us laugh are the budgets.

"John is a full-time recorder player for the local preschool, and Jane works in her office gluing Popsicle sticks together to sell at craft fairs.

Their budget is $3 million!" Maybe on TV a person who earns $300 a week can afford a multimillion-dollar house, but in the real world, the price we pay for real estate must fit within our budget. This is especially true when it comes to buying small multifamily real estate, as the amount of cash you have for a down payment will largely dictate how much you can spend on a property.

But once you know the price range you can afford, you can quickly weed out the noise of all those properties that are either far too expensive or far too cheap. That's why the fourth missing puzzle piece to creating your CCC is the price range you'd be willing to buy within. As we've said before, by weeding out time-wasting options through creating your CCC, you'll have more time and effort to put toward finding your perfect investment.

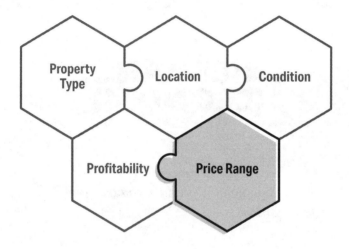

To do this, we want to identify your maximum purchase price (MaPP) and your minimum purchase price (MiPP). Let's start with the MaPP.

Setting Your MaPP

Step one in determining your MaPP is to determine exactly how you'll be financing your next property. This means that if you plan to use a traditional loan from a bank, you'll need to be clear on what that bank's down payment requirements are. Realize that 20 percent down is vastly different from 30 percent down, and either are possible depending on the lender.

Secondly, you'll need to account for the fact that you'll have closing costs associated with buying your property. Closing costs are the various fees, commissions, and prepaid expenses that must be paid at the time of closing. This includes title fees, attorney fees, inspection fees, prepaid insurance costs, prepaid taxes, and often most significantly, fees associated with obtaining your loan. Closing costs vary by location and property type, but typical costs range from $2,000 on a property purchased for less than $100,000 to $30,000 or more on a large apartment complex. For a quick and dirty estimate, we like to use 2 to 3 percent of the purchase price as a rule of thumb for closing costs.

Furthermore, you'll have to decide how much money you'll need in reserves. For example, if you have $50,000 to invest in a small multifamily real estate deal, it's unlikely you'll want to spend all $50,000 on a down payment. That would leave nothing in your bank account as a cushion if something were to go wrong with your property. Furthermore, most lenders actually *require* reserves. Although the exact amount of capital differs among lenders, most require that you set aside an amount of money equal to six months of what your payment (the principal, interest, monthly taxes, and monthly insurance) would be.

On small multifamily deals, you can be usually keep this money in your own bank account or even within a 401(k), though on large deals, the bank may insist on holding this money for you. This obviously changes the amount of money you'll need to close on a real estate transaction, so it's important you begin having conversations with your lenders about how much they require in reserves. Once you've determined these three numbers, you'll have a pretty good indication of how much you can spend on a potential investment property via a traditional lender. To determine your limit, simply follow this formula:

$$\left(\begin{array}{c} \text{Total Cash on Hand} - \\ \text{Closing Costs} - \text{Reserves} \end{array} \right) \div \begin{array}{c} \text{Required Down} \\ \text{Payment Percentage} \end{array} = \text{MaPP}$$

Maybe that's a little confusing, so here's a quick example.

Let's assume you have $60,000 in cash on hand. You decide that having $15,000 in reserves for this property would be ideal, and you've also talked with a title company and assume closing costs will run around

$5,000. Finally, you speak to your local lender, who tells you they can do an investment property loan with a 25 percent down payment. Using the formula above, we get:

$$(\$60,000 - \$5,000 - \$15,000) \div .25 = \$160,000$$

In this case, the most you can spend on an investment property with that lender (and no outside investment) is $160,000. It's just math!

You might be thinking, "Well, I don't have that much cash." Not to worry. Remember, this example applies only to those obtaining a traditional loan on an investment property—in other words, plain vanilla investing. But if you have less cash, there are alternatives, including the BRRRR strategy or partnerships that allow for more creative financing. We'll explain these in depth in Chapters Sixteen and Seventeen. For now, let's just be sure you are clear on how to determine your MaPP when it comes to traditional financing. Use this section to practice determining a comfortable MaPP for yourself.

Setting Your MiPP

Of course, it's helpful to establish not only your maximum purchasing power but also your *minimum*. After all, deals of a certain size may not be worth the effort, so set a lower limit to avoid looking at deals that simply waste your time or won't give you the biggest bang for your buck. This is especially true as you begin to scale your business.

For example, Brian and I invest in large mobile home parks and have an MiPP of $3 million. Does this mean no property under $3 million makes sense financially? Not at all—there are many good deals on the lower end of the price range. However, we have the financial ability to buy much, much larger deals, and the amount of effort that goes into buying a million-dollar property is actually shockingly similar to the amount of work that goes into buying a hundred-million-dollar property. Yes, you read that correctly: At many levels, the larger deals require the same—or even less—work as the cheaper deals. Theoretically, for the same price we could purchase:
- Nine properties for $1 million each
- Three properties for $3 million each
- One property for $9 million

Regardless, we're spending $9 million on real estate, but the first option would require nine times more effort! For this reason, we decided to draw a hard line at $3 million for our MiPP so we don't waste time looking at deals that, although they may pencil out, are simply not worth the effort at this stage of our investing journey.

This applies to smaller deals as well. The amount of time that goes into buying a hundred-thousand-dollar fourplex is about the same as for one that costs $400,000—but there's a good chance the latter will have much higher rents, be in a much better area, and attract much better tenants. Only you can determine what your MiPP is, or whether you even want to have one. It can be zero dollars if that fits your strategy. Just identify it! Get crystal clear on your price range and focus only on properties that fall within it.

Next, we'll delve into the fifth and final CCC puzzle piece: profitability. In other words, let's get really clear on how to spot a great deal by using good math. The next chapter is the longest, and likely the most important, in this book. So put on your thinking hat and let's get nerdy.

KEY TAKEAWAYS

- Rather than look at every property, it's important to get realistic about how much you can afford as well as how small you want to go. This is known as setting your maximum purchase price (MaPP) and your minimum purchase price (MiPP).
- Take a look at your cash on hand, research lenders, and learn about closing costs to determine how much you can reasonably spend on a property.
- Small deals can often take the same effort, if not more, as big deals, so if you have the capital and experience, don't be afraid to aim higher.

Chapter 8

PROFITABILITY & ANALYSIS (CCC NO. 5)*

*AKA THE MOST IMPORTANT CHAPTER IN THIS BOOK—AND THE LONGEST!

"One man's trash, that's another man's come up."

—MACKLEMORE, "THRIFT SHOP"

Everyone wants their small multifamily investment to make money. But how much *should* a multifamily property make? Is $100 per month a good amount of cash flow? How about $500? Or $10,000?

Of course, it depends on several factors. What might be a good deal to you might not be a good deal to me. Maybe I want a higher return and am willing to work harder or smarter or longer to achieve it. Maybe I'm okay with a smaller return because I know that, since I'm just getting started, it's more important to begin building momentum, rather than try to get everything perfect (not a bad mindset to have!). Maybe I'm somewhere in between.

Furthermore, what if I invested only $2,000 to buy a property and make $500 every month from that investment. Sounds decent, right? But what if, instead, I put in $1 million as a down payment. Suddenly, $500 a month seems kind of small, doesn't it?

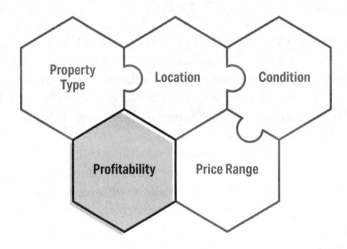

This is why deal analysis—and by extension, establishing your knowledge of what a good deal is—matters so much. What would make you want to pursue a deal or drop it? This is the fifth and final piece to the CCC puzzle. You must establish some go and no-go standards, minimum profitability thresholds that will help you make decisions based on math rather than emotion.

It's easy to get caught up in the moment, the excitement, the thrill of landing a deal. And while excitement is normal, sometimes it leads to bad decisions. At the end of the day, even the best and brightest minds are made up of two sides: the emotional and the logical.

When it comes to putting together a deal, you need *both* the logic (problem-solving ability) and the emotion (instinct and feeling). Logic alone will never provide you the courage or enthusiasm to pursue anything even remotely risky, but emotion alone can drive you straight off a cliff. How do we align emotion's thrill of the chase with logic's careful guidance? By establishing profitability thresholds.

Getting excited about a deal is okay—in fact, we encourage it. After all, we're excited about every single deal we do. But having clearly defined profitability metrics allows us to get excited about the *right* deal and avoid getting carried away by anything less than ideal. By establishing hard-and-fast rules for what makes a good deal, you'll gain the confidence needed to take on deals outside your comfort zone. The more confident you are in your math, the more confident you'll be in making offers. And with the confidence (and victories) you've earned, you'll become more effective when talking with lenders and negotiating with sellers. Most importantly, by establishing your profitability threshold, you will be able to quickly work backward on any potential investment to determine the exact purchase price that aligns with your long-term goals.

You see, every property has a price that *could* make it a great deal.

Highlight or underline that sentence—because it's important.

Maybe that price is a million light-years away from what the seller is asking for a property, but the number exists nonetheless. (And, yes, sometimes that number is negative. We've encountered many properties for which the seller would have had to *pay us* a sizable stack of money to acquire their property!) Determining that number begins with knowing how much you want to make on your next purchase—your profitability goal.

To establish your profitability goal, we are going to look at two basic metrics: pure cash flow and cash-on-cash (CoC) return, while setting a minimum threshold for each. Don't worry; we'll keep the math pretty simple.

Pure Cash Flow

We talked briefly about cash flow back in Chapter One and defined it as the profit earned after paying all expenses. When dealing specifically with rental properties, cash flow is the profit left over after we subtract the total property expenses (taxes, insurance, utilities, repairs, reserves, upkeep, mortgage payments, vacancy, and so on) from the total income (all rent and other income sources). Therefore, the formula is:

$$\text{Total Income} - \text{Total Expenses} = \text{Cash Flow}$$

Sometimes, when investors share their minimum metrics for cash flow, someone else inevitably brags about how they get so much more cash flow from their rentals. "Oh, you only make $300 per month on your rental? Wow. I make $1,000." But if you dig into their math, you'll see that what they call "cash flow" is actually just the rent they are charging minus the mortgage payment. I call this "phantom cash flow" because it might seem real, but it's just an illusion! In reality, their cash flow is much, much lower. So, to differentiate between what most people mean by cash flow and what we do, we're going to take some liberties here and invent a new term: "pure cash flow."

Pure cash flow means the profit a property produces after factoring in both *fixed* expenses (such as the mortgage, taxes, and insurance) and *variable* expenses (things that may not happen monthly but do happen and should be accounted for, such as repairs). So, how much pure cash flow is appropriate? How much should you aim for? What is not enough?

When setting a minimum threshold for pure cash flow, we find it helpful to quantify this number as monthly cash flow per unit (which we'll abbreviate as MCFPU). In other words, if your minimum threshold is $100 per month, per unit, then a fourplex should make $400 per month in pure cash flow, while a ten-unit should make $1,000. On the other hand, if your MCFPU goal is $300 per month, per unit, then that fourplex should be providing $1,200 per month in pure cash flow and a ten-unit should spit out $3,000 per month. So, in terms of MCFPU, what's the ideal amount?

To illustrate, let's go back to the example of our friend who brags about making $1,000 per month in cash flow. When he explains his math, this is what he shows:

Rent:	$1,800
Mortgage Payment (including taxes and insurance):	-$800
(Phantom) Cash Flow:	$1,000

But in reality, here's a more accurate breakdown of the reality of his monthly situation:

Rent:	$1,800
Vacancy (5%):	-$90
Repairs:	-$150
CapEx Reserves:	-$120
Property Management:	-$200
Utilities:	-$200
Mortgage Payment (including taxes and insurance):	-$800
Pure Cash Flow:	$240

Note: The only expense we don't include when it comes to cash flow is your personal tax liability from that profit because it differs for every person. Yes, when you make money from rentals, that money is taxed. However, there are many ways of reducing or eliminating your tax liability completely, which we will discuss in a later chapter. For now, just consider that cash flow "pretax," but hang on to the hope that you might not have to pay any taxes on that money!

Now that we're clear on what cash flow is and isn't, let's dive into setting your profitability goals for pure cash flow.

Pure cash flow profitability is closely tied to the market in which you've chosen to invest. Your market may provide greater or less pure cash flow, depending on your rents, the cost of buying a property, and the expenses the landlord is responsible for.

For example, here's a look at two real-life triplexes I own:

- **Property 1:** Unit A rents for $2,800 per month. Unit B rents for $2,700 per month. Unit C rents for $1,500 per month. Therefore, in total, I receive $7,000 in gross rents on this property. My total expenses, including vacancy, repairs, mortgage, and more, come to around $4,600 per month when I average them out, leaving my final cash flow around $2,400 per month, or $800 MCFPU.
- **Property 2:** Unit A rents for $600 per month. Unit B rents for $500 per month. Unit C rents for $525 per month. Therefore, in total, I receive $1,625 in gross rents on this property. My total expenses, including vacancy, repairs, mortgage, and more, come to around $1,100 per month when I average them out, leaving my final pure cash flow around $525 per month, or $175 MCFPU.

When comparing Property 1 to Property 2, the difference is night and day. Why would Property 1 produce more than 450 percent more cash flow per unit? Does this mean Property 2 was a "bad" investment and Property 1 is a "good" investment? Should my pure cash flow goal be $800 per unit? Not necessarily! You see, Property 1 is located in Maui (average cost of a home: $700,000), and Property 2 is located in the small coastal town of Hoquiam, Washington (average cost of a home: $150,000). A person couldn't find a property in Hoquiam that produced $800 of cash flow even if they had no mortgage at all. It's just not possible.

The same is true for your market. To a large extent, your market will determine what a good pure cash flow is and what MCFPU you should aim for. You'll discover ranges within your market and be able to set goals based on those ranges and how aggressively you plan to pursue incredible deals. Are you hunting only for that rare home-run deal, or is a base hit perfectly acceptable? Only you can define this.

However, we can give you some guidance based on ranges. Please don't rely 100 percent on these numbers; they are simply a rule of thumb based on our experience. But hopefully this gives you a place to start. The left column represents the approximate value of the property divided by the number of units, giving us the price per unit. The second column gives you a target MCFPU to aim for. And remember: This is pure cash flow, not phantom cash flow!

PROPERTY VALUE PER UNIT	TARGET MCFPU
$0–$40,000	$100
$40,000–$75,000	$150
$75,000–$100,000	$200
$100,000+	$300+

Based on this chart:
- If you acquire a fourplex for $100,000, that means each unit is worth $25,000. Thus, the MCFPU to aim for is $100 per unit, or $400 for the fourplex as a whole.
- If you acquire a triplex for $350,000, that means each unit is worth $117,000. Thus, the MCFPU to aim for is $300 per unit, or $1,200 for the triplex as a whole.
- If you purchase a ten-unit for $600,000, that means each unit is worth $60,000. Thus, the MCFPU to aim for is $150 per unit, or $1,500 for the ten-unit as a whole.

Next, let's dig in deeper to see exactly how this number is derived. Pure cash flow is one of the most important metrics for gauging the long-term success of an investment. It's the number behind the financial freedom to retire early, buy cool cars, pay for your vacations in Bali, and sleep soundly each night knowing your bills are covered. Therefore, read the following section carefully: It covers what might be the most valuable skill a real estate investor can ever gain.

To analyze a deal, we're going to use a tool we call the Four-Square Method. This is a simple four-step process for analyzing a deal to determine pure cash flow and cash-on-cash return (which we'll explain below). We simply work through four boxes to determine whether or not to pursue an investment. Those four squares are:

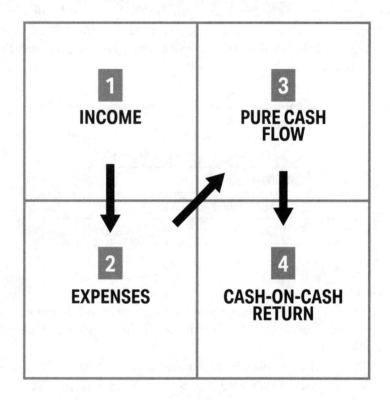

The rest of this chapter is designed to help you work through each of these four squares, starting with income and expenses, which will tell us our pure cash flow, and finally ending with our cash-on-cash return. We've left the boxes in the Four-Square diagrams throughout this chapter blank, so you can fill them in and practice with your own numbers and calculations. Check out Chapter Seventeen for our analysis of a property using this method!

Square 1: Income

The first box in the Four-Square Method, the upper left corner, is the income box. This means we need to get an accurate idea of just how much total revenue this property will bring in. Income includes rent, of course, but may also include other sources of revenue, such as laundry machines, storage rentals, parking, and more. We want to get really clear on the total monthly income the property is expected to produce when running our numbers, so be sure to account for all potential income sources.

If the property is currently rented to tenants, you can easily find out the current rental rates by talking with the seller (or the agents involved in the deal). However, it's possible that the current rents are significantly lower than "market" rents, so it's important to see what rents are possible by looking at similar listings in the area. This same principle applies if you're buying a vacant property and you will be advertising those units for rent.

Rents vary by location, of course, and depend upon numerous factors, like the number of bedrooms in the unit, the neighborhood, the street, the location of the unit within the building, the building's condition, the unit's condition, whether the tenant pays for utilities, and more. Therefore, to determine what your potential unit will rent for, you need to find similar units in the same area and make slight adjustments based on what your unit has or doesn't have, with the most important factors typically being specific location, bedroom count, and condition.

To get an idea of what other units rent for in the area, you'll need some data. To get this data, we typically turn to one or more of the following:

- **Property Managers:** Local property managers are in the business of renting out units, so they usually have a solid grasp on what local rental rates are. Call a local property manager to discuss your units and ask their opinion on rent. This is also a good time to begin meeting local property managers and get a feel for how they operate, just in case you decide to hire a professional manager.
- **BiggerPockets Rent Estimator Tool:** If you are a BiggerPockets Pro member (sign up at www.biggerpockets.com/pro), you have unlimited access to the BiggerPockets Rent Estimator. BiggerPockets has created this easy-to-use tool that employs a vast amount of data to determine the average rent for a property. Simply type in the address with the number of bedrooms and bathrooms, and you can

determine the median rent in that area (plus you'll get other unique insights about the property and location).

- **Craigslist/Facebook Marketplace/Zillow/Apartments.com:** These large online classifieds websites are a great place to look for rental comps. See what properties are currently available and find properties similar to yours in a similar location. You'll quickly be able to spot trends in pricing across your target market.

Once you have a number of comparable rental properties, determine whether your property is better, worse, or about the same as those currently available. Ideally, you'll find several units that are almost identical to yours in bedroom count and condition, and the rental rate will be obvious. If not, you might need to make small adjustments based on the closest comparable rentals you can find.

The good news is that over time, you'll get a good feel for rental rates in your target market. You'll immediately know what a two-bedroom apartment on X street will rent for, and what a three-bedroom on Y street can get. That said, rental rates change often, so even if you're an experienced investor, it's helpful to look at where rental rates are *every time* you rent out a unit. Rents may have gone up significantly since the last time you looked, and a few moments of research could be worth thousands of dollars in additional income.

What if Rental Rates Are Too Low?

Of course, if you're buying a property with existing tenants, you may find that the rents the tenants are paying are far below what you believe their units can rent for. Although you may want to, you might not be able to immediately jack up those rents to market rate because the tenants likely have signed a lease (a legal document that defines how much their rent is for a set period of time).

Even though you are a new owner, the old lease goes with the property, not the previous owner. Therefore, you will be bound by the same lease terms as the previous owner and can raise rent only when a lease term expires. This can be both a source of opportunity (ability to raise low rents) and a source of potential headaches (having to follow someone else's terms until the lease expires). Moral of the story: Always check the existing leases before purchasing a property.

Additionally, even if their leases are expiring or tenants are simply on a month-to-month agreement, you may not want to raise rents right away. Although common, rent raises are a good way to lose tenants. Tenant turnover is part of the game, of course, but it's not something you necessarily want immediately after buying a new property. Imagine buying a fourplex and, upon purchasing it, you raise the rent on all four tenants and all four leave. Now you have four units that are producing no income and probably need to be refreshed or even fully rehabbed before you can rent them out again. Unless you have significant capital set aside for this purpose, you may want to stagger your rent raises over several months, so you don't lose your tenants all at once. We've found that most tenants don't leave just because of a raise in rent. They might grumble, but if you are raising rent only to the market rate, they will quickly discover that rents everywhere else are similar to the new rate and decide that moving isn't worth the hassle and expense.

What About Rent Control?

Finally, let's briefly talk about rent control. In some areas of the country, cities have enacted a policy known as rent control that dictates how much an investor can raise rent on an existing tenant, usually capping the raises at less than 5 percent per year. If you buy a property in, let's say, Los Angeles and the current rent is $2,000 per unit, even if market rent is $3,000 for those units, you may only be able to raise it to around $2,100 per month during the first year, then to just over $2,200 the second year, and so on.

Keep in mind that rent control typically stops rent raises only on current tenants, not new ones. Therefore, if a tenant vacates a property, the landlord can typically re-rent the property at market rate. Rent control is not always a bad thing for landlords, and strategies do exist for real estate investors to make large profits by investing in rent-controlled properties.[8] However, it's vital that you know whether your area and building will be subject to rent control, and plan accordingly.

Now that we have a final number for total monthly income, we'll fill it in at the bottom of Box 1.

---

[8] https://www.biggerpockets.com/show280

1 INCOME	**3** PURE CASH FLOW
Rental Income $ _____ Laundry Income $ _____ Late Fees $ _____ Utility Income $ _____ Storage Income $ _____ Other Income $ _____ **Total Monthly Income** $ _____	
2 EXPENSES	**4** CASH-ON-CASH RETURN

Square 2: Expenses

Next, we move down a square to tackle expenses by looking at some of the most common ones. Of course, every property is unique, and some will have all of these expenses while others may have very few of them. You will need to look at each property separately and determine which expenses are applicable and which aren't. In the beginning this might feel overwhelming, but a few simple questions to the owner or the real estate agent is usually all it takes to identify current expenses. The following are the nine most common multifamily expense items:

- Utilities
- Snow Removal/Landscaping/Other Contract Services
- Property Taxes
- Insurance
- Mortgage Payment
- Vacancy

- Property Management
- Repairs
- Capital Expenditures

Keep in mind that we're focusing on only the most common expenses. However, we recently asked BiggerPockets members on the BiggerPockets Facebook page what other regular expenses they've encountered, and they listed dozens of items, such as annual city permits, pool maintenance, city inspections, pest control, propane, homeowner association fees, and even membership fees to a local fire department for fire protection. To determine what nonstandard expenses you can expect in your market, connect with some local landlords or property managers, and look over the expense reports supplied by the seller to see what they've paid for in the past.

Let's delve into each of the most common multifamily expenses listed above. This might be the most important section of the most important chapter in this book, so please read slowly and carefully to absorb this critical information. When you can accurately predict the expenses, you'll be much more likely to buy great deals that deliver incredible results—and avoid investing in a money pit.

Utilities

To determine your pure cash flow, we need to determine what utilities you are responsible for paying as the landlord. In some small multifamily properties the owner pays the majority of their tenants' utilities, while in others the tenants do. You'll need to find out the current state of utilities and figure out whether there are ways to adjust this in the future.

Start by looking at all the possible utilities for the property and asking the current owner (or the real estate agent) for copies of all recent utility bills. Typical examples of utilities include:

- **Water:** All residential homes have water access, and while this might cost next to nothing for those on a private well, most water is supplied by local municipalities, which charge based on usage. The more water consumed, the higher the water bill. Most multifamily properties have one water meter, usually located in the yard, by the street, or in an alley. From there, the pipes usually go throughout all the units, with no clear separation between units. In some cases, each unit's water supply lines are separated with meters (or have the ability to be separated). If you, the landlord, are physically and legally able to separate the meters and thereby shift the water charges to the tenants, we recommend it. You may be able to eliminate the entire cost of water to your property, increasing and stabilizing your cash flow.

- **Sewer:** In most areas sewer charges are typically bundled with the water bill and not a separate item. However, your local municipality may be different, or your property may be on a septic system. Septic systems are large containers held underground that need to be pumped out by a septic pumping company when they get filled, usually every few years.

    If your property has a septic tank, once a year be sure to set aside around one-twentieth of the cost of replacing one as part of your capital expenditures (CapEx) reserve, because eventually they do need to be replaced, which can cost tens of thousands of dollars. Also set aside several hundred dollars per year for the cost of pumping out the tank.

- **Electricity:** In most cases, the electricity supplied to a multifamily property is already separately metered to each unit, and tenants pay their own electricity bill. However, this is not always the case, especially with older homes that have been converted into small multifamily properties. Check to make sure each unit has its own electric meter. If not, talk with the agent, owner, or utility company to find out what the average cost of electricity has been for the landlord over the past several years. It is possible to install new meters, but the cost can be tens of thousands of dollars, and the local zoning/building departments would have to approve, which complicates things.

- **Heat:** Unless you live in an area that never gets cold, most multifamily properties have a source of heat. Heating sources differ greatly by location, but the most typical are natural gas, propane, heating oil (rare), or some kind of electric heat such as baseboard or a heat pump. Find out how the property is currently heated and who pays for heat, and factor this into your analysis.

- **Garbage/Recycling:** Garbage is typically the responsibility of the landlord in multifamily properties, but in some cases this expense can be shifted to the tenants. This is most common on small multifamily properties where several individual houses sit on one lot and there is room for several garbage bins, so each house can have its own. Additionally, keep in mind that some municipalities include the cost of garbage disposal with the property taxes, so it is essentially free. But even if your area does this, be sure to double-check that this "free" garbage disposal includes multifamily properties; often it does not.

- **Other Systems:** In addition to the utilities listed above, you may also find that some properties have other costs associated with ownership, such as cable or satellite TV, internet access, telephone systems, or security systems. Although these are rare, you should definitely check for them. If you find any of these expenses, you can often eliminate them after taking ownership to increase cash flow.

Snow Removal/Landscaping/Other Contract Services

At most multifamily properties that experience harsh winters, the landlord is responsible for the removal of snow on common walkways, driveways, and parking lots. In addition, the landlord will likely be responsible for expenses to maintain any grass or landscaping. These items will differ greatly based on the layout and location of the property but must be accounted for.

Check with the agent or current owner to see how they currently handle these expenses and what they typically pay. If you're running the numbers on a monthly basis, as we are doing here, you'll want to average the annual cost across twelve months. For example, you may find that the current owner pays around $1,200 per year for snow removal and $800 per year for landscaping. Combined, that's $2,000 per year. We will divide that by twelve to get $167 per month.

Property Taxes

Property taxes are essential to local governments, as they're typically used to fund schools, streets, public safety (police/fire), sanitation, and common spaces, such as public parks. As a landlord, property taxes will be your responsibility, and if you don't pay them, the county can seize your property and sell it to make sure they get paid.

Property tax rates differ wildly depending on location, just as home prices do. For example, in Hawaii, property taxes average 0.27 percent of a property's value, whereas in New York, property taxes average 1.68

percent of a property's value.[9] The rate can also vary by county, so it's important to look at the actual tax amount for the specific property you are analyzing.

Thankfully, the aforementioned information is available online on your local tax assessor's website, and you can typically find the current and past property tax amount in minutes with a quick Google search. Simply type in the applicable county and state and the phrase "tax assessor" and you'll find their page. Then, dig around until you find the property records search (often called the parcel search), which will give you the current and previous years' annual property tax amounts.

Although you typically pay these taxes twice a year, and the assessor will likely list the value as an annual amount, we want to determine the monthly cost of those taxes, so we'll look at the total annual charge and divide by twelve. But we're not quite done yet. Knowing the current tax situation is usually fine for a quick-and-dirty analysis, but bear in mind that property taxes do go up over time. And in some locations, they can increase suddenly when a property is purchased. After all, property taxes are based on property values, so if the assessor believes your property is worth significantly more than what they had previously thought, those taxes could increase, sometimes dramatically.

For example, you might buy a duplex where taxes are $2,000 per year, or $167 a month, but as soon as you buy the property, the assessor uses the new, higher amount you paid (which was much higher than what the previous owner paid years ago) and your taxes are suddenly $4,000 per year, or $333 per month. That's a pretty large difference and could turn a good deal into a bad one. Not all counties reassess the value when a property is sold; many reassess the value every few years.

The best way to determine how taxes are computed and when properties are reassessed is simply to go the local assessor's office and ask. A fifteen-minute conversation will help you determine the specifics in your area and make sure you accurately account for future property tax increases. The point is this: Don't analyze for what the previous owner paid—analyze for what *you* will need to pay. Over time, as you analyze more and more deals in your market, you'll be able to estimate property taxes in seconds. Don't panic if this feels overwhelming—it will become second nature.

---

9 "Property Tax Calculator," SmartAsset, https://smartasset.com/taxes/

Insurance

Some of the most common questions we get from individuals who are considering investing in real estate run along the lines of "What if the building burns down?" and "What if a tornado hits?" These fears are not unfounded—Brian and I both have owned properties that sustained severe fire damage. Thankfully, real estate investors are largely protected against losing money should something catastrophic happen: Insurance will step in and cover the losses. But insurance is not free, of course. Therefore, we want to calculate the insurance payment, at a monthly level, when analyzing a deal.

Before we talk about the cost of insurance, let's talk about the types of insurance. As a multifamily owner, you'll be purchasing rental property insurance, which is similar to a homeowner's policy that you would buy for your primary residence, but with a few key distinctions:

- Rental property insurance typically covers only the structure and landlord-owned items like major appliances, *not* the tenants' belongings. We always encourage tenants to obtain their own renter's insurance to protect their personal belongings.
- Rental property insurance often includes "loss of rent" coverage, which can help reimburse you for lost rent should damage to the property occur and the home is rendered unlivable.
- Rental property insurance includes extra liability protections, so if someone gets injured on your property and sues, insurance may cover your loss.

Keep in mind that rental property insurance does not typically include protection for floods (we're not talking about water leaks here). Floods do happen, most often in areas known as flood zones, which are defined by the U.S. government. If you purchase a property in a designated flood zone, your lender will require that you obtain flood insurance, a separate policy that can be at least as expensive as the rental property insurance. Therefore, it's important to know whether your prospective property is located in a flood zone, and if so, to get an estimate from an insurance broker on the cost of this extra insurance. You can check whether your property is located in a flood zone on FEMA's website, at www.msc.fema.gov.

How much will insurance cost you? Rates differ according to numerous factors, including location, property type, property age, and your personal history when it comes to insurance claims. While you might not be able to predict with 100 percent certainty how much your insurance will cost, you can get a close-enough estimate by talking with a local insurance agent. You won't need a formal quote until you're in the process of closing on a property, so simply call an agent or two in your market and get a feel for average rates in that area.

Mortgage Payment

A mortgage payment is made up of both the principal (which pays down the loan) and the interest (which is the lender's profit). We want to determine the exact monthly payment for your prospective property. Fortunately, there are plenty of mortgage calculators online, although we're partial to the one at www.biggerpockets.com/mortgage-calculator. To determine your payment, you need to know:

- **The Loan Amount:** This is the amount you'll be borrowing, not the purchase price. For example, if a property is $100,000 and you'll be putting down 20 percent, then the loan amount will be $80,000.
- **The Interest Rate:** Call a local lender to find out what the going rate is for your property type. Consider adding half a percent to that number; lenders love to get you in the door by promising low interest rates, but these often increase slightly after a lender has reviewed a deal.
- **The Term:** How long is the loan amortized (spread out) over? Typically, investors use thirty-year loans but other term lengths are possible.

Now we simply plug these three metrics in to a mortgage calculator and—bada-bing, bada-boom—we have your monthly payment.

Calculator Results

Total Monthly Payment:	$429.45
Monthly Principal + Interest (P&I)	$429.45
Monthly Taxes	—
Monthly Insurance	—

Loan Amount*	Loan Period (years)*	Interest Rate*
$ 80000	30	5 %

Vacancy

Let's say you own a nice fourplex. It's in good shape and your tenants enjoy living there. Each unit rents for $700 per month. You might believe that your income is $2,800, and in a perfect month, you might be right. But people move. A unit is considered vacant during the period of time it remains empty between a change in tenants. This is when you (or a contractor) will repair any damage done by the tenant, clean, update photos/advertising, and show the unit to prospective tenants.

While the unit is vacant, it generates no income. Of course, it's hopefully not going to sit empty forever. You'll get it re-rented as quickly as possible, but you've still lost some income from rent. Assuming you re-rent the unit within a month, for the month it was vacant, you will have received rent from three of the four units. That's a vacancy rate of 25 percent (and an occupancy rate of 75 percent). Once you rent that unit you'll be back up to 100 percent occupancy, until another tenant decides to move and the cycle starts over.

Let's say there are only six vacant months at the fourplex throughout a two-year period. That might not seem like a lot, and it isn't, but let's do some simple math:

$$2 \text{ years} = 24 \text{ months}$$

$$24 \text{ rental months} \times 4 \text{ units} = 96 \text{ rental months}$$

$$6 \text{ vacancies over } 96 \text{ rental months} = 6.25\% \text{ average vacancy rate}$$

In other words, during this two-year period, your fourplex was empty, not making any money, 6.25 percent of the time. By the way, according to the U.S. Census Bureau, the national average vacancy rate in properties of at least two units was 7.6 percent in 2019.[10]

You might *believe* that each month you are receiving a total of $2,800 per month from the fourplex, but when we apply a 6.25 percent vacancy rate, you're actually making $2,625 per month, on average. That's a difference of $175 per month in lost revenue, or more than $2,000 per year. Yet most real estate investors completely ignore this number! However, pure cash flow takes this average vacancy rate into account.

Property Management

Next, you'll need to adjust your cash flow to account for property management. Property managers are individuals or companies who do most of the day-to-day handling of the property once it is available for rent. This includes finding and screening tenants, signing leases, scheduling maintenance work, and keeping track of the accounting. This service is not free—and rightfully so.

Of course, it's perfectly acceptable to manage your own property, and in the beginning, most landlords do. However, we still advise that you add a line item to your expenses for property management. Even if you're doing it yourself, your time isn't free!

At some point, you'll want (or need) to transition to professional property management. (After all, you didn't get into the real estate game to manage properties forever, did you?) When you do make the transition, it would be a shame to discover that all your profits are going toward paying that property manager. That's why when calculating pure cash flow, we always assume a cost for property management. Then, if we want to pay ourselves for rendering that service, it's fine. But the investment should stand on its own without you needing to manage it. If not, you've bought

---

[10] "Housing Vacancies and Homeownership," Table 5, "Annual Rental Vacancy Rates by Structure: 1968 to Present," U.S. Census Bureau website, https://www.census.gov/housing/hvs/data/histtabs.html

more of a job than an investment!

Property management fees differ slightly based on location and property type and size, but for most small multifamily properties, the average cost is between 8 and 10 percent of the total rent. Assuming you found a property manager to handle your new triplex at 10 percent of gross rents collected and each unit rents for $800 per month, then:

$$\$800 \times 3 = \$2,400$$

$$.10 \times \$2,400 = \$240$$

You'd be paying about $240 per month for property management.

In addition to the monthly property management fee, property managers also typically charge a leasing fee when a new tenant moves in, which helps cover their cost of finding, screening, and placing a tenant. This fee is typically either half of one month's rent or one full month's rent, depending on the property manager. A rule of thumb for calculating the total cost of property management is to add 1 percent to the property management percentage we looked at a moment ago. This will give you a more accurate estimate of how much property management will cost you in the long run. In our example, the property manager charged 10 percent of gross rents collected for the triplex, so we're going to increase that amount to 11 percent and use that figure when calculating our pure cash flow, which brings the property management expense to $264.

Repairs

Holes will get punched into walls. Cabinet doors will fall off. Bottles of contact lens solution will accidentally get flushed down toilets. Repairs are a necessary part of a landlord's life and must be properly budgeted for when buying rental properties. Like vacancies, repairs occur irregularly. But you must include them in your calculations, because even if they don't happen each month, they do happen. The more rental units you own, the more regular those repairs will look on paper, as they tend to even out across your entire portfolio. When you own just a few units, you might go three months without a single maintenance call and then get hit with a leaky pipe that causes $2,000 in damage. Therefore, when we run the numbers on a multifamily property, we want to treat repairs the same way we treat vacancy: with an amount allocated for that expense each month, whether or not any repairs actually occur.

This begs the question: How much should you set aside for repairs? The amount depends on a number of factors that can increase or reduce what repairs will cost. In the past, most landlords relied on their gut or just blind guessing, when not ignoring this number altogether. However, we realized while writing this book that whenever landlords rely on their gut for this, they are actually (often subconsciously) running an algorithm in their head, giving certain factors more or less weight to try and determine a final number. We figured why not take this out of the landlord's gut (which is prone to errors, lapses in judgments, mistakes, and emotional influence) and create a mathematical algorithm to make a more informed decision.

We developed the Multifamily Repair Budget Algorithm, or MRBA, because we couldn't find another tool like it. In fact, looking back at our own real estate journey, we can both say that this tool would have made the difference between success and failure on many deals. The MRBA can be found in Appendix A, and to make this easier, we also built a free online tool, the Multifamily Repair Budget Algorithm Online Edition, to help you perform this calculation, which you can access at www. biggerpockets.com/mrba.

CapEx

A different type of expense closely related to repairs is that of capital expenditures, which we've mentioned a few times now. CapEx, also sometimes referred to as improvements, refers to replacements, installations, or construction of large systems on the property. In other words, CapEx is not simply fixing something that broke, but replacing the item altogether for long-term use. Replacing the roof on your property with a brand-new one falls under CapEx, as would installing a new water heater, laying new carpet in a unit, or repainting the entire exterior of your property. CapEx is different from repairs because you're generally making updates or adding something *new* to the property as opposed to fixing something previously installed. The line between repairs and CapEx can sometimes get blurry, but here are a few examples of when you'd apply one over the other:

- When a handyman fixes a burner on a stovetop, that's a repair. When you replace the entire stove, it's a capital expenditure.
- When a plumber fixes a leak with a short new section of pipe, that's

a repair. When you upgrade from cast-iron pipes to PEX pipes in an entire unit, that's CapEx.

- When a tenant punches a hole in the wall, patching the drywall is a repair. When they destroy the entire unit and it needs to be completely remodeled with new pretty much everything, the entire project would be considered CapEx.

Why CapEx Matters

Imagine going through all the hard work needed to save up for the down payment, find a real estate deal, close on it, manage it, and then have to do the taxes every year. It's a fair amount of work, but this is what we do as real estate investors. Now imagine this property produced $10,000 in cash flow during the first year. Not too bad, right? In the second year, it produced $10,000 again. You're on fire! Year three—you guessed it—$10,000. Killing it! Three years in and you've already made $30,000.

At the end of year three, you finally get around to installing a new roof on the property. After obtaining several bids, you hire a team to get the job done. Total cost for that roof? Thirty thousand dollars. Wait a second... that was all your profit for the first three years! Oh well, it happens. It was a one-time thing. In year four you make $10,000, and in year five you make another $10,000. But at the end of year five, you need to completely repaint the property, and—oh no—it's going to cost $20,000. Now you're five years in, and you still haven't made any money. Next year you'll need all-new carpet. The year after, all-new appliances. And the beat goes on.

The sad truth is that this story is not just a story—it's a way of life for millions of real estate investors who thought they were buying a property that would cash flow, but instead are continually losing money due to ongoing CapEx. Here's a list of the thirteen most common CapEx offenders, aka items that need to be regularly replaced in a property. Next to each, we'll also list the length of time these items generally last:

Roof	25–30 years
Water Heater	7–10 years
Appliances	7–10 years
Driveway/Parking Lot	50 years
HVAC (heat/AC)	20 years
Flooring	5–15 years
Plumbing	30 years
Windows	50 years
Paint	10 years
Cabinets/Counters	20 years
Structure (foundation/framing)	75 years
Components (doors, locks, lights, gutters, etc.)	15 years
Landscaping	10 years

Looking at the list above, you might be thinking, "Most of those will last a decade or longer, so why worry?" Because unless you are buying a brand-new property, many of these items are probably in the middle of their life span; some might even be at the end of it. For example, your cabinets might last twenty years, but were they installed twenty years ago? Your CapEx bill might be coming up now. This applies across all thirteen CapEx categories. Each year one or two or more of these items will probably reach the end of its useful life and need to be replaced.

CapEx will kill your cash flow if you don't plan for it. That's why we want to be sure we're setting aside money for those big CapEx expenses when calculating pure cash flow. Otherwise, you won't truly know whether you're going to make money on your investment.

As with repairs, the amount of money you set aside for CapEx is going to depend on numerous factors. (You knew we were going to say that, didn't you?) In fact, many of the *same* factors we looked at with repairs will also affect your CapEx amount. But this time, the more units in a property, the more those systems are shared, thus the less CapEx per unit you'll need.

It's time to introduce you to the Multifamily Capital Expenditure Budget Algorithm, or MCEBA, which you'll find in full detail in Appendix

B. We also built a free online tool, the Multifamily Capital Expenditure Budget Algorithm Online Edition, to help you perform this calculation, which you can find at www.biggerpockets.com/mceba.

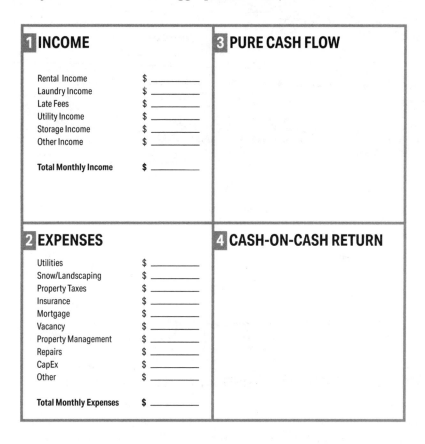

Square 3: Pure Cash Flow

Let's quickly revisit pure cash flow in relation to the Four-Square Method. As discussed earlier, pure cash flow is the profit received *after* paying all the bills and setting aside money for future repairs and CapEx. In reality, by accurately estimating the income (Box 1) and then accurately estimating the expenses (Box 2), we can easily determine the pure cash flow by taking the total monthly income (the number at the bottom of Box 1) and subtracting from it the total monthly expenses (the number at the bottom of Box 2) to determine our monthly pure cash flow.

1 INCOME

Rental Income	$ _____
Laundry Income	$ _____
Late Fees	$ _____
Utility Income	$ _____
Storage Income	$ _____
Other Income	$ _____
Total Monthly Income	$ _____

3 PURE CASH FLOW

Total Monthly Income − Total Expenses

$ _____ − $ _____

=

Monthly Pure Cash Flow

$ _____

Annual Pure Cash Flow (above × 12)

$ _____

2 EXPENSES

Utilities	$ _____
Snow/Landscaping	$ _____
Property Taxes	$ _____
Insurance	$ _____
Mortgage	$ _____
Vacancy	$ _____
Property Management	$ _____
Repairs	$ _____
CapEx	$ _____
Other	$ _____
Total Monthly Expenses	$ _____

4 CASH-ON-CASH RETURN

Square 4: Cash-on-Cash Return

We just spent a considerable amount of time discussing income, expenses, and cash flow—and for good reason. Cash flow is the lifeblood of financial freedom. With enough little oil wells pumping money out of the ground each and every month, you can quit your job, explore the world, spend more time with family and friends, and still pay all your bills without the stress of a job.

However, one aspect of cash flow we haven't discussed is the role of your down payment. Think about it: If you pay 100 percent cash for a property, you will have no mortgage payment, which is usually a rental property owner's biggest expense. On the other hand, if you put no money down on a deal, you'll have a much higher mortgage payment and thus lower cash flow until the mortgage is paid off.

Put another way, would you like $10,000 in pure cash flow per year? Sounds pretty great, right? What if that pure cash flow was only possible after you'd invested $1 million in a deal? Suddenly $10,000 doesn't seem like such a great number compared to the amount you invested. If you were able to get that $10,000 with an investment of only $2,000, that would a *great* return on your investment. Put in $2,000 and get five times that out in the first year? Sign me up!

You can see that pure cash flow paints only part of the picture when it comes to the profitability of a property. It's also important that we look at the return we are getting on our investment. Specifically, we will look at a metric known as cash-on-cash (CoC) return. This is the fourth and final box of the Four-Square Method.

CoC return is a simple ratio that tells us what percent of our investment we are receiving back in pure cash flow. The formula is:

Total Annual Pure Cash Flow ÷ Total Investment = CoC Return

You already know how to calculate pure cash flow, and the CoC return simply looks at that number on an annual basis. Let's focus, for a moment, on the "total investment." This number includes the down payment for the property, of course. But it also includes any other money paid to acquire the investment, such as closing costs and repairs.

1 INCOME

Rental Income	$ _____
Laundry Income	$ _____
Late Fees	$ _____
Utility Income	$ _____
Storage Income	$ _____
Other Income	$ _____
Total Monthly Income	$ _____

3 PURE CASH FLOW

Total Monthly Income – Total Expenses

$ _____ – $ _____

Monthly Pure Cash Flow

$ _____

Annual Pure Cash Flow (above × 12)

$ _____

2 EXPENSES

Utilities	$ _____
Snow/Landscaping	$ _____
Property Taxes	$ _____
Insurance	$ _____
Mortgage	$ _____
Vacancy	$ _____
Property Management	$ _____
Repairs	$ _____
CapEx	$ _____
Other	$ _____
Total Monthly Expenses	$ _____

4 CASH-ON-CASH RETURN

$$\frac{\text{Annual Pure Cash Flow}}{\text{Total Cash Invested}} \quad \frac{\$ \_\_\_\_}{\$ \_\_\_\_}$$

Cash-on-Cash Return   _____ %

For example, let's say you are purchasing a fourplex for $250,000. Your local bank will do the loan for 20 percent down, which would be $50,000. In addition, you need approximately $10,000 for closing costs and fees and another $20,000 for a much-needed paint job. In total, here's how much you've invested:

Down Payment:	$50,000
Closing Costs:	$10,000
Paint	$20,000
Total Investment:	**$80,000**

Now we simply look at the pure cash flow the property produces and plug that into our CoC return formula, giving us our result. Let's assume this fourplex generates $500 per month, or $6,000 per year, in pure cash flow. Therefore:

$$\$6,000 \div \$80,000 = 7.5\%$$

CoC return tells us whether the amount of cash flow we are receiving is good, bad, or somewhere in between. We can set a minimum threshold that makes a deal worth pursuing, giving us the ability to easily determine our MaPP. For example, if you are aiming for a 10 percent return, you will be able to find a target purchase price with any property that will give you that exact return.

Additionally, CoC return allows us to compare our investment to other investments, real estate or otherwise. For example, over the past fifty years, the S&P 500 has produced an average annual return of around 8.7 percent.[11] We like to outperform what we could get passively from the stock market. What CoC return is ideal? The answer is, it depends. What do *you* consider a good return? Like cash flow, this number will depend on numerous factors, both internal and external, but we'll try to give you some guidance so you can make that decision for yourself. Then we'll give you some benchmarks that we shoot for.

Fair warning: Some markets provide significantly less returns than others. Investors in appreciation-heavy markets along the coasts—like Seattle, Los Angeles, or New York City—are often willing to accept a lower percentage return on their investment in the short term due to strong competition and the belief that appreciation will help them in the long run. After all, if you knew your property was going to quadruple in value next year, how much would a 1 percent versus a 10 percent CoC return really matter? Of course, no market is going to appreciate that fast, but the point is the same: Some investors are willing to sacrifice CoC return now in exchange for appreciation later. If you're not in immediate need of cash flow, you're in a great financial position to make that wager and it could be a risk worth taking. But appreciation is not a given, and most people want to ensure at least some level of return on their investment for the work they're about to put into finding, buying, and managing a multifamily property.

In less-expensive and lower-growth markets, double-digit returns are

---

[11] "S&P 500 Historical Annual Returns," MacroTrends, https://www.macrotrends.net/2526/sp-500-historical-annual-returns

the norm. Appreciation may not lift the investment to fantastic heights, so profit is needed on an ongoing basis. The suggested CoC return goals we list below assume a fairly simple, straightforward purchase typical of small multifamily investments, meaning you put a 20 percent down payment on a property not needing a significant level of work. (Also, keep in mind that these suggested return percentages make sense for us in today's economy at the time of publication. However, times change and "normal" return expectations will as well, depending on what investors can get elsewhere.)

PROPERTY CLASS	CASH-ON-CASH RETURN GOAL
A	5%–7%
B	7%–9%
C	9%–12%
D	12%–20%

That said, there are exceptions to every rule. Sometimes you can find deals that provide great cash flow even in appreciation-friendly markets. Other times, you can work to improve the cash flow, and thus cash return, of a property by buying fixer-uppers or adding features that allow you to increase income or decrease expenses.

Finally, remember that manipulating CoC return is easy because it's based on how much money a buyer puts down. If you use the BRRRR strategy (which we'll explore in Chapter Seventeen), you could end up having almost no money left invested in a real estate deal. Then your CoC return could be triple digits or even infinite. (If you have no money at all in a real estate deal, every penny you make is essentially an "infinite" return.)

That's why it's important to rely on *both* of the metrics we've discussed in this chapter: pure cash flow and CoC return. By itself, each metric can be manipulated to make a property look good when it's not. But when you set a strict minimum purchase threshold for both pure cash flow *and* CoC return, you ensure that you're not simply "buying" cash flow with a large down payment. In fact, you are actually getting a substantial amount of return on your investment, bringing you closer to financial independence.

Setting Your Criteria and Next Steps

We're really proud that you've made it through the longest chapter in this book. But don't stop here! It's one thing to read a book on basketball, and another thing entirely to go out afterward and shoot a hundred free throws. Knowledge is not power—it's only the *potential* for power. Now your job is to go out and begin practicing your new superpower.

This chapter focused on defining profitability, in other words, what makes a deal a deal. At this point, we hope you have two metrics you can use for just that. What pure cash flow will you aim for, and what cash-on-cash return will you accept? These two profitability metrics will guide your decisions, ensuring you avoid emotional purchases and buy some home-run deals.

Learning and understanding pure cash flow and CoC return will lay the important foundation for mastering more advanced metrics like internal rate of return (IRR), which we cover in Volume II.

We highly recommend that you take some time to investigate the BiggerPockets Rental Property Calculator, which will help you perform the calculations in this chapter and more—all in less than five minutes per property. It is a fast, efficient, and accurate way to run the numbers and determine your maximum purchase price (MaPP) on a property. We promise you'll love it, and it was designed with small multifamily investors in mind! Check it out at www.biggerpockets.com/calc.

Yes, this chapter was a beast. We fully admit it, but as we mentioned earlier, it's probably the most important chapter in the book as well, because knowing how to analyze a multifamily deal is the key to success in multifamily investing!

At this point you might be saying to yourself, "Okay, now I know how to determine cash flow and cash-on-cash return—but what about the *value* of a property?"

All right, I know you weren't thinking that. Probably more like, "Thank goodness this behemoth of a chapter is over. I need a nap!"

But you *should* get excited about how to determine what a multifamily property is worth, because increasing a property's value is one of the essential components toward becoming a multifamily millionaire.

It's almost magical how fast you can build wealth when you combine the knowledge gained in this chapter on multifamily analysis with the phenomenal power of value-add investing—especially as you begin to scale your business. In the next chapter, we're going to explain exactly how that combination works through a process we call the Multifamily Millionaire Model. This is going to be fun!

KEY TAKEAWAYS

- Don't fall for the trap of "phantom" cash flow. Instead, your metric should be pure cash flow—cash flow that has been purified by truthfully acknowledging and accounting for *all* expenses, even future irregular ones. Don't go by your gut estimates. Rely on tried-and-true equations to help you make smart investments.
- The Four-Square Method is a four-step process designed to help you estimate the total income, total expenses, monthly pure cash flow, and cash-on-cash return you can expect from a multifamily property.
- Deal analysis is one of the most important skills an investor can have, but it must be learned and practiced.

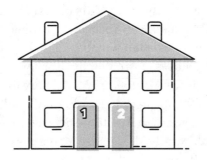

Chapter 9
THE MULTIFAMILY MILLIONAIRE MODEL

"The money you make is a symbol of the value you create."

—IDOWU KOYENIKAN

The previous chapter may have been the most *important* chapter of the book (and the longest!), but this one, we believe, is the most *fun*. That's because we're going to tie together the lessons you've learned so far and show you how to generate *big* wealth simply by increasing a property's income and lowering its expenses. You're about to discover the secret to building millions of dollars in wealth in single properties, a process we call the Multifamily Millionaire Model. You'll discover exactly how to determine the value of a midsize-to-large multifamily investment as well as how to manipulate that valuation to grow to unbelievable heights. If you've dreamed of having a multimillion-dollar net worth, this chapter is the playbook to make it happen.

The Vital Differences Between How Properties Are Valued

First, let me make one thing clear: This chapter and the model you're about to learn are almost entirely focused on properties with *more than four* units. We sincerely debated whether to include this chapter at all, being that this book focuses on smaller deals. However, we've decided to introduce the Multifamily Millionaire Model here for two good reasons:

1. As noted at the beginning of the book, small multifamily real estate includes properties with five, ten, and even twenty units. In other words, the Multifamily Millionaire Model does apply to those reading this book. If you ever plan to purchase a property with more than four units, this information is going to matter.

2. The Multifamily Millionaire Model is going to excite you, motivate you, and (if you're like us when we first discovered this concept), blow your mind. We couldn't help but include it here. We're *that excited* to share this with you.

First, let's establish how to determine the value of multifamily properties with up to four units and how to determine the value of those with five or more. It's a subtle difference, but a vital one.

When it comes to single-family houses, and even duplexes, triplexes, and fourplexes, a property's value is based on what other similar properties have recently sold for. If your neighbor's property just sold for $250,000, then it makes perfect sense that your property, which is almost identical to your neighbor's in this example, would be worth about the same. Maybe your house is a tad nicer, so it might be worth a bit more. Or maybe your neighbor's house has a pool, which now makes that house worth a little more. Determining the value of a property based on recently sold comparable properties (comps) is what residential appraisers do for a living. To establish how much your house is worth, they look at a few comps and then add or subtract some value based on what your home has or doesn't have compared to the comps. Makes sense, right?

Now let's go over why this *doesn't* work well for larger multifamily properties. Imagine for a moment you want to determine how much a small apartment building is worth. Maybe the property has fifteen total residential rental units: a mix of one-bedroom and two-bedroom apartments with a couple of studios thrown in for fun. Oh, and there's a few mini storage sheds that rent for $50 a month. In total, the property brings in $12,000 every month in rental income.

I can almost guarantee that you're not going to find another fifteen-unit property with the same mix of units that rent for the same amount in a nearby area. Commercial real estate is just too diverse, and so we have to determine its value differently. (As we explained in Chapter One, mortgages for multifamily properties with more than four units are handled by lenders' commercial loan departments, so we'll refer to those properties as commercial real estate.) How would someone determine what this property is worth if there are no comparable properties?

How about instead of comparing the property itself to other properties, we compared the *profit* generated by the property to that of other properties? After all, real estate investors are the only ones really buying these properties, and what they care about is profit, that is, getting a good return on their investment. Trying to compare your fifteen-unit property to my thirty-unit with totally different rental rates would just be silly, but comparing the profit generated by different investments? That's apples to apples.

For example, if your fifteen-unit property made you $30,000 in profit this year and my thirty-unit property also made $30,000 in profit this year, to an investor, these are pretty similar investments, correct? Both make the same amount of money, so you'd assume they'd be worth the same, right? Almost. You see, it's not quite enough just to compare the profit you made. Here's why.

If you paid $1 million cash for the property and have no mortgage payment but I put 25 percent down (let's say $250,000) and have a large mortgage payment, who's *really* making more profit? Or more accurately, which project is more profitable *based on the amount of money we've invested?* You're making $30,000 a year but you invested $1 million. I'm making $30,000 per year and I put in only $250,000. Clearly, my deal is pumping out way more profit per dollar invested, because although we're making the same cash flow in terms of dollar amount, my deal has a large monthly mortgage payment to consider and yours doesn't. If I didn't have that mortgage payment, I'd be making *way* more than $30,000 per year.

Let's clarify this before I drop the most life-changing truth about making millions through the Multifamily Millionaire Model. You really have to understand this point to understand everything that follows, which is why we're spending some time explaining this. It's not super complicated, but if this is your first time walking through this, it might take a few moments to internalize it and let it sink in. You might even have to go back and read the last few paragraphs again. But once you get this, your life will never be the same.

We know the following facts about our example:

1. Each of us is making $30,000 per year in cash flow on this deal.
2. You invested $1 million to get that $30,000.
3. I invested $250,000 to get the same amount of cash flow.

How can someone trying to determine the *value* of a property—what it's truly worth—compare my deal to your deal?

Simple: *We ignore the mortgage.* We leave it out.

Think about it: You had no mortgage, so your deal stays the same. You are making $30,000 in profit after all your bills have been paid. Let's assume my mortgage payment is $100,000 per year. Although I'm clearing $30,000, just like you, if we ignore my mortgage payment, I'm actually making $130,000 per year. I simply add back in the mortgage payment (principal and interest), which is $100,000 per year, to my $30,000 and I'm at $130,000.

This amount of money, $130,000 for me and $30,000 for you, is essentially the cash flow not including the mortgage payment. Another way of looking at this is how much money you have left to pay the mortgage with, after all the bills have been paid. This metric, this amount of money left to pay the mortgage, is known as your net operating income (NOI). NOI is *so* important when it comes to any kind of commercial real estate deal, that it's imperative you understand this. In its most basic definition, NOI is the profit you've received in a year, excluding your mortgage payment.

Written out as a formula, it looks like this:

$$NOI = Revenue - Operating\ Expenses$$

Here's where things start to get fun.

An Introduction to Cap Rates

An appraiser can now look at the amount of money you paid for your deal ($1 million) and say, "They paid $1 million for this property and it's making them $30,000 in net operating income. They are receiving a 3 percent return on investment."

Whoa! Wait a second. Where did they get that from?

If you invest $100 in anything, regardless of what it is, and you make $10 in profit during the first year, that's a 10 percent return on investment. That's all we're saying here. In mathy-math formula terms, it looks like this:

Total Profit ÷ Total Investment = Return on Investment

For the purposes of evaluating a commercial real estate deal, we want to see the *return* that different deals produce, on paper. We're going to slightly modify the above return on investment calculation to get us to the finish line. We're simply going to ask ourselves how much profit we made (not including the mortgage payment, to allow us to compare apples to apples) compared to how much we paid for the property. (Since we are ignoring the mortgage, the price we paid for the property *is* the total investment.)

Your property's profit, its NOI, is $30,000, right? And you paid $1 million for the property. The formula looks like this:

$$\$30,000 \div \$1,000,000 = 3\%$$

That 3 percent is known as the capitalization rate, or cap rate. You've probably heard this term before, and the last few sections of this book have been an attempt to explain the theory and reasoning behind what the cap rate is and why it matters. Cap rate is the rate of return an investor would buy a property at, not considering the mortgage payment.

The cap rate is a number that represents risk for an investor. If a property is extremely risky, you'd want a higher return on your investment. If you're going to toss your money into an investment that has very little chance of paying you back, you wouldn't choose one in which the best-case scenario is a 3 percent return. You'd probably just put your money into a savings account or the stock market instead. Therefore, the higher the risk, the higher the potential reward, and the higher the cap rate. Conversely, the lower the risk, the lower the cap rate. This is why super-nice properties in Class A neighborhoods usually sell for exceptionally low cap rates (currently below 3 percent in some markets) but a nasty fixer-upper in a Class D neighborhood might sell for a cap rate of 10 percent or more.

The official calculation for cap rate, therefore, is:

$$\text{NOI} \div \text{Property Value} = \text{Cap Rate}$$

Commit that to memory, pin it on your wall, and tattoo it to your forehead (backward, of course, so you can read it in the mirror). This is one of the most powerful formulas in all of real estate and will make you a millionaire many times over if you work it right. But more on that in a moment.

We've determined that you bought this property at a 3 percent cap rate. That's the number that you, a normal real estate investor, were willing to buy this property at.

Now let's talk about my property. My profit was also $30,000, but because we're ignoring the mortgage, thus adding it back into our numbers, my NOI, the profit I had left with which to pay the mortgage, was $130,000. Then what did I buy *my* hypothetical property at? For the sake of this example, let's say that I paid $3.7 million for my property.

Math quiz time! If my NOI was $130,000 and I bought the property for $3.7 million, at what cap rate did I buy the property?

Let's do it together, rounding the final number to three decimal places:

$$\$130,000 \div \$3,700,000 = 3.5\%$$

I was able to buy my property at a 3.5 percent cap rate. Here's the big deal, the thesis we've been building toward:

To determine the value of a single-family house, you compare it to what other similar houses in similar condition in the same area have sold for. To determine the value of commercial real estate—which includes any multifamily property with more than four units—you compare it to what other properties of a similar asset type in similar condition with similar cap rates in the same area have sold for. Therefore, we can compare the fifteen-unit apartment with the thirty-unit apartment, even though the rents are totally different.

By just looking at the *data* of commercial real estate investments in a given area, you can determine what an area's average cap rate is for a given asset class. Of course, that's not typically your job, as a great commercial real estate broker or lender will have a much more thorough grasp on the data in a given market. You can confer with them and get a list of comps, then look at what cap rates those properties have sold for to determine what your property would sell for.

For example, let's say you do some research by talking with a local commercial real estate broker and they send you some data on recent sales of apartment complexes in your area. Here's what you see:

501 L Street	21-unit apartment complex	4.5% cap rate
2912 First Street	40-unit apartment complex	4.9% cap rate
98490 County Road I	64-unit apartment complex	4.2% cap rate
832 Hill Road	33-unit apartment complex	4.3% cap rate
4999 Beaker Avenue	12-unit apartment complex	5.9% cap rate
12 Hometown Avenue	99-unit apartment complex	3.3% cap rate

You can definitely see a trend here. Most of these deals have sold at around a 4.5 percent cap rate. But you also notice a few outliers, properties that didn't quite fit the norm. If you recall from a moment ago, cap rate is a measure of risk. Cap rates, even within a given area, can be higher or lower than average based on the perceived risk of a given property. For example, maybe you asked the broker some questions and discovered that 4999 Beaker Avenue was located in a really crummy area of town and needed significant repairs. That would make that property much riskier to the average investor, which is why the cap rate was higher. You also researched 12 Hometown Avenue and found that it was a brand-new, top-of-the-line property in the best part of town. Because these property types attract the best tenants and require fewer repairs due to age, they are considered much less risky to investors, so the cap rate is much lower than average.

Hopefully at this point you have a solid grasp on how to determine the cap rate of a property. But keep this in mind: Although you should always dig in and verify any estimates you get from brokers, a great real estate broker should be able to advise you on an appropriate cap rate to use for your calculations in a given area. Commercial lenders and appraisers also tend to be very familiar with this metric, so don't be afraid to ask what the prevailing cap rate in an area is.

How does this cap rate make you millions? After all, you're not reading this so you can be the best commercial real estate appraiser around.

You want to *use* this information to create personal wealth. Let's start tying it all together.

Simple Math

Here's the formula for determining the cap rate we looked at earlier:

$$NOI \div Property\ Value = Cap\ Rate$$

This formula could also be written as:

$$NOI = Cap\ Rate \div Property\ Value$$

or

$$Property\ Value = NOI \div Cap\ Rate$$

All three formulas tell the same story, and as long as you know *two* of the variables, you can solve for the third. For example, let's say there is a property for sale—a fifteen-unit apartment complex—and you want to buy it. Based on data you've discussed with your broker, you know the average cap rate in a given area is 5 percent. You also know the NOI of that property is $40,000 because it appears in the marketing materials. Because we know two of the variables (cap rate and NOI) we can solve for the third, property value. Let's do that now.

$$NOI \div Cap\ Rate = Property\ Value$$

Therefore:

$$\$40,000 \div .05 = \$800,000$$

This property should be listed for sale at around $800,000, because this is probably the same methodology the seller is using to price their property. (I say "probably" because, let's be honest, sometimes people just list their property at whatever price they want. Or maybe the property needs a ton of fixing up, so it will be priced lower to reflect that.)

Now that you know how cap rates work when buying a property, I'm going to say something a little bit shocking: Buying a property based on a cap rate is not recommended. In fact, it's often just plain stupid. You can't look at a property and say, "Well, that's selling for a 5 percent cap rate, so I'm going to buy it," or "That one is a 10-cap. It must be a good deal!"

Wait... what? Didn't we just spend, like, forever to determine that number? I thought that was what we were building up to? Yes, it's an important number to understand. The reason it's not all that important is because you don't necessarily care about what the property's NOI *has been.* You care about what the NOI *will be* once you own it.

Let's revisit the previous example, where the prevailing cap rate was 5 percent and the property's current NOI (the amount of profit left over after all the bills, except the mortgage, have been paid) is $40,000. As we just said, that would likely lead the listing broker to price the property around $800,000. But what if you could improve the NOI? At the end of the day, NOI (as we saw earlier) is your total income minus your operating expenses. Let's make some assumptions as to what exactly makes up the NOI:

$$\text{Revenue} - \text{Operating Expenses} = \text{NOI}$$

Let's say your revenue was $100,000 and your operating expenses are $60,000 per year, leaving you with the following:

$$\$100,000 - \$60,000 = \$40,000$$

Let's say the income was far lower than you think it could be, because the current owner had not raised rent in ten years. After buying the property, you raise the rent by $50 per month per unit. There are fifteen units in this complex, so that's an additional $750 per month in extra income (because $50 × 15 = $750), which works out to an extra $9,000 per year in income.

Let's also assume that during this time, you were able to reduce the property's operating expenses, perhaps by installing LED lighting and renegotiating the cost of the garbage bill and property management, saving a total of $500 per month, or $6,000 per year, in expenses. Within no time, your revenue has gone from $100,000 to $109,000 and your operating expenses have dropped from $60,000 to $54,000. Using the same calculation for NOI, we can see:

$$\$109,000 - \$54,000 = \$55,000$$

By raising rent slightly and reducing expenses slightly, you've increased the NOI by $15,000 per year. Maybe you don't think that's impressive. I mean, what's $15,000 per year going to do for your life? Well, let's find out what happens when we plug your new $55,000 NOI into the original valuation formula:

$$\text{NOI} \div \text{Cap Rate} = \text{Property Value}$$

$$\$55,000 \div .05 = \$1,100,000$$

Wait just one minute—did you just raise the value of that apartment building by $300,000 by slightly increasing the rent and slightly decreasing the expenses?

Yes, you did. It's just math. It's the Multifamily Millionaire Model— and it's powerful.

The Multifamily Millionaire Model

As you can see, cap rate is a number that is generated when you buy a property, because you are going to pay a certain price and the property has a certain NOI. Math will tell us that you paid a certain cap rate, and the property was valued at that price usually because of the trend in cap rates in that area for that asset class. However, I'm far more interested in what the property can become in the future. This is why we don't usually ask investors what cap rate they paid for a property. The answer doesn't tell the whole picture.

Yes, cap rate is an important metric for establishing a midsize-to-large multifamily property's value. But it won't tell you whether a property is a good deal. Cap rate is simply a metric that showcases the ratio between current income and current value.

Hopefully at this point you're starting to see the connection between NOI, cap rate, and *your wealth*. Once you've bought a midsize-to-large multifamily property, you can raise its NOI by increasing income and decreasing expenses, which will raise the property's value. You really can make millions of dollars in real estate from one single deal if you can find ways to up that NOI!

Of course, that's not the only thing working for you. Ideally, when you buy a good multifamily investment, you're also getting consistent monthly cash flow, as well as slowly paying down the loan and getting huge tax write-offs. Win-win-win-win!

Let's look at one final example. The Ale Street Apartments are a fifteen-unit complex located in a decent suburb (a solid Class B– neighborhood where cap rates average 5 percent) of the city you live in. The property is listed for sale at $1.3 million. Currently, the average rent per unit is $900 per month, for a total gross monthly rent of $13,500, or $162,000 annually. The seller provides a list of income and expenses for the trailing twelve months (T-12), and this is what you see:

	Total Potential Income:	$162,000
	Vacancy (5%)	-$8,100
	Actual Income	$153,900
Expenses:	Advertising	$1,500
	Cleaning	$2,600
	Maintenance	$2,500
	Insurance	$7,500
	Legal	$3,100
	Other Professional Fees	$1,500
	Management Fees	$15,390
	Supplies	$2,100
	Property Taxes	$11,400
	Electricity	$2,230
	Water/Sewer	$22,000
	Garbage	$7,000
	Bank Charges	$250
	Licenses and Permits	$200
	Pest Control	$3,000
	Phone and Internet	$4,000
	Repairs	$6,200
	Total Operating Expenses:	$92,470

In other words, last year it cost $92,470 to operate this property and it brought in $153,900 in total gross rent. This does not include the mortgage payment, nor does it include capital expenditures, which (for several reasons that we'll explain in Volume II) are not included in the operating expenses.

With $153,900 in income and $92,470 in operating expenses, this puts our NOI at $61,430. Remember, our formula for determining the value of a commercial property is based on knowing the NOI and the going cap rate in an area (we are assuming 5 percent). Therefore:

$$NOI \div Cap\ Rate = Property\ Value$$

$$\$61,430.00 \div .05 = \$1,228,600$$

Notice that, based on a 5 percent cap rate, the property is worth only $1,228,600. Then why would you consider paying $1.3 million for this property— $70,000 over the value? *Because of the long-term play.* You know this property can be improved. You don't care as much about *today's* value, because today's value doesn't tell you about the property's possibilities. Some investors might think you were crazy for buying this deal for more than it was apparently worth. You're not worried because you didn't buy it for today: You bought it for the future. You even "overpaid" for this property, based on its current condition, because you wouldn't have gotten the deal any other way.

Additionally, you ran the numbers using the Four-Square Method, the strategy we covered in the last chapter, and you know you will still get a healthy cash flow right away—even if you paid slightly more than the property is worth today. Because you've been analyzing so many properties in this market, a few things stand out to you as opportunities to save money:

- You know the current owner could charge more for each unit, as there are many properties in worse shape in this neighborhood getting more than $1,000 per month.
- The legal fees are high because of frequent evictions, which is due to improper tenant screening. You know you can do better.
- Your local property manager can manage for 8 percent of the received rent, not the 10 percent the current owner is paying.
- There are three "storage closets" on the property near common

areas that are currently being used for miscellaneous junk storage by the owner. You believe you could clean these out and rent them for $50 per month each.

- Finally, you discover that the landlord has been supplying internet for the property for the past decade, even though no one else in the market offers this. You know tenants won't love having to pay for their own internet, but because tenants everywhere else in the area do, you can cut this expense out entirely with no long-term financial damage.

At the end of the analysis, you realize this is a great deal and you pull the trigger, buy the property, and get to work. You get the exterior painted, you raise the rent slowly over the first year, and your expenses drop across those areas you targeted for improvements.

Let's compare year one with year two, looking at your numbers compared to the previous owner's:

	YEAR 1 (PURCHASE YEAR)	YEAR 2
Total Potential Income	$162,000	$189,000
		($1,050 per unit average)
Vacancy	-$8,100	-$7,560
		(4 percent, due to better management)
Other Income	$0	$1,800
		(3 storage closets, rented)
Actual Income	$153,900	$183,240
Expenses:		
Advertising	$1,500	$300
Cleaning	$2,600	$2,600
Maintenance	$2,500	$2,500
Insurance	$7,500	$6,500
Legal	$3,100	$2,000

Other Professional Fees	$1,500	$1,000
Management Fees	$15,390	$14,659
Supplies	$2,100	$2,100
Property Taxes	$11,400	$12,400
Electricity	$2,200	$1,500
Water/Sewer	$22,000	$17,000
Garbage	$7,000	$6,000
Bank Charges	$250	$200
Licenses and Permits	$200	$200
Pest Control	$3,000	$2,500
Phone and Internet	$4,000	$0
Repairs	$6,200	$8,000
Total Operating Expenses	**$92,440**	**$79,459**

Take a look at the differences between year one and year two. The rent was raised by year two, and many of the expenses were decreased by *caring* and *trying* to find ways to decrease all expenses without negatively affecting the tenants' experience at the property. As a result, the total received income went from $153,900 to $183,240, while the cost to operate the property dropped from $92,440 down to $79,459. These are not uncommon situations when buying problem properties from burned-out landlords!

Of course, after subtracting the operating expenses from the income, we discover our new NOI:

$$\$183,240 - \$79,459 = \$103,781$$

Here's a quick quiz to see how well you've been paying attention: Is this $103,781 the amount of money you get to keep each year? Is it your profit? Nope! Remember, NOI does not include the mortgage payment (principal and interest), nor does it include CapEx. Don't get me wrong—the cash flow would have increased dramatically, but not to $103,781!

Let's get to the moment you've been waiting for. What is this property, with an NOI of $103,781, worth now? By using that same formula we've been talking about, and assuming the cap rate stays the same at 5 percent:

$$NOI \div Cap\ Rate = Property\ Value$$

$$\$103,781 \div .05 = \$2,075,620$$

Reminder: We paid $1,300,000 for this property. It's now worth more than $2 million. But, am I really saying that just by increasing the rent on this property by $50 and decreasing the expenses on a few key items, we've added almost a million dollars in value to the property?

Yes! That's the Multifamily Millionaire Model! You've just added *massive* value to this property. You have truly built immense wealth for yourself and your future generations from one deal—and it's only the beginning! Because over time the rents are going to rise even higher. And the loan is going to be paid down a little more each month. Plus, you get the cash flow each and every month, and you are likely paying almost no taxes on the income thanks to the amazing tax benefits offered by our government. Win-win-win-win-win. (That's a lot of wins!)

As a matter of fact, it gets better. With moderate rent raises over the next few years, this one simple example property could be conservatively worth $3.5 million five years from now. At that point, the mortgage would have been paid down below $1 million, which means when you sell, you could net more than $2 million in profit. Of course, you could pay taxes on this money, stick the remaining in mutual funds, and live on six figures of annual passive income while you sip margaritas on the beach in Mexico. But where's the fun in that?

What if you took this roughly $2 million in profit and and used it to buy a $7 million property, and then over the next five years turned that into a $12 million property, turning that initial $2 million into almost $7 million in profit? And then, could you turn that $7 million in net worth into $10 million, $20 million, $100 million? And in the meantime, you live a fabulous life with the incredible cash flow from these properties like you're winning a slot machine jackpot each and every month. The sky's the limit with the Multifamily Millionaire Model.

Buy property. Increase the income. Decrease expenses. Build wealth. Turn that wealth into more wealth. Raise money from passive investors. Buy more deals with less of your own cash. Scale. Profit. Have a blast.

Travel more. Watch your kids grow up. Take your spouse on luxurious vacations around the globe. Donate millions of dollars to charities that make the world a better place. Donate your time helping those who are less fortunate than you. Share the good news of financial freedom. That's what the future holds for the multifamily millionaire.

KEY TAKEAWAYS

- Residential properties are valued based on comps, what other similar properties have sold for. Commercial properties (which includes multifamily properties with more than four units) are valued based on comparing what profit they generate.
- The cap rate is a way of measuring the return an investor would receive in the first year from an investment, but does not include the mortgage payment or capital expenditures (CapEx).
- By increasing the income and/or reducing the expenses on a property, you will increase the net operating income (NOI) of that property, which can dramatically increase the value of a commercial property.

Chapter 10

THE STRATEGY FOR FINDING GREAT DEALS

*"If I cease searching, then, woe is me, I am lost.
That is how I look at it—keep going, keep going
come what may."*

—VINCENT VAN GOGH

Everything is a funnel. If you're a regular listener to *The BiggerPockets Podcast*, you've likely heard me utter these words more than once. That's because this simple sentence is the fundamental truth that guides the attainment of nearly everything great in life. Spouses. Kids. Jobs. Real estate deals. The secret to achieving any of these things lies in learning how to properly use the funnel. By the "funnel" I mean the process of elimination, whereby many options are available at the top and they get narrowed down so that only a few (or one) come out the other side. For example:

- You may know a hundred available people in your social circle; you may have dated ten of them; you might get serious with two or three and end up marrying one of them.
- There may be 1,000 available jobs in your city; you hear about a hundred of them, you are qualified for thirty of them, you apply for ten of those, and you get one job offer.

Funnels have existed throughout history, in every industry, nation, and situation. (That line sounded like a rap from *Hamilton*!) Even if you don't recognize it, if there is success to be had, there is a funnel that can lead you there. Funnels are exciting because they demonstrate the simple truth that success in anything is not an accident. It's a process. It's a filter. It's a situation that can be controlled. Want to increase your odds of getting married? Define the funnel and work at improving your success at each level by meeting and dating more people. Want to find a new job? Improve your résumé, submit more applications, and do mock interviews. By turning what many consider to be a question of luck into concrete goals that can be measured, refined, and tracked, you turn that luck into a *plan*.

Real estate investing might be the clearest example of this principle in action. Finding great deals is not a question of luck. It's not a mystery. It's not about a good or a bad market. It's about the funnel.

Just this morning, I had two separate conversations with real estate investors. The first investor said, "I have so many deals coming at me right now. I've bought more in two months than in the last two years combined." The second told me, "I look and I look and I look, and I just can't find anything. There are no deals to be had right now."

How can this be? The difference is that the former investor understood the power of funnels, while the latter was relying on luck. The struggling investor was looking around, casually, for a deal. The successful investor was outlining his strategy in exactly the way we're going to show you—by using the LAPS funnel.

The LAPS Funnel

I've talked about the LAPS funnel in previous books, but it's such an important tool for multifamily real estate investing that there was no way I could leave it out of this book. LAPS is an acronym that explains the funnel for finding real estate deals. It looks like this:

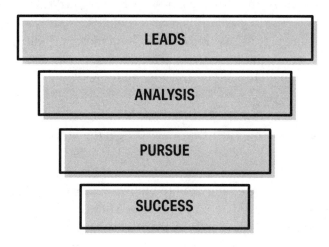

Let's dive a little deeper into each level.

Leads

Leads are properties you can potentially buy. There are several ways to get leads, which we'll focus on in the next chapter. But no matter how you find leads, you have to get in touch with potential sellers (or their agent). You'll never find Mr. or Mrs. Right if you never go on any dates. You have to have options. The same is true for real estate—you must have "deal flow" coming into your funnel!

Analysis

When the phone starts ringing and the inbox begins to fill up with people wanting to sell their properties, most of those leads will be terrible. That's just how the top of the funnel works. No matter how you got the lead or what type of real estate you plan to acquire, most of them will never make you money. The good news is that you can run the numbers on a property to find out what price would make it a good deal. In Chapter Eight we talked all about deal analysis and how you can determine how much you can pay for a property to still consider it a good deal. And once you know what that maximum purchase price (MaPP) is, it's time to...

Pursue

You'll never get the date with that perfect person if you don't ask them out, and you'll never land a great deal if you don't go after it. In real estate, this is usually referred to as making an offer, but I like to use the word "pursue" because sometimes an official offer (for which you sign a purchase and sale agreement) is overkill and a simple phone conversation will do the trick to get a yes, no, or maybe. We'll talk more about strategy and even explore ways you can improve the odds your offer will get accepted later, but for now, remember that you can't get the deal if you don't try.

Success

I get rejected often when it comes to buying real estate. Whether it's a single-family home, a small multifamily, or a multimillion-dollar mobile home park, rejection is part of the game. It's like high school prom all over again. On average, I get about one in ten offers accepted (about my odds with high school prom too). However, while that might seem negative, it's actually one of the most powerful forces in the universe. Every no is just one step closer to a yes. If I'm getting 10 percent of my offers accepted, I know I just need to make more offers and I'll close more deals. It's as simple as that. If you follow the funnel and continually seek to improve every level in your deal pipeline, success is inevitable.

The Bottom Line

When someone complains to us that they cannot find any deals, we walk them through the same four-step funnel we just outlined. *How many offers did you make last week? How many deals did you analyze? How many leads came across your desk?* Rarely is the answer to these questions anything but zero. Even in the rare case where someone is getting leads, or analyzing numerous properties, or making offers, the LAPS funnel allows us to find the problem and correct it. Getting a lot of leads but analysis is showing your offer price is far too low? It's probably time for a new lead source. Making competitive offers but getting rejections? Maybe it's time to brush up on your offering process.

You see, the funnel is designed to showcase the strength of your deal pipeline and to expose any weaknesses. Beginning today, start tracking your LAPS funnel meticulously. You should be able to know, at any given moment, how many leads you are getting, how many properties you've analyzed, and how many offers you've made. Then get to work improving each level of the funnel. In time, you'll have the great problem of finding too many deals and you won't know what to do with all the success at your doorstep! But until that day, keep working your funnel.

Furthermore, set goals for what you need to achieve at each level. For example, at our company, Open Door Capital, we have targeted quarterly goals for the number of leads we get, the number of in-depth underwriting (a fancy word for analysis) we do, the number of offers we submit, and more. As a team, we meet weekly and report on how our numbers are looking compared to the overall quarterly goal. This way, we know each week whether we're ahead of schedule or trailing behind. And the truth is that *it works*. Progress happens through process, not luck. If you want to achieve success in anything, find the process that makes it happen, set goals that will help you carry out that process, track your progress carefully, and watch success unfold.

Now, this chapter is not all we have to say on finding great deals. This topic is so important that we wanted to introduce the strategy first, followed by a deep dive into the tactics you can use to get leads. Let's turn the page and begin with finding deals "on-market." Yes, it is still possible!

KEY TAKEAWAYS

- Finding real estate deals is all about the LAPS funnel: get Leads, Analyze them, Pursue them, and you will find Success.
- Track each level in the LAPS funnel. You should know exactly how many leads you are getting, how many properties you are analyzing, and how many offers you are making.
- Set goals and aim to beat them, meeting weekly with your team (or with yourself) to review your progress and hold yourself accountable to the process that will deliver success.

Chapter 11
FINDING SMALL MULTIFAMILY DEALS ON-MARKET

"For there is nothing lost, that may be found, if sought."

—EDMUND SPENSER, *THE FAERIE QUEENE*

Everyone has a nickname. Some have nicknames they'd rather never be known by, holdovers from a younger, less-intelligent version of themselves. It's one of the latter that I am about to share with you today. But you have to swear to never call me by this in public. Deal?

I met Wendy in third grade, and from the moment I laid eyes on her, I knew it was meant to be. She, on the other hand, had no idea who I was nor any interest in finding out. I think I said three words to her in third grade. But fourth grade—that would be the year I finally won her heart.

And then tragedy struck: We were placed in separate classrooms. I was devastated. My agony multiplied when I learned that not only was Wonderful Wendy placed across the school from me, but we would not even share the same recess each day. But I, never one to give up, discovered an opportunity: Wendy's classroom was located on the first floor and overlooked the playground. While the rest of my class ran around playing four square and dodgeball, I stood by myself, six inches from the window to Wendy's classroom. And stared.

Day after day, I would find myself at Wendy's window as her teacher taught her the basics of multiplication and division and how Christopher Columbus somehow "discovered" America even though there were already people living here. I thought I was stealthy, staring at her through that window. The kids in the classroom, of course, began to notice the peculiar child standing in the grass inches from the window, and thus my nickname was born: the Window Kid.

Fourth graders are weird. And I may have been the weirdest one. But there's something to be said for my willingness to gaze into that classroom, fully committed to what I wanted. And that's my hope for you as well—that after defining your CCC, as we did earlier, you are prepared to fully commit to finding the thing you truly want: an incredible deal.

When it comes time to search for that incredible small multifamily real estate deal, you have two options: You can search on-market or off-market. What's the difference, you ask? And what exactly is "the market?" The market is what we call the Multiple Listing Service, or MLS. Properties that are officially listed for sale on the MLS are placed there by real estate agents, and agents are able to search and sort the listings to get detailed information about properties in their area with their (paid) access to the MLS. In other words, the MLS is like the classroom where my not-meant-to-be love of my fourth-grade life resided. You can peer through the window, but you can't get inside the classroom and see the object of your affection close-up (unless you're an agent).

To clarify further, the MLS is not one list of properties—it's hundreds of lists. You see, back in the day before computers, TikTok, and chai lattes from Starbucks, real estate brokers actually kept physical paper lists of all the properties they were selling. They would then fax or otherwise share these lists among all the real estate agents in town. Therefore, different regions across the country developed different lists.

Over time these lists merged and split and merged and split again, and, of course, with the advent of the internet, they all moved online. But the concept of the regional list still exists. In fact, there are more than 600 different "lists" in the United States, and when we combine them all, we simply call the conglomeration the MLS. Just as in the past, agents join their local (regional) MLS, and the regional MLS licenses their data so they can show their clients all the properties for sale in a given area.

Getting into the Classroom

That might sound amazing, and it is. The data in the MLS is phenomenal and updated continually so you can see details, photos, and status updates on any of the "listed" properties in your area. However, sadly, the MLS is a lot like that classroom. If you're not a real estate agent, you're not getting in. But, hey, it's not all bad—you have a couple of options. Even though you can't enter the classroom, you can still lay your eyes on the prize in one of two ways.

First, make friends with someone in that classroom who can go in and out and tell you what's going on there. In other words, get a real estate agent. This is a no-brainer for real estate investors because in most cases, it's entirely free. Why? Because the seller of the property pays the commission to the agent.

But there's another way to get yourself into the room: Like I did, you can simply look in the window. The "windows" that look into the MLS classroom are known as portals. These portals are independent companies that have licensed the use of the MLS data so you, the consumer, can view all the properties for sale in a given area. These companies include Zillow, Realtor.com, Redfin, Trulia, and even BiggerPockets.com.

Keep in mind that different regional MLS groups have better or worse relationships with different portals. One region may not give Zillow any of their data while another region gives it all. You won't know what the best portal in your area is until you begin searching, so start digging in today. A portal is no substitute for a good agent, though. When buying a property, you'll still want a real estate agent to perform a variety of tasks for you, including:

- Provide you access to property details not accessible through a portal
- Give you insight on local market trends and growth patterns
- Supply you with comps, data on recently sold properties, and opinions on the current and future value of your investments

- Bring you "pocket listings" that have not been entered into the MLS yet
- Help you overcome fear and limited thinking
- Advise you on negotiation strategies and tactics
- Refer you to great lenders, contractors, home inspectors, and other professionals
- Fill out all the paperwork for making an offer
- Set you up with automatic emails for new listings
- Physically take you to tour properties
- Navigate the due diligence process
- And *so* much more

A good real estate agent basically holds your hand through the entire process and can save you (or make you) tens of thousands of dollars. On the other hand, a bad agent can drive you nuts while leading you toward bad deals and connecting you with the wrong industry professionals, stalling your progress for years. What makes a great agent for real estate investors, and how can you find one? We recommend seeking out agents who are "OnFire."

OnFire Agents

There are potentially hundreds of problems that lie between *wanting* to invest in real estate and *actually* investing in real estate. Enter the real estate agent, someone whose sole job is to get you from *wanting* to *actually* investing smoothly.

But not all agents are the same. In fact, you'll commonly hear that 20 percent of the more than 2 million real estate agents in the United States are responsible for 80 percent of the transactions. Around 85 percent of those who call themselves agents will quit within the first five years. Furthermore, the funnel gets even tighter when you are a real estate investor, someone with different needs from the average home buyer. Therefore, to help you distinguish a top agent from an average or below-average one, we're going to use a simple acronym that spells out the seven traits your agent should exhibit: OnFire.

Organized

Real estate transactions get complicated, especially when purchasing multifamily investment properties. An agent who is not extremely organized (or lacks an assistant to keep them organized) will forget appointments, fail to return calls, make mistakes, and lessen your ability to find great deals in many other ways. The sad fact is that many, if not most, agents are simply not well organized. They run their business as a hobby, not as a professional business. A great agent should have a reliable system in place to handle the entire transaction—from searching for deals to scheduling appointments to making offers, negotiating, and closing. Top agents stand out because they have systematized everything and leave little to chance.

Networked

One of the primary responsibilities of a real estate agent is to introduce you to other professionals who will help make sure your deal happens. Specifically, your agent should be able to connect you with great lenders, property managers, contractors, title companies, attorneys, inspectors, and more. They should also have a broad network of relationships with other agents that they can leverage to help you find the best deals—sometimes before the deals even get entered into the MLS.

Therefore, the second trait in the OnFire acronym is "networked," meaning the agent has lived and worked in an area long enough to know the best of the best. As David Greene, the author of *Long-Distance Real Estate Investing*, likes to say, "Rock stars party with other rock stars." In other words, if your agent is well networked in the local real estate industry, they will know the best vendors to connect you with.

Focused on You

A great agent is focused on delivering you a real estate investment that meets your CCC, not just something that makes them a commission or appeals to their desires. True, most agents don't make any money unless a deal closes, but an OnFire agent takes the time to understand your needs, your desires, and your intentions so that the closing will be a win-win for both of you. They listen more than they talk. They probe deeper, asking questions like, "You say you want a duplex, but would you be interested in a triplex or should we ignore them?" Because at the end of the day, they are fully focused on you.

Furthermore, an OnFire agent is literally focused on you by being *present* when they are physically with you. They are not talking with several other clients at the same time, glued to various text exchanges, or constantly looking at their watch because they scheduled another meeting while yours is still going on. They are engaged and demonstrate through their behavior that you are a priority. You have their full attention when they're with you.

Investment-Savvy

Follow any average real estate agent as they offer a tour of a property, and you'll likely hear comments like this: "You'll absolutely love this kitchen! Check out the beautiful travertine tile, the gorgeous bar sink, and the cutest little doggy door ever!" As an investor, you have needs, but a cute doggy door isn't one of them. Many agents are simply not accustomed to working with a real estate investor and don't know what it is you actually care about (which ties into the previous point about finding an agent who is focused on you). Most agents simply are not trained to understand the somewhat complex world of real estate *investing*. And most agents are not investors.

That doesn't mean your agent must own their own rental properties (though that wouldn't hurt). However, at a minimum, an OnFire agent should be familiar with the property and location concerns that matter to investors. Rather than opinions about the look of the property, investors crave information like: *This part of town tends to attract higher rents. This bonus room could easily become a fourth bedroom. I called ahead and found out that the water meters have already been separated on this duplex.* That is music to our ears!

Responsive

In the competitive world of the MLS, great deals go quickly. You must have an agent who is responsive to your needs. This means they return calls quickly, can answer questions via text, can be reached at the times you need to reach them, and can take you to see a property the same day it is listed, or at least the next. If a new property hits the market on a Tuesday and the agent's next availability is Saturday afternoon, you need to find a different agent. Great deals don't wait.

Some agents have begun to add "showing assistants" to their team. A showing assistant is someone who works for the agent and will meet you at the property to give you the tour. While it might turn you off to see a property without your agent, we oftentimes appreciate this setup because it means the agent is competent enough to have built a system for getting showings done efficiently. The only downside for new investors is that a less experienced showing agent might miss things about the property that a more experienced real estate agent would notice and point out during the showing.

Experienced

Finally, an OnFire agent is typically not a *new* real estate agent. We feel bad saying this, because there are many, many great individuals out there who are just beginning their career as a real estate agent and could do an excellent job for you. They aren't going to learn unless someone gives them a chance, but, to be frank, we'd rather let someone else give them that chance. We're not running an internship program here; we're creating wealth and financial independence through small multifamily real estate investments.

When buying investment properties, you really need an agent who is experienced with the process: someone with demonstrated mastery of the local market's dynamics, a solid understanding of the property type you're pursuing, and the ability to adeptly solve (or better yet, proactively *avoid*) the dozens of problems that can pop up between showing and closing. A new agent simply doesn't know what they don't know!

OnFire agents exist in every market. However, they are in the minority, and they don't always stand out. How do you find them?

The key is to understand that like many things in life, it's all about the funnel. The more leads you get into the top of your funnel, the greater the likelihood you'll find a great option at the bottom. If you know of only one agent (such as your sister's hairdresser's boyfriend), what are the odds *he'll* be a great agent? Slim. But if you have a list of twenty different real estate agents in your market, and you sift through and interview these, what are the chances you'll find an OnFire agent? Pretty good.

Therefore, the first step is to create your list of prospective agents. From there, you'll be able to begin interviewing them to find the ideal OnFire agent. Here are four ways to begin compiling your list:

1. **Referrals from Friends and Family:** Jump onto your Facebook feed. (Or do the old-school thing of actually *talking* with your local family and friends... like, on the phone.) Ask if they can recommend any agents in your town, especially ones they have personally worked with. Be on the lookout for people you trust *selling you hard*

on a particular agent. You see, almost anyone can identify an agent to help you out. You're looking for people who really *love* their agent. There's a big difference between "Sharon is an agent" and "OMG! You just *have* to talk to Jamal! He did *such* an amazing job finding us our last house! In fact, let me introduce you to him now!" See the difference? Go find Jamal.

2. **Check out the BiggerPockets Agent Directory:** BiggerPockets is the world's largest real estate investors' network, with millions of real estate investors congregating on the site each month. Therefore, if someone is fairly active on the BiggerPockets forums, it stands to reason they might be more investment-savvy than the average agent. Head to www.biggerpockets.com/findanagent to search a network of top quality agents in every state to talk to. You can even see how often they've posted on BiggerPockets as well as how many times their posts have been liked or reviewed. A high like-to-post ratio indicates they are providing value to others in the investment space.

3. **Cold-Call Brokerages:** Most large real estate brokerages have a person manning the phones at all times. Do a quick Google search and find some of the popular brokerages in your market. Call them up and simply ask, "Who are the top three real estate agents in your office in terms of purchase volume?"

4. **Monitor Active Listings:** Oftentimes a small handful of agents will account for a disproportionately large percentage of the rental properties coming to market. These agents are likely to be more investment-savvy, and their listing activity demonstrates hustle. A great way to assess these agents is to schedule a viewing for one of their listings. This will give you a chance to ask them questions that test their knowledge and determine whether they might be a good fit for you.

After getting agents in the top of your funnel, it's time to begin narrowing your search. Begin interviewing prospective agents using the Agent Interview Form[12] and look for an agent who not only passes the OnFire test, but is someone you think you'd get along with. You may be spending a lot of time with this agent over the coming months and years, so having a great relationship will be key.

---

[12] https://www.biggerpockets.com/agentinterviewform

A Word About You

Before beginning your search for the perfect (or almost perfect) agent, let's talk about *you*. We've just spent several pages on how to find an agent who is aligned with *your* goals, but what about your agent and *their* goals? (This is a two-way street, after all.) If you want to work with the best agents (or contractors or property managers), you yourself will need to be the best possible buyer or show them you're making all the effort you can to get to that level. Since agents don't get paid until you buy something, you need to be worth their time. They are investing in you too, after all. How do you show your agent you're worth the investment (especially as a first-time buyer)? Here are some ways:

- **Pick the right kind of agent:** This was already covered in the "Investment-Savvy" section above but bears repeating: Find someone who is already working with investors. You'll save everyone time and headaches by choosing the right person for the job.

- **Be responsive:** You want your agent to send you all the hottest deals the moment they hit the MLS, right? Well, *respond* to them! Did you like the location but not the layout? *Tell them!* Did you run an analysis and not quite hit your target returns? *Let them know!* A great agent will go above and beyond to find what you're looking for, but you need to help them by giving timely feedback and showing that this is as important to you as it is to them.

- **Give back:** This applies to agents as well as most professionals you'll end up working with. There's one simple question that will blow them away: "What can I do to help your business?" About 99 percent of the time this is by referring other potential clients to them. This might not seem like much, but it goes a long way toward showing you care about an agent and making sure they do well too.

Once you establish a solid relationship with an agent, don't expect them to spend forty hours per week with you. They probably have many other clients (as well as a personal life), so remember: Their job is to assist you, not to do all the work for you.

Four Tips for Finding Deals on the MLS

The biggest problem with the MLS is that it's just so darn accessible, especially today. When anyone can jump online and search Realtor.com or Redfin or one of the many other portals, great deals can be tough to find. However, there are still deals to be had on the MLS. In fact, in a recent BiggerPockets survey of real estate investors on the site, nearly 60 percent of those who purchased a property in the past six months found their deal on the MLS. The key is being savvy about *how* you use the MLS. In this section, we're going to lay out four techniques for finding and buying great deals directly from the MLS.

1. Set Up Automatic Alerts

With so many people searching the MLS, speed is the key to success. Our goal is to make an offer before anyone else even knows the property is for sale! The best way to do this? Get set up with automatic email alerts for properties that meet your CCC. Any real estate agent worth their salt can set you up with alerts based on criteria like number of units, property types, price range, and more. You can also set up automatic alerts on websites like Zillow and Redfin, though we've typically seen faster results directly from an agent's system.

2. Look for Properties with High Days on Market

Motivations change, and the price someone is willing to accept on their property decreases the longer that property sits on the market. Many times real estate investors are selling their multifamily properties because they just aren't very good at managing those properties. They deal with constant headaches, repairs, angry tenants, vacancies, trashed units, and the ever-present fear of losing more money. Therefore, one great way to land a home run on the MLS is by pursuing properties that have been listed for many, many months. In agent language, this is known as days on market, or DOM.

When searching for properties, you can specifically sort "oldest to newest" on most portals or with the help of your real estate agent. Put extra effort into pursuing deals that have been listed a long time, keeping in mind that they haven't sold for a reason: The asking price might be too high, or the property could have some inherent problem that will cost a lot to fix (such as a foundation or roofing issue) or can't be fixed (such as a bad neighborhood). But the good thing is that because these properties have been listed for a long time, fewer investors are likely to be interested in them, so you can be more aggressive in making a lower offer.

Never assume that the price a property is listed for is the price the seller is willing to take. You might make an offer that's $100,000 below what they are asking, and because the seller decided just the day before that they'd finally had enough, they could be newly motivated to take whatever they can get. If you let fear of rejection stop you from making that offer, you could miss out on some incredible opportunities!

3. Look at a *Lot* of Deals

The MLS is tough. As we mentioned moments ago, we typically lose out on 90 percent or more of the deals we pursue. Therefore, one of the most important strategies for landing deals on the MLS is to be persistent and consider a lot of properties, combing the MLS daily to find something that everyone else has missed. Of course, we're not telling you to spam out fifty offers a week at 50 percent of asking price (even though some investors use this very strategy). You can still be selective when pursuing deals and focus on the ones where there's at least a marginal chance that your offer will be accepted. Offering $200,000 on a fourplex listed last week at $500,000 is probably a waste of everyone's time (and sure to irritate your agent), but offering $400,000 on a $500,000 fourplex that's been on the market for sixty days is completely reasonable.

4. Look for Hidden Potential

"At least I don't have to be an insurance salesman," thought the slender University of Michigan quarterback when he was drafted into the NFL as the 199th draft pick. Many of the 198 other players who were chosen before him would never play a single game before being dropped by their team. This young quarterback was placed on the bench for the New England Patriots, not as a backup, but as a backup to the backup to the backup. During his entire first season, he completed just one pass, for six yards.

But then, in his second year, something began to change. When the starting quarterback got injured, this young man, thanks to his hard work, was given an opportunity to show his worth. By the end of that season, Tom Brady was wearing a Super Bowl ring. Over the course of the next eighteen years, Brady would lead the Patriots to nine Super Bowls (winning six of them), and many consider him to be greatest quarterback to ever play the sport.

All this from a man the owner of the Patriots once called "a skinny beanpole." Tom Brady is a prime example of hidden potential in sports, and he's not the only one. Many athletes have been late bloomers whose true potential wasn't evident from the get-go. The same is true for real estate deals. There is hidden potential out there—and your job is to find it.

Hidden potential is something about a property that doesn't immediately stand out to most buyers but can dramatically affect its value or rental rates. Ask yourself: Could this property actually be a Tom Brady in disguise? Hidden potential comes in many forms. The following are some of the most common ways to unlock a multifamily property's hidden potential:

1. **Rehab:** The most common examples of hidden potential are properties that sell at a discount because they need to be remodeled. Ugly properties simply don't rent for as much as nicer properties, so by improving the aesthetics of the units (inside and outside), you can dramatically increase the rent. I purchased a fourplex where rents were around $500 per month. After rehab, each unit rented for $750–$800. That's more than $1,000 in additional monthly revenue.

2. **Add Bedrooms:** Properties with more bedrooms typically rent for higher amounts. For example, consider a fourplex that consists of four one-bedroom units, each with a "bonus room." With a few thousand dollars of work, you could turn those bonus rooms into bedrooms and end up with a fourplex of two-bedroom apartments. If the average two-bedroom rents for $150 more than a one-bedroom, that's an extra $600 per month in income with few additional ongoing expenses. We like to look for properties that have basements or attics that can (legally) be converted into additional bedroom space.

3. **Add Units:** Sometimes you can add an extra unit or several units by reconfiguring the layout of a small multifamily property. For example, a large three-bedroom unit could potentially be turned into two separate units (a one-bedroom and a two-bedroom) to achieve higher rent overall. Or perhaps an attic, garage, or basement could be turned into a separate rental unit. Just be sure to obtain the necessary permits and abide by zoning laws before adding units to a property.

4. **Raise Rent:** Many landlords resist raising rent because they're fearful of losing their good tenants and being forced to deal with the hassle of turnover. Other landlords simply have not kept current with rental rates in their area and have no idea they could be charging more. As a result, you can often uncover hidden potential by understanding what market rents are and comparing them to what you find in the properties listed on the MLS.

For example, you might find an eight-unit property for sale on the MLS that at first glance doesn't seem to be a great deal. Upon further digging, you learn that each unit is rented for $1,300 per month, but you *know* that market rent is $1,600 minimum for that part of town. You purchase the property, raise rents over the first year, and soon are bringing in nearly $30,000 per year in additional income with no additional expenses— simply because you saw the hidden potential in the low rent.

5. **Shift Utility Responsibility:** Many landlords continue paying the water, sewer, gas, and sometimes even electricity bills just because that's how they've always done it. Or perhaps the property's current setup makes it impossible to have the tenant pay their own utilities. But, as we've discussed several times already, in some property types, you can shift the responsibility for paying the water bill to the tenant by simply submetering the water. While not every multifamily can accommodate this strategy, when you find a property that can, it presents an opportunity to increase your cash flow significantly.

6. **Change Strategy:** Is the property currently being operated at its *highest* and *best* use? In other words, is there another strategy you could employ to bring in additional revenue or increase the value of the property? For example, the property may be rented as a traditional rental for $1,000 per month but is located in an area where many people travel for business and vacations. Could you turn one or more of those units into short-term rentals, getting $250 *per night* in revenue and potentially doubling, tripling, or even increasing your income tenfold?

    Perhaps a property is currently being used as a college rental, but you discover that you could rent it out through the government's Section 8 program, getting guaranteed rent that's higher than the college kids are paying. Or vice versa—maybe it's currently a Section 8 rental but you can turn it into a rent-by-the-room college rental and increase income that way? Study your market and speak with a lot of local investors (as well as investors in other areas) so you can begin to identify these creative opportunities.

7. **Look for Listing Mistakes:** Many real estate agents list properties in a hurry and make mistakes. This is especially true when it comes to small multifamily real estate, as agents are largely unfamiliar with how multifamily works and how to properly enter the information.

Furthermore, the MLS is really designed for single-family houses, so it's hard to accurately enter information specific to multifamily properties. For example, the MLS typically specifies only "number of bedrooms." But does this mean the *total* number of bedrooms or the number of bedrooms *per unit*? It's anyone's guess!

Therefore, another way to find hidden potential is by digging deeper on any multifamily real estate deal listed on the MLS. Look for the possibility of mistakes with square footage, number of units, number of bedrooms, and so on. In fact, just today, I was searching Realtor.com for multifamily properties in Tulsa and stumbled upon a picture of what appeared to be a duplex. However, it was listed as having just two bedrooms and one bathroom in total. Upon further investigation, I discovered it actually had two bedrooms and one bathroom *per unit* and was in fact a triplex. Another time, I bought a five-unit property that was incorrectly listed as a four-unit. Learn to recognize these mistakes and you'll find hidden potential all over the MLS.

8. **Add Income Sources:** Finally, many properties have the potential to earn extra income, but the current owner has failed to do so. The two most common examples are adding coin-operated laundry machines and adding rentable storage space for current tenants or other residents in the neighborhood. You could also add vending machines, charge ongoing "pet rent" or pet fees, charge extra for a garage stall, and more.

There *are* hidden deals on the MLS, and the more you dig in and learn about the possibilities, the greater the chance you'll recognize these for the gems they truly are.

The MLS Is Not Dead

From time to time, we hear real estate investors lament that there are no deals on the MLS. But there is a big difference between none and few. Yes, the MLS is competitive, but it's full of people who honestly don't know what they are doing. You have more knowledge than most, just because you've made it halfway through this book.

In fact, for new real estate investors, we almost always recommend starting with the MLS, even if you can't hit a home run on every deal. Just get the momentum going by purchasing a few base-hit deals on the MLS and you'll be well on your way to becoming a multifamily millionaire.

Commercial Brokers and Marketplaces

The MLS has very few listings for properties with five units or more. That's because the MLS was designed to be used for residential properties, and as we've discussed before, units with more than four units are considered commercial properties. You might be wondering whether there's another MLS for these commercial properties. The short answer is no. You see, commercial real estate operates *very* differently from residential. Or, more accurately, the commercial world operates a lot like the residential world did *prior* to the coming together of all the MLSs to create today's MLS.

To sell a commercial property—even small and midsize multifamily properties—a broker will typically put together a detailed marketing pamphlet with information about the property and send that out to all their clients. Rather than listing it, they'll usually try to broker the deal themselves, potentially getting both sides of the listing commission. If that fails, they will often send the deal out to other brokers in their network, and finally, if a buyer still cannot be found, they will advertise the property for sale through an online marketplace like LoopNet or CREXi.

If you're looking for a small multifamily property that has more than four units, you will want to begin building relationships with the top commercial brokers in the area where you are hoping to invest. Keep in mind that commercial brokers are similar to residential real estate brokers in that a small percentage of the brokers do the majority of the business. Therefore, it's important to ask around to find out who the top players are for your particular niche. You can locate active commercial brokers in your area by searching Google or websites like LoopNet (at www.loopnet.com/commercial-real-estate-brokers), theBrokerList (at www.thebrokerlist.com), or even BiggerPockets.com. As usual, you'll probably get your best contacts by asking for referrals from other successful real estate investors and interviewing brokers to find someone who is OnFire.

When you find a commercial broker, it's vital that you be crystal clear about what it is you're looking for and that you present yourself professionally in all your interactions. Commercial brokers are very different from residential real estate agents, so be prepared to showcase your professionalism and ability to buy so that the broker knows you aren't just another tire-kicker.

Should You Get a Real Estate License?

You do not need a license to invest in real estate, especially if you're investing in single-family homes or small multifamily properties. As you buy larger and larger properties, you may find that not having your real estate license can actually be an advantage. This is because many listing agents and brokers would prefer to deal directly with investors so they don't have to split their commissions.

But could it help? After all, being a real estate agent can get you direct access to the MLS. While that's nice, as we said earlier, an OnFire real estate agent can provide you with a lot more value than that. They assist with negotiations, referrals, and headaches that will pop up mid-transaction and can be a great sounding board when fear, doubt, or uncertainty creeps in. In addition, earning and maintaining a real estate license can cost several thousand dollars a year and it only applies to individual states, so if you're investing long-distance, it won't come in handy.

KEY TAKEAWAYS

- The MLS, or Multiple Listing Service, is a compilation of all the residential (single-family and small multifamily) properties currently offered for sale by real estate agents in a given area. Only other real estate agents have direct access to the MLS, but investors can use portals, such as Redfin and Zillow, or a real estate agent to get limited information from the MLS.
- You need a great real estate agent, but great agents are hard to find. Search until you locate one who is OnFire—Organized, Networked, Focused on you, Investment-savvy, Responsive, and Experienced.
- To find great deals on the MLS, look for hidden potential, meaning something that doesn't immediately stand out to most buyers but can dramatically affect the value or rental rates of a property.

Chapter 12

FINDING SMALL MULTIFAMILY DEALS OFF-MARKET

"And above all, watch with glittering eyes the whole world around you because the greatest secrets are always hidden in the most unlikely places."

—ROALD DAHL

In the last chapter you learned how to find deals on-market, so it's time to start looking off-market. In other words, it's time to stop being the Window Kid. (You remember that anecdote, right? Wait, that's a silly question. How could you forget it?) It's time to start looking for that fourth-grade love of your life outside the classroom. Because some of the best options are not in the classroom at all—they are on the playground with you.

At any given time, there are approximately 5,700 small multifamily properties for sale on the MLS. However, there are more than 4 million small multifamily properties in the United States,[13] which means there are plenty of owners out there who may not be actively looking to sell but would entertain the thought if someone were to approach them—especially since many of them may be tired of the headache of maintaining their property.

Most small multifamily properties are owned by real estate investors, the bulk of them being mom-and-pop landlords (as opposed to large multifamily properties, which tend to be owned by large institutions). These owners are not always sophisticated or skilled investors, and many of them never intended to be landlords. Maybe they are burned out. Maybe they have tenants they are tired of dealing with. Perhaps they inherited the property, or perhaps they attended a weekend real estate guru bootcamp and got excited, but the honeymoon ended long ago.

Or maybe there are no headaches there at all. Nonetheless, the owner may have reached a point in their investor journey at which selling the property makes the most financial sense, even though they haven't made the conscious choice to sell yet. A few years back, I received an inquiry from another investor who contacted me through my property manager and wanted to know if I would sell my twenty-four-unit apartment complex. Honestly, the thought had not really occurred to me, but the more I mulled it over, the more I realized that I would love to take all my equity and reinvest it in some other types of real estate—and so I did. I sold it to the gentleman who'd called me—without ever listing the property for sale. Sure, maybe I could have sold it for more by selling on-market, but it was such a convenient and hassle-free way for me to shift my real estate strategy that getting top dollar didn't matter as much.

I took that money and bought a mobile home park and another apartment complex out of state, which led me to where I am today, with more than 2,000 rental units. That initial twenty-four-unit apartment complex may not have been a headache, but it was time for me to move on. The buyer got a great deal with some meat still left on the bone, I got to move on, and the entire transaction was *off-market*.

When a seller deliberately decides to sell a property, usually with an agent, that seller knows they can get a higher price by fixing up their

---

13 "United States Multi-family Homes," Reonomy, https://www.reonomy.com/properties/multi-family-home/us/1

property, increasing their rents, reducing their expenses, and buttoning up their management. But that's also what *you* want to do! You can increase your chances of swooping in to grab these properties by contacting owners directly. You might be able to reach them before they've taken the steps toward selling their property, while also saving them the hassle of doing any work.

Furthermore, buying a property off-market doesn't mean you're "stealing" a property from someone who has no idea what their property is worth. Many times, especially in competitive markets where a single MLS-listed deal gets a dozen or more offers, our goal is simply to get in before the competition. Because an off-market deal has no real estate agent (agents are typically involved only in on-market listings, so off-market deals are truly buyer to seller), the seller can potentially save tens of thousands of dollars in commissions by selling directly to you. Or, better yet, you can get a discount worth tens of thousands of dollars, while your seller ends up with the same amount of cash after closing as they would have by selling through an agent.

Finally, and this is super important, buying off-market doesn't guarantee you'll be getting a great deal. Yes, we are big fans of off-market small multifamily deals, but like single-family homeowners, many owners of small multifamily properties are proud of their work and have pie-in-the-sky opinions of what their property is worth. You must still do the math to make sure you will have the right numbers at the end of the day, as you learned how to do back in Chapter Eight.

While we want to explain the primary off-market strategies you can employ in your search for your next great small multifamily deal, we recommend that you not try to master all of them to start. Instead, focus on becoming an expert at one of the following six strategies. Then, once you've optimized that marketing channel, add additional channels as needed. In this case, it's better to be a master of one strategy than a hack of all trades!

Off-Market Strategy No. 1: Driving for Deals

Most multifamily properties are not hard to spot. With their multiple front doors and numerous cars in the driveway, multifamily properties tend to stand out. Next time you're driving around, take a few side streets and look for small multifamily properties. But don't just drive by—jot down some information, like the address, the approximate number of units, and the condition. Put that information into a simple CRM (customer relationship management) program, such as Pipedrive, Asana, or even just a well-organized spreadsheet, and begin to connect with these owners.

To get in touch, you could always knock on the door, but because these are multifamily properties, there's a good chance that the person who answers won't be the owner but rather a tenant, who may not give up their landlord's name or even know it. Instead, armed with addresses, go home and research the owners of all the properties you've identified.

You can look on the county tax assessor's website to see who owns the property as well as the mailing address where the tax bill gets sent, since these typically go to the owner and not the property. From there, you can either send a letter to the owner (direct mail) or attempt to find their phone number and reach out. There are several smartphone apps that can automate this process, such as Driving for Dollars and DealMachine, as well as many online resources for researching ownership information including phone numbers, alternate names, and lien details.

Off-Market Strategy No. 2: Direct-Mail Marketing

Talk with any high-volume real estate investor and they'll tell you they're using some type of direct-mail marketing in their pursuit of deals. Direct mail is one of the most scalable ways to get the phone ringing from prospective sellers and fill your funnel. Ideally, the more mailers you send, the more calls you get, which you can convert to deals. But we're getting ahead of ourselves, so let's go back to basics.

Direct mail is the art and science of sending a large volume of mail, usually postcards or letters, to potential sellers with the intention of having a small percentage of them call you with the desire to sell. The process can be boiled down to five steps.

1. Build Your List

Imagine going out to your mailbox, peering inside, and pulling out a large glossy postcard with a photo of a big, smiling dog. It says, "Get Your Pooch the Smile He Deserves!" with the phone number of a local veterinarian's office that specializes in teeth cleaning for pets. How you respond to that ad will depend entirely on your situation. If you have a dog with yellowing teeth, you might rejoice at your good fortune and call the number immediately. If you don't have a dog, you'd mutter something about junk mail and toss it immediately into the trash. You see, the response to this direct-mail piece is going to depend entirely upon *whom* it was sent to. If the veterinarian is sending it to a list of dog owners, success! Sending to people without dogs? Failure. That's the importance of building a strong list.

You'll need an actual list of names and addresses for individuals who may be in a position to take advantage of whatever you're offering. If you're looking to buy a property, you'll want to build a list of owners who may be in a good position to sell. Where do you get your list? While you can begin building one by driving for deals in your area, there is a much faster way: You can buy the list. Some of the most popular list brokers for real estate investors are ListSource (great for residential), Reonomy (great for larger commercial properties), and PropStream (great for both). Simply visit the website, define the criteria you wish to sort by, and then purchase the list. Of course, these websites change often, so rather than list step-by-step instructions here, we recommend that you visit www.biggerpockets.com/listbuilding for an up-to-date video on how we're currently building our own lists.

But this now begs the question: What kind of list should you buy? How do you decide which list is the right list? After all, you don't want to send doggy-dental postcards to the cat lady! Direct-mail marketing can get incredibly intricate, as you'll hear on many episodes of *The BiggerPockets Podcast*. You can buy or build very niche-level lists, and the right list can give an investor an edge over the competition. The most highly specific lists are necessary for single-family houses because few of their owners are ready to sell.

Thankfully, we're not focusing on buying single-family homes. Because most small multifamily real estate is owned by investors, nearly *any* multifamily owner can be a prime candidate for direct mail. Therefore, the simplest list you can mail to is "people who own multifamily real estate." If you want to drill down further, you could narrow down your list by targeting investors who meet any or all of these qualifications:

- Are behind on their mortgage by thirty or sixty days
- Bought their property more than ten years ago
- Live out of state (absentee owners)
- Have 50 percent or greater equity in their property
- Are past due on their property taxes

Of course, the narrower your list becomes, the fewer letters you'll be able to mail. Direct mail is a balancing act between sending enough letters to raise the odds in your favor and keeping your criteria precise enough to not waste money on individuals who will never call. At the beginning, aim for at least 500 owners on your list.

2. Choose Your Method

Next, you'll need to decide what type of direct mail you want to send. As with building your list, there are many options, but the most common are postcards and letters. Some investors swear by postcards because they're cheaper to buy, print, and mail. Others swear by letters because they tend to generate a higher response rate.

Some investors alternate, sending postcards some months and letters other months. I've even heard of some investors sending UPS packages, though you can imagine how quickly that would blow your budget. (But, hey, if it makes them a solid return, don't knock it!) There is no single right way; certain options just work better with different markets, messages, and asset types. You won't know until you test it out yourself.

3. Craft Your Message

Once you've decided on the type of direct mail you'll be sending, it's time to craft your message. Most investors recommend keeping it fairly simple, short, and to the point, but you may find that longer works better. Again, you won't know until you try. When crafting your message, keep in mind these four golden rules of copywriting:

1. **What's in It for Them (WIIFT)?** People are busy and selfish (no offense!) and want to know how something is going to help them. "We buy multifamily properties—fast!" is a clear WIIFT statement. Don't be clever, overly smart, or vague (e.g., "We specialize in solving prodigious problems!").

2. **People Skim; They Don't Read.** Everyone skims almost everything—especially junk mail—so keep it simple. Use short sentences, bold important words, and highlight the most important information. Someone glancing at the document should be able to get the gist of your offering or request in five seconds.

3. **Give Calls to Action.** You must give people a very clear, simple next step. Do you want them to call you? Make sure the phone number

is LARGE and say, "Call us!" Don't assume people will know what to do. Tell them directly.

4. **Sell the Hole.** Good marketers know that people don't buy a drill because they want a drill—they buy a drill because they need *a hole*. The drill is simply a means to an end. What "hole" are you selling? Speed? Easy closing? Peace of mind? No more nasty tenants to deal with? Brainstorm some simple language that, in as few words as possible, explains what you can offer. However, be sure to phrase it so you're selling the hole, not the drill.

Here's an example of a direct-mail letter I commonly use:

Hi [NAME],
My name is Brandon.
I'm an investor in [COUNTY OR CITY NAME] and I'm highly interested in buying your property at [ADDRESS].
If you are interested in selling, please call me at [PHONE NUMBER]. You'll reach either me or my assistant!
I look forward to chatting,
Brandon
www.YOUR WEBSITE NAME.com

P.S. I can buy it even if it's in BAD condition or if it has tenants in the house. I've dealt with it all—and I can pay cash and close quickly!

After deciding on your message, you will decide on the *look* of those words. The most common options are:

1. **Handwriting:** This is, of course, the most time-consuming, but many investors achieve higher open and response rates this way.
2. **Fake handwriting:** You can choose a font that looks a lot like handwriting, but it's tough to fool people when reading up close.
3. **Normal font:** Simply type the letter on a word processor in normal font.

Again, you can find investors who swear by each of these methods; there is no single right way.

4. Settle on a Vendor

Now you're at the stage to decide whether you want to print these yourself or hire someone to handle printing. Unless you have absolutely no money to get started or plan to send fewer than a hundred letters, we highly recommend outsourcing this, as your time is better spent on more valuable tasks. There are many companies that specialize in printing direct-mail pieces, including several who work exclusively with real estate investors. For an updated list of direct-mail companies, check out www.biggerpockets.com/directmailvendors.

5. Mail and Repeat

Finally, it's time to send your mail. However, your job is far from over, because it often takes multiple touches with a seller before they'll pick up the phone and call. Maybe they don't have the "headache" today, but three months from now they might be feeling it when they still haven't received rent from their tenant (because they are too nice to issue a late notice and enforce their lease). At that point they may remember your mailer and be ready to call you.

At the end of the day, you can test hundreds of direct-mail options, fonts, colors, postcards, and lists. But it's more important that you mail consistently rather than stressing over the color of paper you selected. Don't miss the forest for the trees. We recommend mailing your list every single month, changing up the message and the type each time. Mail consistently until (a) they call and tell you to take them off your list, (b) threaten to drive to your house and beat you, (c) you buy the property, or (d) the world ends. Unless one of those three events occurs, mail consistently. You never know when your direct-mail piece is going to land in their lap at just the right moment.

Off-Market Strategy No. 3: Networking with Landlords

As discussed earlier, landlords move through different stages of their business. At one point, they may have loved their small duplexes, but they've since decided either to move on to bigger investments or to scale back and maybe even retire. Therefore, connecting regularly with local landlords and inquiring about properties in their portfolio can be a great source for small multifamily leads.

Landlords are everywhere, but finding them can be tricky. Start by attending local real estate meetups, which you can find advertised on websites like www.meetup.com or at www.biggerpockets.com/events. By networking with those in attendance, you will quickly find out who the real players are and begin building relationships with those people. Don't be weird about it—just make conversation and get to know them. You don't have to ask whether they want to sell their properties in the first conversation.

However, don't stop at meetups. Talk to your friends and family and ask for introductions to *their* landlords. Offer to take those investors out to lunch or dinner, or simply ask if you can schedule a phone call for five minutes to ask some questions about the local market. Use social media to let people know what you're looking for. Consider starting a local private Facebook group or local paper newsletter designed to bring together landlords and address concerns and share advice. Even easier, you can find local investors in your city and connect with them directly on BiggerPockets.com.

These techniques, along with many more, can help you get in front of numerous landlords, and over time, these landlords may offer to sell you their property. Get to work on developing a strong network of local real estate investors. You may not get a deal right away, but as one of our favorite adages says, "Dig your well before you're thirsty." Start digging!

Off-Market Strategy No. 4: Working with Property Managers

Local property managers can be an excellent source for leads on small multifamily properties because they are intimately involved in every aspect of their clients' properties. No, you shouldn't ask property managers for the names, addresses, and phone numbers of their clients, but you can begin building relationships with those managers and let them know that you are aggressively buying small multifamily properties. Tell them that if they provide you with a lead, you'll keep the rental contract with them. You may even be able to offer them a referral fee on any deal they pass your way.

Think about it: Property managers know when owners are struggling. They probably know which properties need a complete overhaul and which owners are refusing to get it done. Those owners are prime candidates for selling, so the property manager might pass your message on to them and you could land a great deal.

Off-Market Strategy No. 5: Working with Local Wholesalers

Real estate wholesalers are individuals who do all the hard work needed to find off-market deals and then connect you with those deals—for a fee. A wholesaler will typically get a property under contract by signing a purchase and sale agreement with the seller. Then they add their fee to what they paid for the property, and you buy the property from them for the higher amount.

For example, a wholesaler might use direct-mail marketing to find a great deal on a triplex but have no interest, or perhaps financial ability, to purchase the triplex for themselves. They get it under contract for $280,000 and then approach you with the deal for $290,000. If you pay $290,000, the wholesaler and you will jump through the legal hoops to make sure the seller gets their $280,000, you pay the $290,000, and the wholesaler gets the difference, which in this example, would be $10,000.

Wholesale fees typically range from a few thousand to tens of thousands of dollars; the amount is largely based on how good the deal is. For example, if someone is willing to pay $100,000 for a property and a wholesaler has it under contract for $80,000, they could potentially earn a $20,000 fee. But if they got that same property for $95,000 instead, the fee might be more like $5,000. The better the deal a wholesaler finds, the more money they make on the fee.

If that concerns you, keep this in mind: A deal is a deal no matter how much someone else is making on it. If a deal makes sense to me at $100,000, I don't care if the wholesaler found it for $80,000, $40,000, or $95,000. It's still worth the same $100,000 to me! Investors often get bent out of shape about wholesaler fees, but the truth is, people get paid in direct proportion to the value they bring. If they bring more value, they get paid more.

How do you find a good wholesaler? It's tough. The problem with finding good wholesalers is the same as with trying to find a great real estate agent. There are a million of them out there, but very few good ones. You see, there's a common myth in the real estate investing world that says wholesaling is a quick, easy way to make a lot of money. Perhaps you even got that impression by reading the last few paragraphs.

The truth, however, is far different. Being able to find incredibly good deals requires an exceptional level of knowledge, hustle, and organization, coupled with great marketing and negotiation skills. Plenty of individuals *claim* to be wholesalers but have never wholesaled a deal in their entire life. Many of these wannabes will give up and move on before ever closing their first deal, or use unscrupulous methods to pretend they have deals under contract (such as simply marketing someone else's wholesale deal and attempting to collect an even higher fee).

Great wholesalers *do* exist, though. Here are a few options for finding them:

- Search members in your area on BiggerPockets.com.
- Attend local real estate meetups.
- Call the phone number on any "bandit signs" you see around your neighborhood. (Bandit signs are those ugly, often yellow or white, corrugated cardboard signs that usually have a simple phrase like "We Buy Nasty Houses" with a phone number. They are often found on telephone poles and street corners. The individuals who use bandit signs are often wholesalers.)
- Look for "We buy property"–type posts on Craigslist.

Next, interview those wholesalers to find out whether they are legit or just wannabes. Of course, there's nothing wrong with working with a new wholesaler, especially since you aren't tied to working with only one (as you would normally be with a real estate agent). You just want to avoid the time-wasting and ethically compromised wholesalers. Start building a relationship with the best wholesaler you find. Since wholesalers deal almost exclusively with single-family houses, you can position yourself as the investor who is willing to look at the larger leads that come their way. Show the wholesaler you are a legitimate buyer and someone who can close. That way you'll find a great win-win relationship that can be profitable for both parties for years to come.

If you can't find a great wholesaler in your market, consider creating your own. After reading this chapter, you should have a fairly concrete understanding of how to find off-market deals. The problem, however, is that *doing* is very different from *knowing*. So rather than relying on your own willpower to go out and drive for deals, send direct mail, or implement any other strategy, you could partner with or hire someone else to do that for you. Perhaps you pay them a salary, or maybe you pay them a commission after they successfully bring you a deal. If you have the knowledge and can offer simple directions, there is a never-ending supply of eager, excited real estate up-and-comers who would love to hustle for you.

Off-Market Strategy No. 6: Online Marketplaces

Finally, there are a number of online sources for off-market deals for commercial-sized multifamily properties. While there is no one website that lists *all* commercial real estate deals out there, let's talk through a few online destinations that list *some* of these deals.

LoopNet

The closest thing the commercial world has to the MLS is LoopNet, a massive listing directory with more than 800,000 listings at any given time. As mentioned earlier, these listings typically wind up on LoopNet because a broker has failed to put together a deal with their own clients and decides to open the buyer pool to a more public audience. This is not to say that LoopNet has no good deals, but the cream of the crop have likely been picked over before landing there, which further reinforces the need for you to build relationships with brokers if you're attempting to buy commercial-sized multifamily properties.

Once you've registered for a free account on LoopNet, you'll gain access to the listing information on many properties, including detailed financials and analysis. This can be a fantastic resource for getting started with larger properties, since you can use those detailed financial documents to analyze commercial real estate deals and, who knows, you just might just find your next deal on the platform.

Also be sure to check out some of LoopNet's competitors, such as CREXi, Reonomy, and Catylist.

Facebook

Facebook is where the world—at least the older demographic—still congregates. Therefore, it can be a great source for off-market real estate deals.

- **Facebook Marketplace:** Back in the day, someone realized they could create a Facebook group, attract a lot of local individuals to that group, and use the group to buy and sell items in a sort-of online garage sale.

This idea caught fire and soon thousands of similar "swap-and-shop" groups sprang up. Facebook took notice of this powerful movement and made it part of the social network. Dubbed "Marketplace," this is where you can buy and sell anything from winter boots to old cars to used socks and more. But Marketplace can also be used to buy or sell real estate. Look for the "Home Sales" category and scroll through the properties. Many of these listings may be from real estate agents, but many others will be "for sale by owner." Check this category daily, because you never know what will pop up.

- **Facebook Friends:** There's no harm in asking your Facebook friends for help in finding available small multifamily properties. Post about your goals on your Facebook feed and maybe one of your local friends will know of an off-market deal for you. This strategy also works with other social media platforms (maybe even TikTok!).
- **Facebook Ads:** For a more advanced strategy, you could create a simple website and drive traffic there using Facebook Ads. Using a service like LeadPropeller.com, Carrot.com, or Vestor.com, you can build a real estate lead generation (lead-gen) website in just a few clicks. Although Facebook doesn't (currently) allow you to specifically target owners of small multifamily properties in your area, you can advertise to a wider local audience and simply announce, "We Buy Duplexes, Triplexes, and Fourplexes!" You could even harness the power of tenants to find deals for you with a promotion that says, "Connect us with your landlord and if we buy the property, live for free for a year!"

Craigslist

You can buy and sell pretty much anything on Craigslist, the largest online classifieds site, including real estate. There are three strategies that work well for finding deals on Craigslist:

1. **Real Estate for Sale:** Owners who don't want to deal with the cost of using a real estate agent often list their small multifamily properties on Craigslist. As an investor, you should be monitoring Craigslist continuously for the occasional deals that pop up. That does not mean spending all day, every day on the site. But you can create customized alerts for certain keywords in this category, such as:
   - Duplex
   - Triplex (and tri-plex)

- Fourplex (and four-plex)
- Quad
- Casita
- Bonus unit
- Multifamily (and multi family and multi-family)
- Multigenerational (and multi-generational)
- Two kitchens
- Mother in law (and Mother-in-law)
- Suite

2. **Real Estate Wanted:** Rather than just waiting for a deal to show up, you can market yourself as a small multifamily buyer by posting in the "Real Estate Wanted" section of Craigslist.

3. **For Rent:** Finally, for the most time-intensive, rarely used tactic, you can regularly visit the "For Rent" section of Craigslist and look for ads for units within small multifamily properties. (You can usually tell it's a small multifamily from the pictures.) Then, simply contact the owner to introduce yourself and ask whether they'd be interested in entertaining an offer on their property. While many will say no, you need just one to say, "Let's talk!" Even if they do say no, always ask this powerful question: "Do you have any other properties you'd be interested in selling?" They just might have another property giving them a headache that they'd love to part with.

Don't Forget the LAPS Funnel

Just as with on-market deals, your success at locating off-market deals comes down to one thing—your persistence at using and perfecting your LAPS funnel: leads, analysis, pursue, success.

Do you have a consistent method for getting leads across your desk each and every day? Can this be automated or outsourced so leads come in without your direct involvement? Next, are you consistently analyzing these off-market opportunities, looking for hidden potential, and running the numbers to determine how much you can pay to help these owners? Then, are you regularly pursuing these deals via offers? Are you seeking ways to improve your offer to get a higher number of owners to say yes?

If so, you will land some incredible deals and reach multifamily millionaire status soon. If not, you know what to do. Now's the time to do it.

KEY TAKEAWAYS

- Many multifamily owners have "headache" properties that they would be willing to sell, even though they haven't decided to do so yet. When you connect with these individuals before they list their properties officially with an agent, you can land some terrific deals.
- Just because you find a property off-market doesn't necessarily mean it's a great deal. You'll need to do the math to find out whether it's the right property for you.
- Find deals by driving for deals, direct-mail marketing, networking with other owners, talking with local property managers, working with local wholesalers, and searching online marketplaces. The deals are there.

Chapter 13

WALKING A PROPERTY— WHAT TO LOOK FOR

"Nothing has such power to broaden the mind as the ability to investigate systematically and truly all that comes under thy observation in life."

—MARCUS AURELIUS

After a busy day of appointments and putting out fires, I was grateful for the chance to relax. I had just enjoyed dinner with a good friend, at which I'd told him about my day. One of those appointments had been to visit a multifamily property I was interested in buying. As the waiter dropped off our check, I was just wrapping up my assessment of the property and the neighborhood.

"Did you used to live there or something?" my friend asked. "It seems like you know a lot about the place."

"Actually, I was there for about an hour today and that was my first visit," I responded, adding, "other than a quick stop the other night."

He looked a little puzzled, so I explained that I always like to see a property and neighborhood at night to get a better sense of what's going on and how it feels after dark. The tenants are also more likely to be home in the evening, so it's the best time to make sure there's adequate parking. And you can sometimes get a sense for the quality of the tenants from the type and state of their vehicles.

"Huh, that's interesting. I never would've thought of that. But what about all that other stuff you told me about?" he asked.

"I just did a lot of digging and asked a lot of questions," I replied.

He looked skeptical, so I explained how I'd heard the property's "story" from the listing agent, carefully reviewed the seller's information, and done my own analysis, which in turn prompted more questions for the agent and seller. I did a lot of other homework ahead of time too: everything from wandering the neighborhood on Google Street View, to looking up the property sales records, to speaking to an investor who owned properties nearby.

The actual property visit had yielded a wealth of additional insights. I showed up about twenty minutes early so I could poke around a bit without the broker. I parked a short distance away so I could get a closer look on foot at what was nearby. When I saw a police cruiser driving past, I waved it down, explained that I was a property investor, and asked the officer for his take on the neighborhood—what kinds of calls typically come in, whether he felt it was safe, and how things were trending. His perspective was super helpful.

It must have been my lucky night because I also caught a contractor just as he was departing the property I was there to see. I engaged him in a brief conversation as well, asking what he was working on, what kinds of work had been done there, and what he thought the property needed. By the time the broker arrived, I had also chatted up a nosy neighbor and felt I had an even better picture of what was going on.

As we toured the grounds, I took careful note of everything, snapping photos and shooting video clips of the landscaping, driveway, sidewalks, siding, porches, decks, roof, and gutters, taking close-ups of anything that looked questionable. I knew that if I got it under contract, there would be a much more thorough inspection, but I wanted to make sure I did the best job I could to value the property based on any work it would require and any value-add potential. While it's difficult to assess all that during a brief visit, having the videos and photos makes it easy to review things later or show them to someone with more expertise.

I repeated the process when I entered the building. I made a conscious effort not only to size up everything from a physical standpoint but also to categorize all my first impressions, including smells, temperature, lighting, and general feeling. I started with the front door, moving on to the lobby, the hallway, and the individual units. I explained to my friend that it's a challenge, but I pay as close attention as I can and try to pick up on as many details as possible. In the end, I felt I knew the property pretty well. Or at least well enough to run my financials and arrive at a price. "After all," I told him, "I'm a pretty observant guy."

As I reached for the restaurant check, I noticed it was already gone.

"Where did the check go?" I asked.

"Um, I already paid for it," he said. "I guess you're not as observant as you think!"

Let's hope you're more observant than I was at that dinner. At some point, you'll need to begin walking around small multifamily properties to size them up. While you can gain a lot of knowledge from the internet and through phone calls or emails, you will need to tour the property personally to observe firsthand the big and small picture of what's at stake. This chapter will give you a checklist of features to consider on your tour. The goal is not to tell you what you should or should not pursue in a property, but to present a list of things to be aware of as you walk through so you can make the best decision possible about whether to pursue a deal.

Neighborhood

You can improve almost any aspect of an investment property except the neighborhood. Without heavy investment and community involvement, you get what you get. Therefore, the first property characteristic to consider is the neighborhood. When you first pull up to the property, take a look around. How does it *feel*? Dangerous? Calm? Busy? Exciting? Does it feel family-friendly? Is it teeming with college students, mostly elderly residents, or a mix? Are the other properties mainly other small multifamily buildings, or is there a mix of single-family or other types of real estate? Does it look like improvement projects are under way? Does the neighborhood appear to be in decline? Consider visiting the neighborhood at different times of day. Sometimes things change after the sun goes down.

Parking

Unless you are planning to buy in a major urban center where the majority of tenants would never dream of owning a vehicle, most properties are going to require parking for tenants. Observe the parking situation. Are a lot of cars parked on the street? Does the property have a surface lot or a garage? Also note the condition of the parking lot or garage if the property has one. Is there enough parking for each tenant to have their own spot? Will you constantly have to monitor the parking lot for non-residents parking there, or is it fairly self-contained? Generally speaking, the more available parking you have for your tenants, the more your tenants will appreciate the property.

Curb Appeal and Landscaping

How does the property look from the front? From the side? From the back? Are the bushes trimmed or growing wild? Do the mulch beds look fresh, or are they faded and bare? When it comes time to fill a vacant unit, will potential tenants simply keep on driving or slow down to check out the updated building? If the exterior isn't looking so hot, you will definitely need to budget for immediate improvements to the property's curb appeal. As we've said before, nasty properties attract nasty tenants, so take an honest inventory of the condition of the exterior and decide what would need to be done.

Entrances and Common Areas

How does a tenant enter the property? Is there a shared common entrance and, if so, is this entrance locked, or does each tenant enter from their own individual door? Next, take a look at any and all shared spaces, such as hallways, courtyards, and laundry rooms. What's their current condition? What would they need to be above average? Common areas must be cleaned and maintained regularly, so be sure to budget and plan for this.

Layout

Take a good hard look at the layout of both the property itself and the individual units. Is there anything that makes it weird? For example, do you have to walk through the bathroom to get to the bedroom (or vice versa)?

While it isn't necessarily a deal breaker, an odd layout (often known as functional obsolescence) can turn off tenants and make a property harder to rent out.

Tenant Quality and Habits

If the property is currently rented to tenants, what does their *stuff* and the condition they keep it in tell you about them and their quality? Do you see old fast food on the coffee table and cigarette butts littered around the back door? "Kill the Landlord" protest signs in the closet? A 5,000-gallon fish tank in the living room on the second floor, just waiting to cause a property-wide flood? Take note, because these tenants might just become *your* tenants. Again, if you don't like what you see, that doesn't mean you shouldn't buy the property. You may simply need to pad your budget with some extra cash and have a solid plan for dealing with these tenants.

Water Submetering Capability

Water may be the most common natural resource on the planet, accounting for about 71 percent of the world's surface, but that doesn't mean it's free! Water bills vary dramatically by location and can easily run into the hundreds or even thousands of dollars for a multifamily property. While the landlord typically pays the water bill, it might be possible to charge each unit for its own consumption, which can add significant cash flow to the landlord's bottom line. The way to do this, if the property's plumbing configuration supports it, is through submetering. What this means is that the water supply lines (the copper, cast-iron, or plastic pipes that bring the cold and hot water into the property) are contained entirely within each unit, allowing for the placement of a measuring device on each unit, either from the street or from somewhere inside the property. When looking at the property, attempt to answer the following:

1. Does the layout of this property imply that each unit has, or easily could have, a completely separate water meter at the street? This would be most common in multifamily properties that have separate small houses on one lot, such as cottages. If you're touring the property with a real estate agent or with the owner, ask them. If you're by yourself, you might need to make some assumptions until you can verify.

2. If submetering at the street does not appear possible (it's usually not in multifamilies), ask yourself, "Would the layout of this property

allow for separation of water supply lines?" In a large, old monster house containing several units that at one point were part of the main house, it would be difficult to separate the water lines, as they are simply too interconnected. On the other hand, in a newer side-by-side duplex, it's entirely possible that the water lines are already separated, or could be.

If you can shift the responsibility for paying the water bill to the tenants, you can turn a mediocre deal into a good one, and a good deal into a grand slam. That's why it's so important to at least consider the possibility of water submetering when you look at a property. Perhaps you'll see that hidden potential when no one else does.

Electricity

Who's paying the electricity bill at the property—the landlord or the tenants? At most multifamily properties, tenants pays for their own electricity, since each unit has its own electrical service, completely separate from other units. However, some multifamily properties (especially older ones and monster houses) are still "master metered," which means that all the electricity flows through one electrical service and is on one bill with the local electric company. Obviously, it's best for the landlord when tenants pay for their own electricity, as you don't need to worry about your bill going up because they are running their AC on full blast all summer while keeping all their windows wide open because they like the breeze. But you need to know for sure.

Besides asking the owner or the agent, take a look for yourself: Does each unit have its own electrical panel? An electrical panel is a metal box, usually in the wall somewhere, that holds all the breakers for the different electrical lines in the house. Power comes into the panel as a single current direct from the power company and is then divided up through breakers. For example, 200 amps may be coming into the unit, with one breaker designated for the stove, another for the dishwasher, another for all the bedroom outlets on the first floor, and so on. If you see electrical panels, each unit has its own electric service.

Alternatively, note whether there are separate meters for each unit outside the property. Although the look may differ slightly in different areas, a meter is usually a metal box with a round glass or plastic dome built into the side. This meter is how the power usage is measured by the local electric company, and there should be a separate one for each unit on the exterior of the property.

In many multifamily properties you'll also find an extra meter and panel that is designated for the common areas. Even if tenants are paying for electricity used in their own units, they probably are not paying for lighting in common areas such as laundry rooms and hallways. Take note of this, and when analyzing your property, be sure to account for your electricity obligations.

Heat

The cost of heating a property can be expensive, so you need to investigate to determine *how* the property is being heated and *who* is paying the bill. This will dramatically affect your cash flow projections. Be sure to talk with the agent or the owner about the heating situation, and while touring the property, take a look at the current situation to see for yourself.

The methods for heating a property differ greatly by location and the age of the property. Here's a quick rundown of the most common methods for heating multifamily properties:

1. **Warm-Air Furnace:** A warm-air furnace is a large device that heats air and sends it throughout a property via metal ducting in the walls, above the ceiling, and below the floor. Furnaces can be heated by gas. (Natural gas is most common, but propane, kerosene, and other types of fuel are found in some areas.) Furnaces are popular for both single-family homes and multifamily properties, though due to the relative difficulty in separating the ducting for each individual unit, as well as the cost of installing a separate furnace for each unit, furnaces are not typically found in older multifamily properties.

2. **Boiler-Radiator System:** A boiler is a large device that heats water (using natural gas, propane, kerosene, or sometimes electricity) to high temperatures and then sends that water throughout the building to have the heat "radiated" into the rooms via metal radiators located in each room. Many older apartment buildings rely on large boiler-radiator systems to heat the entire property, and typically the landlord is responsible for paying for the boiler's operating costs (the cost of the fuel plus ongoing maintenance). If you are buying a property with a boiler, be sure to check its age and condition and factor the cost into your analysis.

3. **Electric Baseboard:** Many apartment units rely on built-in electric baseboards to provide heat. These long, thin, metal heating units typically sit below windows. Electricity heats the metal coils, which then radiate heat out into the room. In reality, baseboard heaters are not much different from a toaster or an electric hair dryer. They are popular in multifamily properties because:

   - They're inexpensive to buy (typically less than $100 each).
   - They're relatively easy to install, maintain, and repair.
   - They operate independently from one another, meaning you can heat via "zones" rather than having to heat the entire property.
   - They can last for decades (no moving parts to break down).
   - The tenant usually pays the electric bill for the baseboard heater's operation.

   For these reasons, particularly the last, electric baseboard heat is very common in apartments, especially in Class B, C, and D properties. However, there is a tradeoff: It is typically the most expensive heating method on an ongoing basis, due to the high cost of electricity. If your tenants are paying for their own electricity, this might not affect you as a landlord, but *they* will certainly be aware of the high cost. We've found that many tenants simply turn off heat in rooms they don't use often, which can lead to mold and mildew, as well as freezing pipes in colder regions. Furthermore, if a tenant has a choice between renting a property with baseboard heat versus another, lower-cost option, they will usually choose the latter.

4. **Electric Wall Fans:** Similar to baseboard heaters, electric wall heaters convert electricity to heat through coils and then use a small fan to blow the warm air into the room. If you've ever owned one of those small portable space heaters with a fan built into it, this is essentially the same thing, but installed into the wall and directly wired into the home. Like baseboard heating, this method can be expensive for whoever is paying the electric bill, but units are cheap to buy and fairly easy to install and maintain. On the plus side, an electric wall fan (the most common brand being Cadet, sold at all major big-box home improvement stores) can warm a room significantly faster than a baseboard heater.

5. **Heat Pump:** A heat pump is similar to a furnace, but rather than using fuel to warm the air, the heat pump actually connects to an outdoor

condenser and pulls heat from the outside air (even in colder temperatures) and transfers it indoors. In fact, a heat pump is really just a glorified air conditioner and uses the same technology, in reverse, to heat a room. (An air conditioner pulls cool air from outside, even in warmer temperatures, and transfers it inward.) The warm air is typically sent throughout the home via ducting, similar to that of a warm-air furnace. Heat pumps can be one of the lowest-cost methods for heating a property, but due to the high purchase and installation cost ($5,000–$20,000, depending on ducting needs), they are not quite as popular for multifamily properties. If your property does have a heat pump, be sure to check its age and determine who pays this bill.

6. **Ductless Heat Pump (Mini Splits):** One of the newest additions to the heating system space, at least in the United States, is the ductless heat pump, often referred to as a mini split system. This heating system uses the same technology as a traditional heat pump but, as the name suggests, does not rely on ducting to deliver the warm air throughout the home. Instead, each unit stands alone and heats (or cools) whatever room it is installed in. Heat pumps also tend to lose the ability to heat or cool in extreme temperatures, so they operate best and are most common in areas with more moderate climates. (Sorry, northern Minnesota!)

   Because these systems do not require special ductwork to install, they can be a good alternative for adding supplemental heat to a space or for heating properties where ducting would be impractical. On the downside, each unit (usually measuring around three feet long, one foot high, and one foot deep) is mounted to the wall in the room, which takes up extra space and might not be aesthetically pleasing, though ceiling-mounted units are available. If the property you're looking at has ductless heat pumps, check on the age of the units; life expectancy is similar to that of a traditional heat pump, about fifteen years.

Although these six heating sources are by far the most common in multifamily properties, you may occasionally encounter solar heating, geothermal heating, fireplaces, trolls in the attic, or some other obscure system. None of the alternative options above should be considered deal breakers, but it's important to identify the heating source so you can adequately plan for the cost of operating it, including ongoing maintenance, repairs, and replacement.

Water Heater

A water heater is typically a tall, cylindrical appliance that heats water (with either electricity or gas) and stores that warm water for use by residents. When you turn on the hot water faucet in the bathroom, hot water (which has been kept hot in the water heater) is sent to that faucet and warm water flows out. Some multifamily properties have one master hot water heater that heats all the water in the property, but in most multifamily properties, each unit has its own individual water heater.

Water heaters are one of the more expensive items to repair and replace in multifamily properties, as the life of a water heater is typically less than ten years and leaks (and the damage that can result from them) can be expensive. When touring a property, take note of the water heater situation.

- Does each unit have its own water heater, or is there one central heater?
- Is the heater placed in a shallow pan to prevent any leaking water from causing damage? To be honest, this is something most landlords skimp on when installing new heaters (but you should rectify this every time you replace a water heater).
- How old is the water heater unit? (The installation date is usually listed on the manufacturer's label.) If the tank is more than five years old, you'll probably have to replace it in the next few years, so budget accordingly.

Laundry

How do tenants get their clothes clean? Typically, you'll find one of three options at your multifamily property.

Some multifamily properties have laundry hookups directly in the unit, which is something nearly every tenant would love. Take note of this when touring the property, and check whether the previous landlord supplied the washer and dryer or the current system is owned by the tenant. If the washer and dryer are owned by the landlord, you'll be responsible for ongoing maintenance of those appliances, so include that in your budget.

Other properties have a central laundry room where laundry machines are shared by all the tenants. Laundry facilities inside a multifamily property can actually be a significant source of extra revenue for a landlord, as coin-operated laundry machines can be installed. If your property has a central laundry room (or rooms), check the age of the washers and dryers (their life span is generally less than ten years) as well as the condition of the facility. Does it need to be updated? Painted? Does it need new flooring? Will tenants *want* to sit in those rooms for hours and do laundry? If coin-operated, are the washers and dryers owned by the landlord, or has the landlord contracted that service out?

Laundry machines are a big business, and there are many companies that can provide the machines, service them, collect the coins, and replace the appliances as needed—for a split of the profits (usually 50/50.) This can be a great choice if your goal is to create a more hands-off investment. But be aware that these laundry companies typically have multi-year contracts that go with the *property*, not the owner. In other words, if the previous owner signed a five-year contract with a coin-operated laundry machine company and you buy the property two years into that contract, you'll have to continue using that company for three years. Also know that these contracts often renew automatically, so if you do want to cancel at the end of the contract, look into the exact process for doing so or you may find yourself saddled with another five-year contract. (Ask me how I know...)

Finally, some multifamily properties have no laundry facilities at all, forcing tenants to use local laundromats. If this is the case, ask yourself whether there is any opportunity to create a laundry room, install coin-operated machines, and collect additional revenue—all while providing your tenants with an amenity they'll greatly appreciate.

In this chapter we've covered some of the most common things to look for when you're walking a small multifamily property. This is not intended to be a comprehensive list, but it's a great start. Every property is different and has its own unique considerations, so stay alert and be as observant as possible. Except of course when you're having dinner with a friend and the check arrives!

KEY TAKEAWAYS

- Visiting a property in person is a vital step on the road to buying a property, and having a checklist of major items to take note of can ensure you are as observant as possible.

- When touring a property, start with the exterior and work your way inside, making note of the overall feel of the neighborhood as well as the condition of all major systems.
- Keep an eye out for items that can or must be improved. This will help you create an accurate estimate of the cost of maintaining the property.

Chapter 14

TRADITIONAL FINANCING FOR SMALL MULTIFAMILY PROPERTIES

"Money is only a tool. It will take you wherever
you wish, but it will not replace you as the driver."

—AYN RAND

What comes first, the chicken or the egg?

Or, in real estate terms: Which comes first, the deal or the financing?

While there is no right answer to this question, both the deal and financing are vital to the success of the transaction. (And note that both the chicken and the egg are delicious.)

In this book, we've chosen to place the chapters on finding deals before this chapter on financing them because once you begin looking for deals, you'll be hooked. Our hope is that, like a hunter on the trail of their prey, you are out there tracking down your own deals right now. However, a hunter without a weapon to take down the target is nothing but a hiker in the woods, and an investor without a plan for financing their properties is nothing but a dreamer. In this chapter, and the several chapters that follow, we want to arm you with the skills and tools you'll need to financially take down whatever real estate beast you encounter.

This chapter will focus on traditional financing—in other words, getting a loan from a bank. Subsequent chapters will focus on some more creative methods for financing real estate deals. But first, let's get you a solid understanding of how traditional loans work, which will provide a solid foundation for your future success with whatever financing method you use.

Debt or No Debt? That Is the Question

You do *not* need enough cash on hand to pay 100 percent of the purchase price of a small apartment building because, thankfully, we have leverage. In the case of real estate, "leverage" refers to using a smaller amount of your own money (a down payment) combined with a larger amount of money obtained from a lender to purchase the property. Leverage allows an investor to buy significantly more real estate than they could afford to buy without it. However, leverage is a double-edged sword. By using a loan, you introduce two significant variables:

1. A monthly payment that *must* be paid
2. A lien on the property, which gives the lender the right to take the property from you if you don't pay

In other words, a loan adds risk to the investment. Because of this, some real estate investors and financial commentators advocate never using a loan to buy an investment property, and instead encourage saving up all the cash needed to purchase a property without debt. This all-cash approach can definitely reduce the risk of failure. If something bad happens (like, say, a global pandemic) and tenants stop paying rent, at least you don't have that massive mortgage payment hanging over your head each month. You can much more easily weather financial storms without a mortgage payment, and you get to keep more of the cash that comes in. All this sounds pretty good, and neither of us would encourage someone *not* to approach real estate in this manner if their gut and risk tolerance tell them to play it safe.

However, without leverage most people simply would not be able to invest in small multifamily properties. Let's say you earn a good salary of $120,000 per year from your job and pay $30,000 in taxes on that money, which leaves you with $90,000. If you are able to live on $60,000 for your own housing, food, clothing, travel, kids' schooling, and your crazy Amazon shopping habit, you've got roughly $30,000 left each year to invest in real estate. That might sound like a lot, but then consider that the average sales price for a duplex in the United States right now is more than $280,000.[14] Even if you save up that extra $30,000 a year, it would take you nearly ten years to buy your first duplex, and that wouldn't even include the extra cash you'd need for closing costs, repairs, and reserves.

Let's say you were able to save up for that duplex by putting away $30,000 per year for ten years, plus one more year to cover closing costs, repairs, and reserves. Finally, you pull the trigger and make it happen. After eleven years of saving, you're the proud owner of a duplex that brings in $1,200 per unit in rent. That's a total of $2,400 in income every month. But as you know by now, not all of that is *profit*. You need to cover property taxes, insurance, water, garbage, repairs, and property management fees, as well as set aside money for capital expenditures and vacancies. After all those bills have been paid and money allocated, you're left with a profit of about $1,500 per month.

Now, $1,500 per month in passive income is nothing to sneeze at; I'm sure we would all love that. However, what did it take to achieve that extra $1,500 per month? Over a decade of saving. And here's the bottom line: If you had to wait a decade to buy each property, how long would it take you to replace your salary and leave your job? How old will your kids be when you're finally able to spend more time with them? How will your health be when that day comes? It could be *decades* away. Of course, you could increase your level of savings, even putting that $1,100 per month toward paying for the next deal, which might shave a year or two off your wait time. But at the end of the day, it will *still* take you decades to earn enough passive income to quit that job.

Sounds depressing, doesn't it? Something tells me "decades" is not a timeline that works for you and your ambitions, dreams, and plans.

Enter *leverage*.

---

[14] Note that this website updates on a rolling 24-month basis and will show more recent numbers than printed in 2021, when we first pulled this data. "United States Duplexes," https://www.reonomy.com/properties/duplex/us/1

Let's go back to that same example and look at what life could be like if you used leverage. You still buy that duplex for $280,000. But this time, you put down 20 percent ($56,000) and obtain a loan for the remaining 80 percent. You set aside another $10,000 for reserves and closing costs, bring your total cash outlay to $66,000. The loan you get from the bank costs you $1,050 per month, bringing your monthly cash flow from $1,500 down to $450.

You might be thinking, "Hold on, $450 per month is *way less* than the $1,100 I was making without a loan." And you'd be right, but it didn't take you a decade to get this deal. It took you just two years of saving. Even more important is what this does for your *return on investment*. Specifically, we're going to look at your cash-on-cash, or CoC, return (remember this term?). As a quick reminder, CoC return is the percentage of your investment that you earn back in a given year strictly from cash flow. Let's compare the COC return in both scenarios:

Total Annual Cash Flow:	$1,500 × 12 = $18,000
Total Investment:	$290,000 (total cost of the duplex, for which you paid all cash, plus closing costs and reserves)

$18,000 ÷ $290,000 = 6.2% CoC Return

Let's compare that to the COC you get if you use a loan:

Total Annual Cash Flow:	$450 × 12 = $5,400
Total Investment	$66,000 (down payment, plus closing costs and reserves)

$5,400 ÷ $66,000 = 8.2% CoC Return

The projected return on your investment from the cash flow in the first year is either 6.2 percent or 8.2 percent.

You may be wondering, "What's the big deal? It's only a few percentage points." True, and maybe a 6.2 percent return is enough to satisfy you, since you would rather receive a smaller return in exchange for less risk. That's your prerogative and no one here is going to fault you for this.

But let's dig a little deeper to understand the massive potential difference between our hypothetical 6.2 percent and 8.2 percent over a long period of time. For this example, we'll assume you have $50,000 to invest. Investment no. 1 would give you an annual growth rate of 6.2 percent, while investment no. 2 would give you an annual growth rate of 8.2 percent. Take a look at the graphs below to see the difference:

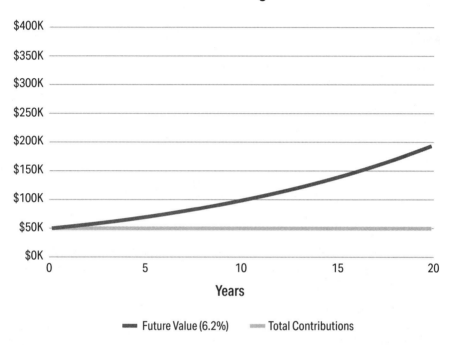

Total Savings

In the above scenario, a 6.2 percent return on your $50,000 investment, compounded annually, will earn you $166,517 at the end of twenty years. When we subtract the original $50,000 investment from this, we can see our profit over those twenty years was $116,517. While that's not too shabby, even after twenty years, let's compare it to the higher interest rate.

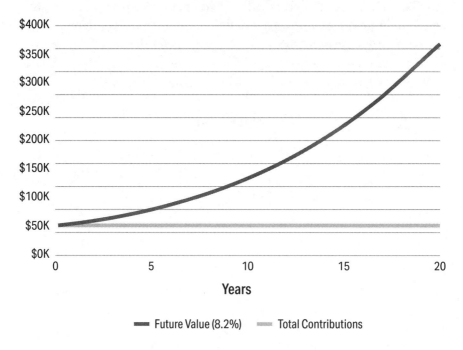

Total Savings

$400K

$350K

$300K

$250K

$200K

$150K

$100K

$50K

$0K

0   5   10   15   20

Years

━━ Future Value (8.2%)   ▓▓ Total Contributions

That same $50,000 investment earning an annual rate of 8.2 percent would turn into $241,832 over that same twenty-year period, earning you $191,832 in profit, which is more than 60 percent growth over the 6.2 percent interest.

That's more than double the profit from the higher interest rate over time. But the higher return is not the only reason to consider using debt. Remember, in the all-cash scenario, it took eleven years to even begin investing in your first deal. During that time, your money was likely earning next to nothing in a savings account. In the debt example, however, you saved for just two years to be able to buy that first property, so your investment begins generating a return much, much sooner.

Also, keep in mind that your entire monthly mortgage payment does not go straight into the banker's pockets. A mortgage payment is typically split into two parts: interest and principal. The interest is the profit the lender makes, but the principal is the loan balance of your property that you are *paying down* over time. You might owe $150,000 this month, but next month you might owe $149,500. If you have a thirty-year mortgage, you will owe nothing to the bank at the end and the property will be worth a sizable amount. Although the CoC return on investment might be 8.2 percent in the example above, your actual overall return would be more than double that if you account for the wealth you are building every month as you pay down the loan balance.

Finally, and perhaps most importantly, leverage allows for a faster "do-learn-repeat" cycle, which is a simple three-step process for mastering virtually any skill. Want to get better at golf? Do it (play the game), learn from what you did, and repeat. Mastering real estate is no different. It's not easy, but with practice, it becomes easier and easier. At the beginning, you may not buy the best deals. You might make mistakes. You could even lose money (though we hope not). But if you learn from what you do and repeat the process, you'll steadily improve and become a powerhouse millionaire multifamily owner!

However—and this is where the debt discussion comes in—if you make only one purchase every five or ten years because you are waiting to save up money for each subsequent purchase, your do-learn-repeat cycle moves so slowly that it may take decades for you to master real estate. By purchasing more properties more quickly, you can accelerate that cycle, improving each time. Then, as you get into larger multifamily properties, you'll have learned enough to make sure those are highly profitable and provide you with significant wealth and passive income.

But, it bears repeating: loans do add risk—a lot of it. If don't receive enough income to cover your required monthly mortgage payment, you might not be able to make that payment. Miss enough required monthly payments and you could be foreclosed on, lose the property, lose your home, lose everything. However, that risk is the reason you get a higher return. As the saying goes, "No risk it, no biscuit!" You will need to determine what your risk tolerance is and evaluate what's best for your personal financial situation. Also, taking on debt is not an all-or-nothing proposition. Maybe 20 percent down feels over-leveraged to you. There's nothing to say you can't put down 40 percent or 60 percent. You do you.

If you're among the more risk averse, rest assured that there are ways to substantially lessen your risk. After all, it's risky to drive a vehicle, but we do it anyway and protect ourselves with seatbelts and airbags. The same goes for investing in multifamily properties. There will always be a degree of risk (even without a loan), but you can do the following to mitigate it:

1. **Know Your Math:** When you carefully evaluate potential properties, you can get a good indication of their future performance. Good math leads to good deals, and good deals lead to financial freedom. Therefore, the better your math, the lower your risk. How do you get better at math? The do-learn-repeat cycle. Start analyzing deals every single day.

2. **Find Great Deals:** When you buy a mediocre or bad deal, the chance of losing money increases greatly. If your property's expenses are $2,000 a month and the property brings in $2,000 a month, you can see how easily that could turn bad. This is why it's important to build your lead-generating skills. You need to find ways to generate leads that allow you to find the needles in the haystack. Of course, the strategy laid out in Chapter Ten will give you a great start, but don't let this book be your only education on lead generation. Talk to other investors, listen to podcasts, read other books, and continually find new ways to generate leads for your business.

3. **Start Small and Scale:** Back in Chapter Two we talked about the power of The Stack method for building wealth. When you start small, you learn a tremendous amount about finding deals, analyzing deals, managing properties, financing, and more. And you *will* make mistakes during this process. However, by starting with smaller, inexpensive properties, you can survive those mistakes, learn from them, and scale with your newfound knowledge and experience.

4. **Harness the Experience of Others:** One of the great things about investing in real estate is that it's just so *common*. Millions of people invest in real estate, and you can learn from their mistakes and experiences. One of the best ways to reduce your risk is by partnering (or even just becoming friends with) more experienced investors and harnessing their expertise. Never let your ego get in the way of asking for guidance.

5. **Get the Right Loan:** Many people point to the horrible events of 2007–2012, when the real estate market crashed, leading to millions of foreclosures, as a reason for not using debt. It's a solid argument, and as Dave Ramsey is famously quoted as saying, "One hundred percent of foreclosures happen to people with mortgages." However, before the Great Recession, many mortgages were created with provisions that made paying them almost impossible.

For example, it was entirely possible to obtain a loan for 25 percent more than the value of your home, and the interest on that loan could jump from 4 percent to 29 percent overnight. When that happened, borrowers with this type of loan suddenly owed way more on their home than their home was worth, and their monthly payment jumped thousands of dollars.

Not all loans are created equal. The *type* of loan can help reduce the risk of borrowing. The most stable mortgages are typically fixed-rate loans with payments that extend over a long period of time (say, thirty years). With a fixed-rate mortgage, you know your monthly payment isn't going to change, and you can more accurately estimate your future expenses.

6. **Manage Effectively:** Even if you buy a good property, it's not guaranteed to make money. Math is irrelevant if you don't back it up with proper management. Therefore, one of the surest ways to reduce your risk is to manage your investment effectively. This means controlling costs, increasing revenue, handling problems, filling vacancies, and keeping accurate records. This also applies if you plan to hire a property manager. In fact, it might matter even more, as you'll need to monitor the work your property manager is doing on a regular basis to make sure your property is performing as you intended. A great deal, managed effectively, is a long-term low-risk deal. We'll talk more about being a great manager in Chapter Twenty.

If you follow the six guidelines above for reducing your risk, you'll be fine. You'll make mistakes, sure. But you'll get through them. You'll learn. You'll do more. You'll learn more. And you'll succeed. Should the worst happen and by some horrible set of circumstances you end up in financial trouble, can't make your mortgage payments, and lose the property, you won't go to debtor's prison (thankfully, that's not a thing anymore). Your banker won't show up with a Louisville Slugger to break your kneecaps. You'll be okay. You'll learn. It might hurt, but you'll get back up and try again, using your newfound knowledge to become a multifamily millionaire even faster.

The Loan Process

If you've decided to use debt to finance your next multifamily investment, understanding the basics of how loans work in this sector will help you navigate the often tricky mortgage application process with ease. You'll be able to talk the talk with bankers, ask the right questions, get the right information, and look like a pro, even if it's your first deal. First, let's review several key loan attributes you need to know.

1. Amortization and Term Length

Different loans are spread out over different lengths of time. The shorter the length of time you have to pay back the loan, the higher the monthly payment. The longer the term, the smaller the monthly payment, but the longer it will take you to pay off the loan. The length of time that the loan is spread out over is known as the amortization. The amortization of your loan will depend on two factors:

1. **What the bank will allow:** Banks typically have a maximum amortization length, which is usually thirty years for residential and twenty-five years for small commercial loans in the United States, though some exceptions can be found. In Canada, for example, the most common residential amortization length is twenty-five years.

2. **What amortization length fits your goals:** If your goal is monthly cash flow (profit), you'll probably want your loan amortized over as long a period of time as possible, keeping your payment lower and your cash flow higher. But if your goal is to pay off your property as fast as possible, you may prefer a shorter amortization.

Although a loan may be amortized over twenty-five or thirty years, that doesn't necessarily mean you can keep that loan for all those years. This is because of another important term: "term." (See what we did there?) The term of a loan is the period of time for which you are legally contracted with the lender to make regular payments to them. The term *may* actually be shorter than the amortized length.

For example, you might have a thirty-year amortized loan, but the term is only five years. In this case, you would be required to get a brand-new loan at the end of those five years and pay the existing loan off completely. This sudden end to the loan is known as a "balloon payment" because the size of the payment *inflates* at the end of the term to pay off the remaining principal balance. While balloon payments on residential loans are rare, they are much more common with commercial loans. Therefore, if you're shopping for a commercial mortgage, be sure to investigate both the term and the amortization period to make the best choice for your investment and risk tolerance.

To determine the actual amount of money you'll need to pay each month on your loan, knowing the term and the loan amount isn't enough. We need a couple more pieces of information.

2. Principal and Interest

When you obtain a loan on a piece of real estate, the total monthly payment usually consists of two separate parts: principal and interest. The principal is responsible for issuing detention and controlling the school's budget... er... sorry, that's a different kind of principal. In loan terminology, the principal is the part of the payment that actually pays off what you owe, which normally decreases each time you make a payment.

The other part of the payment is the interest, which is the profit the lender makes each year. In real estate, this number is expressed as a percentage. Because of the math behind mortgage payments (known as "amortization"), in the beginning of a loan, the majority of the payment goes toward interest and very little goes toward paying down the principal balance. However, over time, that changes. The longer you have a loan, the larger the chunk of payment going toward the principal is. And don't worry about trying to do this math in your head: Simply use the BiggerPockets mortgage calculator (www.biggerpockets.com/mortgage-calculator) to see your payment.

Some loans don't include any principal to be paid down; these are known as interest-only loans. This means if you get that $100,000 loan today and pay 5 percent interest, you'll pay that $5,000 a year for many years and still, at the end, owe $100,000. That's a bummer, but this type of loan has its uses. For example, if you are flipping a house and don't really care about paying down the loan slowly over time, an interest-only loan might be great. Or, as is common in the commercial real estate space, lenders often offer interest-only payments for a short period of time at the beginning of the loan period, usually for the first one, two, or three years, as a way to boost cash flow during the early years of the investment (more on that in Volume II of *The Multifamily Millionaire*).

When you're shopping for a loan, the lender will be able to tell you what the going interest rate is. This number fluctuates based on many different factors, including the general state of the economy, the lender's policies, the policies of the U.S. Federal Reserve, and current supply-and-demand dynamics. (When lenders are overwhelmed with loan applications, rates typically climb because there is so much demand.)

For residential mortgages, this interest is usually "fixed," meaning it doesn't change. A fixed-rate mortgage is great for making long-term projections on your property, as the amount you pay this month will be the same amount you'll pay ten years from now. However, another option exists: variable (or floating) interest rates. These rates can fluctuate, which as you'd assume, will change your monthly payment. The rate you pay is typically tied to some common rate like the U.S. prime rate (the interest rate banks charge their most creditworthy customers), with some kind of margin baked in, which lenders refer to as the spread. For example, if a lender offers you a rate of "prime plus 2 percent," that means that if the prime rate is at 3 percent, you would pay a total of 5 percent. If the prime rate dropped to 1 percent, your interest rate would drop to 3 percent, but if it jumped to 7 percent, you would pay 9 percent.

When you obtain a loan, many banks will give you the option of a fixed or a variable rate. (However, especially in the commercial loan space, you may not be given an option.) If you believe rates will increase over time, a fixed-rate loan might be your best option, as the only way to go is up (and "up" is not a good thing when talking about rates). But if you believe rates will drop, a variable rate could be a good bet, as your payment could decrease over time. In general, we recommend obtaining a fixed-rate loan whenever possible to reduce risk, but the choice is yours. Just keep in mind that the direction of interest rates is notoriously difficult to predict.

To further complicate things, some loans combine several of these options into one loan product. For example, you may get a "variable" loan that is "fixed" for a certain amount of time. On one of our recent multifamily acquisitions, we obtained a variable-rate loan that was fixed for the first ten years. After that, the rate will reset based on whatever the going rate is ten years from now. Our gamble is that either we'll sell or refinance the property before those ten years are up, or our property will be able to support a higher mortgage payment if the interest rate rises.

Earlier, when we talked about the risk inherent in obtaining loans, we noted how back in 2007–2012 many foreclosures occurred because the interest on many variable-rate loans jumped from reasonable to crazy high, causing monthly payments to skyrocket. In an effort to prevent this from happening again, more than half of all U.S. states have passed so-called usury laws that place a cap on how high those variable rates can go and how fast they can increase. These laws help reduce the risk of variable-rate residential loans.[15] Each state dictates the maximum legal rate lenders can charge. Therefore, when shopping for a variable rate loan, check to find out how high those rates can go. Recently, when shopping for a variable-rate loan on a duplex, I found one with a maximum rate of 11 percent; however, the rate could increase by only 1 percent per year—and it started at 4 percent. I looked at the worst-case scenario and decided that even if my rate *did* jump to 11 percent, it would take nearly seven years to get there and my payment would increase by just a few hundred dollars per month on a property that provides more than $1,000 per month in cash flow. I decided that this was a risk I was 100 percent confident taking.

3. P&I versus PITI

In addition to principal and interest, many mortgage payments include an allocated amount of cash for the taxes and insurance to be paid. This is known as escrowing the taxes and insurance and is very common for loans on residential (one- to four-unit) multifamily properties. Essentially, the bank is collecting one-twelfth of the annual property taxes and one-twelfth of the annual insurance premium each month. They will then make the payments for you when those bills are due.

No, the lender is not just doing this out of the goodness of their heart—they're protecting *their* investment. If the bank makes the payments for you, you can't "forget" to pay those bills and face more serious problems down the road. It's in the bank's best interest to combine them all into one monthly payment, known as the PITI payment, which stands for principal, interest, taxes, and insurance. When discussing a "mortgage payment" it's important to know whether the lender is talking about just the principal and interest (P&I) or also including the taxes and insurance with this amount (PITI).

We recommend generally ignoring the PITI model, because we want to have a separate line item for taxes and insurance when we run the numbers. However, in conversation, many individuals do wrap it all in together and simply call the entire number "the mortgage payment." There's nothing wrong with this; just be sure that you and the other person are on the same page.

---

15 Richie Bernardo, "Usury Laws by State, Interest Rate Caps, The Bible & More," WalletHub, June 14, 2014, https://wallethub.com/edu/cc/usury-laws/25568/#:~:text=Usury%20laws%20cap%20the%20interest,its%20own%20maximum%20legal%20limit

4. Prepayment Penalties

Many loans, especially on the commercial side, include a prepayment penalty. This provision in the loan paperwork essentially forces you to pay a fee if you were to pay off the loan prior to a certain predefined date. For example, a lender may include a four-year prepayment penalty that requires you to pay a fee of 2 percent of whatever the loan balance is if you refinance before the four-year mark. When shopping for your mortgage, be sure to ask whether there's a prepayment penalty, and if there is, get the details to ensure they make sense within your plan.

The Lender's Combination Lock

A lender's primary goal is to not *lose* money, which happens when borrowers don't pay back their loans. To avoid this, the bank sets up certain criteria that must be met in order to fund your deal. Once you meet all those requirements, the loan is approved and the deal is funded.

Many people feel that a bank's decisions are personal, when in fact, a loan is much more akin to a safe's combination lock. Enter the right combination, and the safe will open. Check all the right boxes for the lender, and the money will flow. In this section, we want to give you a basic overview of those requirements, so you can begin talking with your lender about them and make sure your deal can unlock the bank's safe!

1. Loan-to-Value Ratio (LTV)

The lender will look at the worst-case scenario and ask themselves, "If this borrower decides not to pay and we are forced to foreclose on the property, how do we make sure we don't lose money?" The answer is the loan-to-value ratio, or LTV. This simple ratio looks at how much of a loan they are giving out compared to how much the property is worth. In basic math language, it looks like this:

$$\text{Loan Amount} \div \text{Property Value} = \text{LTV}$$

For example, if a lender is willing to give a 70 percent LTV loan, it means they want to make sure the total loan amount does not exceed 70 percent of whatever the property appraises for. If a property is worth $250,000 and the lender agrees to 70 percent of that, you would be able to borrow $175,000 ($250,000 × .7 = $175,000).

Keep in mind that most traditional (bank) lenders will look at both the appraised value *and* the purchase price, basing the LTV on whichever number is lower. For example, if you are attempting to buy a $250,000 triplex and that property appraises at $300,000, the bank will base the LTV (in this example, 70 percent) on the purchase price. Of course, different lenders have different policies, so if you find yourself with a property that appraises much higher than what you are buying it for, be sure to ask.

What is a "normal" LTV when buying small multifamily properties? As with most things, it depends. If the loan is for a residential property and you plan on living in one of the units, you could get up to a 96.5 percent LTV loan, with just a 3.5 percent down payment. However, for most investment properties, 65 percent to 80 percent LTV is average. There can be exceptions depending on the property's condition and, therefore, the inherent risk in the property. In general, the more risk a lender is taking, the lower the LTV.

2. Debt-to-Income Ratio (DTI)

When you apply for a residential mortgage, the bank isn't overly confident in your ability to be an effective landlord. *Yet.* They want to know that you have other income that can cover the mortgage if something goes wrong or the property sits empty for a while. To determine this, they use what's known as the debt-to-income ratio, or DTI. This simple equation compares your total monthly debt payment obligations (mortgage, car payments, credit cards, student loans, etc.) to your gross income from your job.

$$\text{Total Debt Obligations} \div \text{Total Income} = \text{DTI}$$

For example, let's say that you made $10,000 last month and had $3,000 in debt payments. That would be a DTI of 30 percent. Although the number fluctuates with changes in banking regulation, lenders typically want to see a DTI below 43 percent.

Of course, you can imagine the problem with this: If lenders don't count your rental income as income but *do* count the mortgage on that property as debt, you will quickly surpass the DTI threshold. For example, if you buy a fourplex for $400,000 and your mortgage payment is $2,200 per month, that's a lot of debt for not adding any income.

Yes, this is a challenge for new real estate investors—but after owning rental properties for two years, the lender will count your rental income as part of your income, which can dramatically increase your documentable income and, as a result, lower your DTI to an allowable level. Also, DTI is primarily an issue for residential, not commercial, loans, so as you build your portfolio using The Stack method and begin buying properties with five units or greater, this will quickly become a non-issue. And finally, rest assured that there are many creative financing options to get around strict bank rules, which we'll cover in the coming chapters.

The bottom line on DTI:

- Keep your debt low. Pay off credit cards and student loans. Don't get car loans unless you have to (and pay them off quickly). Don't buy the most expensive house for yourself to live in.
- Make as much income at your job as you can.
- Start *now* and in two years, when your DTI won't be as much of an issue because you're bringing in great rental income, this won't be a problem.

3. Debt Service Coverage Ratio (DSCR)

If you're about to buy a multifamily property with five units or more, the debt service coverage ratio, or DSCR, is going to be an important number for you to know. Exclusive to commercial investing, DSCR is used by a lender to look at the property's ability to generate cash flow each month. The DSCR compares the Net Operating Income (NOI) for the property (which, if you'll remember from back in Chapter Nine, means the money you have left to pay the mortgage after all the bills have been paid) to the total debt payment. In other words:

$$DSCR = NOI \div Debt\ Service$$

For example, if a property's NOI is \$100,000 per year and the total debt payment is \$100,000 per year, the DSCR would be one because \$100,000 ÷ \$100,000 = 1. This means, essentially, that the property would break even. You have \$100,000 left to make the mortgage payment, and the mortgage payment is \$100,000. Probably not a great deal for most people, nor is it a good enough deal for most lenders to want to fund. Although DSCRs can fluctuate based on location, property type, and other factors, a good rule of thumb to shoot for is a DSCR of at least 1.2, meaning that after all the expenses are paid, you show a profit of at least 20 percent.

4. Capital Reserves

Lenders have been around the block. They know that rental properties encounter problems: water heaters break, roofs leak, foundations crack. And because their number one goal is to not lose money, they want to make sure you have sufficient capital reserves (that is, money sitting in the bank) to cover any big problems that come up. The actual amount required differs based on the lender and the property, but a good rule of thumb is to have the equivalent of six months of PITI payments for all your properties in a savings account somewhere. (We are now seeing some lenders who require reserves equal to up to twelve months of PITI payments, so be sure to check with your lender to make sure you have enough capital for your next deal.)

How to Find a Great Lender and the Perfect Loan

If you want to enjoy a good fast-food burger, you have lots of options. You could get a simple dollar-menu cheeseburger if you need a light snack, or you could get the quadruple pounder animal-style monstrosity if you're in the mood for a heart attack. In both cases, you're getting a burger, but the end result is very different. The same is true about shopping for a loan for a small multifamily property. Money is money, just as a burger is a burger, but there are infinite ways to make the loan work for you. To help you select the best lender and the best loan for your next multifamily property, we put together a seven-step process.

1. Decide What You Want

What kind of burger are you in the mood for? What suits your appetite? Answering this question will narrow down your restaurant choices. And, you guessed it, this is exactly how the loan process works as well. You need to know *what* you want before you can decide *where* to get it.

When it comes to real estate, loans can be complicated. There are numerous factors to weigh and negotiate to make sure you get the best loan for your property. And especially when dealing with multifamily lending, it's not just the interest rate that matters. Therefore, the first step in obtaining a great loan is to decide what's most important for you and your investment. Then you can approach a lender with a clear picture of your needs and avoid wasting everyone's time if they can't accommodate them. Ask yourself:

- What type of property am I obtaining a loan for, and where is it located?
- How's the condition of the property? (Some lenders will lend only on properties that are in great shape.)
- What term length would be acceptable?
- What amortization length do I need?
- How much money do I want to put toward a down payment?
- How much do I plan to have in reserves?
- What maximum monthly payment would help me achieve my monthly cash-flow goals?
- How much money do I have for closing costs?
- And how do all these factors fit into my overall goals, my CCC, and my plans for financial freedom?

The goal is to have a clear understanding of the kind of loan you are looking for. At the beginning, you might not know exactly what is possible, and that's okay. Ask plenty of questions, speak to a lot of lenders, and soon you'll have a pretty solid grasp on the situation.

2. Gather All Necessary Information About Yourself and Your Deal

Lenders are busy. When it comes time to talk with a lender, the more prepared you are as a borrower, the more responsive and capable they'll be. It's not that they don't want the business, but when they have a dozen loan applications to work through, human nature is going to direct them to handle the easiest one first. Show up with the necessary information. At a minimum, bring the following in an organized three-ring binder and send a digital copy to the lender as well:

- Previous two years' W-2s from current and past employers
- Previous two months of pay stubs
- Previous two years of tax returns
- Any 1099s you've received in the past two years
- Proof of alimony or child support
- Bank statements from all substantial bank accounts for the previous two months
- Retirement or investment account statements for the previous two months

The lender will probably have their own list that includes the above items and more, so gather this information, keep it well organized, and get all documents to the lender fast.

3. Make a List of Potential Lenders

Once you've decided what's important to you and you've prepared the necessary documents, it's time to make a list of potential lenders that may fit the bill. There are several avenues for creating your list of potential lenders.

- **Your Bank:** Start by talking with the lender wherever you do your personal or business banking. Remember, if you're attempting to obtain a loan on a property with five or more units, you'll need to talk with the commercial lending department. If obtaining a loan on a property with four units or fewer, the residential lending department is what you want. Banks value loyalty, and if you've been a loyal customer for years, you may find favorable loan terms as well as a great working relationship.

- **Local Banks and Credit Unions:** In addition to the institution where you do your banking, look at other banks and credit unions in the area. Lending is often a very location-specific practice, meaning lenders in one town don't generally want to fund deals in another town. Therefore, check out all the banks and credit unions in your area and add them to your list. If you don't have any luck there, you can also try the local branches of national and regional banks.

- **Referrals:** Ask other real estate investors in your market who they are using for loans on their multifamily real estate deals. You can also talk with local real estate agents who are selling properties similar to your ideal investment type to see who they recommend. After all, a real estate agent gets paid only when the deal closes, so a good lender who can actually close deals will be important to an agent.

- **Mortgage Brokers:** Let's quickly revisit the hamburger analogy. Let's say you really want a hamburger and there are dozens of fast-food restaurants in town, but you're not sure which hamburger tastes the best and who has the lowest price. You recruit a friend to go out and find the best hamburger for you. (As a reward, maybe they get to keep the fries.) The analogy might be stretching a little thin at this point, but you get the idea: A mortgage broker is someone who goes out and consults with numerous lenders to find the best loan product for you. They will talk with you to discover your needs (the first step in this process), help you put together your paperwork (the second step in this process), and then help with the rest of the steps we haven't touched on yet.

Mortgage brokers can take a lot of the hassle out of finding the ideal loan, but their services don't come free. (Are you sensing a pattern?) They will typically take a fee that you'll pay at the time of the loan closing, typically 1 to 2 percent of the loan amount. Mortgage brokers can be found in almost any market; they often have the word "mortgage" or "loan" or "lending," rather than "bank" or "credit union," in their name. For example, First Place Lending is likely a mortgage broker, while First Place Bank is probably a direct lender.

- **Online:** Just like many other industries, the mortgage industry has moved largely online, so you can shop for mortgages without ever putting on your pants! A Google search will bring up numerous potential lenders, as can searching websites like LendingTree and BankRate. You can also search at www.biggerpockets.com/loans.

4. Fill Out Lender Call Sheets

For each bank or lender you speak with, jot down the most important information they give you so you can compare and contrast the different options available. Trust us, once you've spoken with four or five lenders, the details will begin to blur and you'll forget the subtle differences between their loan programs.

To assist you with this, we created a simple checklist called the Lender Call Sheet that serves two purposes. First, by filling out this sheet as you talk with a lender, you'll remember to ask all the right questions. (Don't you hate it when you hang up the phone with someone and *then* remember something you forgot to ask them?) Second, this sheet allows you to compare the different options side by side, so you can make the best decision for your investment. And remember, it's not always just about the total monthly payment or the interest rate. You can download the following form, and all the forms used in this book, by visiting www.biggerpockets.com/multifamilybonus .

	LENDER			
	1	**2**	**3**	**4**
Do you lend on investment properties?	☐ Yes ☐ No	☐ Yes ☐ No	☐ Yes ☐ No	☐ Yes ☐ No
Do you keep your loans in-house, or are they Fannie Mae or Freddie Mac loans?	☐ Yes ☐ No	☐ Yes ☐ No	☐ Yes ☐ No	☐ Yes ☐ No
What down payments do you require for non-owner-occupied investment properties?	_____	_____	_____	_____
What are the going interest rates on investment property loans right now?	_____%	_____%	_____%	_____%
What credit score requirements do you have for investment property loans?	_____	_____	_____	_____
How much would I expect to pay in closing costs?	$_____	$_____	$_____	$_____

As you speak with lenders and fill out the Lender Call Sheet, you'll undoubtedly find that some lenders just won't work for your particular situation. That's fine. Make note of this, but don't abandon all hope of ever working with this lender. Keep your Lender Call Sheet(s) on file even after choosing a lender, so you can refer back to those lenders for other deals. Just be sure to update your sheet regularly, as loan rates, terms, and requirements change often.

You may be thinking, "Geez guys, this sounds like a lot of work. Do I really have to speak to a bunch of different lenders? Why can't I just find one and go with them?" You absolutely could. And then that lender could pull out at the last moment, leaving you high and dry and forcing you to start the process all over again. Or maybe they'll finish the loan for you without a problem, but what if a competing bank down the road could have shaved a quarter percent off your loan? A quarter of a percent might not sound like a lot, but consider this: On a $300,000 loan, an extra quarter of a percent of interest could amount to an additional $16,000 over the life of a loan. What's a few hours of your time worth?

5. Shop Your Loan to Those Who Appear Most Promising

A friend once shared his best dating advice: "It's a game of numbers," he said, "and there's no downside to playing the odds to find the right one." We won't comment on how well this works when dating, but we can say that when it comes to shopping for loans for multifamily properties, his advice is spot-on. Of course, you don't want to disingenuously "date" multiple lenders, stringing them along for weeks and making them put in hours of work when you have no intention of working with them.

But sometimes there will be several good lending options and since you've done all the work to collect your financials, it wouldn't hurt to run your deal past several of your top lending choices to see who is most excited about working with you and vice versa. Remember, many lenders *say* they can do something for you, but they can't truly offer you a loan until they've looked at all the paperwork. Therefore, rather than spending a week going back and forth with one lender only to possibly be rejected after all that work, play the odds and shop your loan to several lenders to see who comes back with the best rates, terms, and conditions.

6. Make Your Choice

Now it's time to commit and begin working with one lender. Going back to the dating analogy, at some point, it's time to get serious and date each other exclusively! If you have only one workable loan option in front of you, you may be forced to settle for whatever you can get, but you'll probably have several good options available. Weigh those options, and pick a lender who not only has the ability to fund your loan with the right product but is also responsive and professional. A bank with an amazing loan will be worthless if your contact at the bank is unresponsive, rude, or difficult to work with. You want both: a solid loan from a solid lender.

7. Be Responsive

Finally, even though you may think you've already given the lender all your financial information, be prepared to supply four times as many documents once underwriting gets under way. The underwriter's job is to process your loan by checking hundreds of boxes on dozens of forms, and they're relying on you to deliver them the documentation they need to check off those boxes accurately. To ensure that the process goes smoothly, you need to be incredibly responsive to your lender's requests. When they ask for a document, get it back to them the same day, if not the same hour.

At this point, you have all the knowledge necessary to begin talking with traditional lenders to learn about your ability to qualify for a loan. Don't worry if you don't qualify right now, because a good lender will help you design a program to get your debt, credit score, and any other important factors up to their standards so you'll be "lendable" in the future. And if you find yourself unable or uninterested in obtaining traditional lending, don't quit this book yet. Creative financing is the art of putting together a deal using other-than-traditional means, and in the coming chapters you'll learn how to do just that.

KEY TAKEAWAYS

- While some investors choose to build their real estate portfolio using no debt, most use traditional financing. Debt does add risk, but it also adds the leverage needed to get started sooner, boost returns, and grow a portfolio quickly.
- Understanding how a loan works is the key to unlocking a bank's financing options. Once you know the right questions to ask, you'll get the answers needed to get your loan. You'll also know to come prepared to your meeting with your lender by providing all the necessary documents.
- There are many lenders out there, but different lenders offer different types of loans. Do your due diligence and interview several lenders to find one who is both responsive and able to help you get your next loan with the best rates and terms possible.

Chapter 15
CREATIVE FINANCING PART I: HOUSE HACKING

"Without pain, without sacrifice we would have nothing. Like the first monkey shot into space."

—CHUCK PALAHNIUK, *FIGHT CLUB*

This book began with me collecting rent in cash and looking sketchy to my neighbors. As you may have gathered by now, I was house hacking.

"House hacking" is a term used to describe the process of combining your primary residence (where you live most of the time) with an investment property. (True story: This term originated in a blog post I wrote years ago titled "House Hacking: A Beginner's Guide to Hack Your Housing and Live for Free."[16] It's actually the post that introduced Scott Trench (current CEO and fellow house hacker) to BiggerPockets and has

---

[16] https://www.biggerpockets.com/blog/2013-11-02-hack-housing-get-paid-live-free

been read by tens of thousands of people since its publication.)

The most common way to do this is by purchasing a small multifamily property with two, three, or four units and living in one unit while leasing out the other units. However, as with most things real estate, there's more than one way to do it.

Types of House Hacks

1. **Traditional House Hack:** The traditional house hack involved buying a duplex, triplex, or fourplex using an owner-occupied loan from a traditional lender. You live in one unit (for at least a year) while the tenants in the other units pay you rent, which goes toward paying your mortgage and expenses, allowing you to live for cheap or for free, or maybe you even get paid to live in your home. Someday you'll move and rent out your unit, your cash flow will increase, and you'll have a solid investment foundation for future wealth creation.

2. **BRRRR House Hack:** Not all small multifamily properties are in great condition, and if you're willing to tackle a rehab project, you can turn a small multifamily house hack into a cash cow. Based on the BRRRR strategy (buy, rehab, rent, refinance, repeat, which we'll cover in depth in Chapter Seventeen), this approach involves buying a small multifamily property in need of significant work. While traditional lenders refuse to lend on such properties, you may qualify for a special rehab loan from the famed 203(k) program—which I'll address in a moment and requires just a 3.5 percent down payment on the total cost plus rehab. Or you could use a short-term financing option, such as cash, a hard-money loan, borrowing from family, or borrowing from a 401(k).

   You then rehab the property, doing what you can to fix anything broken or outdated and improving both the interior and exterior to attract the best tenants and collect the highest rent. After the rehab has been completed, you'll rent out each unit to great tenants at higher-than-average rents. Then you'll be able to refinance the property, unless you obtained a 203(k) loan or similar long-term loan that allows you to bypass the refinance entirely. If the rehab was successful and you increased the property's value, you may be able to pull out all the cash you invested in the property and repeat the process, maybe with another house hack.

3. **Bedroom House Hack:** Although this is a book about multifamily real estate investing, don't forget that house hacking can also work for single-family homes if you are willing to treat the other bedrooms as "units" and rent those out as you would a traditional multifamily property. While having "housemates" doesn't work for everyone, a bedroom house hack can be an effective way to live for free in any market.

   Craig Curelop, author of *The House Hacking Strategy*, successfully accomplished this several times, even choosing to rent out his own bedroom while living in the living room, hanging up a sheet to create a new "bedroom" in the corner so he could maximize his income. While such extreme house hacking may not work for most people, it does show that there are many options available for those willing to sacrifice some luxury (and privacy) for a better financial position.

4. **ADU House Hack:** In Chapter Four, we discussed the ADU, an extra unit added onto a primary residence to make it a small multifamily, which has become increasingly common as a way for homeowners to generate more income. The ADU house hack can be a fantastic solution for those who love the idea of house hacking but highly value their privacy or are committed to a location where small multifamily properties are difficult to find. Although ADU laws differ by location, many cities allow for their construction as a state-approved solution to the rising cost of home ownership. After all, not only are you building more housing without taking up more land, you are also providing a relatively low-rent house for the town's residents, improving your property's value, and helping yourself afford to live there. You win, the tenant wins, and the city wins.

   The ADU house hack requires that you either own or purchase a single-family home with a lot large enough to accommodate (both physically and legally) the construction of an ADU. You then hire a licensed professional contractor to build that ADU (or build it yourself), rent it out to great tenants, and suddenly you are house hacking! If you find a single-family home that already has an ADU, so much the better.

   Finally, if you're in a hurry to obtain financial freedom, you could rent out the main house and live in the ADU yourself. The primary home should rent for significantly more than the ADU, maximizing the cash flow from your house hack.

5. **Vacation or Short-Term Rental House Hack:** Vacation rentals have existed for as long as vacations themselves, but in recent years companies like VRBO and Airbnb have completely changed the game. As a result, vacation rentals are no longer just for quirky Aunt Betty who loves to meet new people—they are now an option for anyone with a smartphone. Of course, in 2020 the COVID-19 pandemic rocked the vacation rental market. Nonetheless, vacation rentals remain a viable option for individuals looking for a temporary place to stay. If you live in an area where vacationers are common, buying a small multifamily investment property or a single-family home with an ADU could give you the option to rent out that extra unit (or units) as a short-term rental, increasing your income (often dramatically) while giving you the opportunity to meet people from around the world. But, please check your local laws and zoning before diving in!

    Don't automatically assume your location doesn't fit the "vacation area" bill. Any semi-major city, as well as the cities that surround it, can be a vacation destination, since people travel for conferences, weddings, funerals, and just to see a new place.

6. **College Rental House Hack:** If you live in a college town, renting your small multifamily units to college students can be a significant way to increase your cash flow, with the added benefit of the occasional landlord-tenant beer pong challenge in the front yard. (Or maybe not.) Regardless of your choice of after-work activities, renting the other units in your small multifamily house hack to college students can be a highly profitable venture—if you manage those students correctly.

    College students, as you can imagine, can be rougher on rental properties than other types of tenants, so plan for that and use more tenant-resilient materials in your property. Also be sure to have the parent(s) cosign the lease, so you can collect for any damage from someone who has a job outside the school cafeteria. Additionally, because college classes typically run from September to June, we recommend having your tenants sign a full one-year lease so their rent is paid year-round, even if they leave during the summer (no landlord wants to have two or three months' vacancy each year). Often students who will be away for the summer know that in advance and are able to find a sublet to take their place. That way, you won't lose any cash flow. Just make sure you vet any new tenants before they move in.

7. **Mixed-Use House Hack:** A mixed-use building is a property that serves both residential and commercial tenants. For example, there may be a mom-and-pop shop on the first floor, with several apartments on the second. You could live in one of the residential apartments while your commercial tenants pay the rent. Although financing on this type of property for an owner occupant can be harder to find than traditional owner-occupied loans, it is possible.

    Just recognize that this type of house hack requires you to master two largely separate sets of skills: managing residential tenants and managing commercial tenants. Commercial real estate is an entirely different animal, and while it's not impossible to learn, you definitely will need to do so if you choose to be a mixed-use house hacker. On the plus side, commercial tenants tend to pay their own repair and maintenance costs and generally stay for much longer lengths of time, giving you fewer expenses to worry about.

Why House Hack?

House hacking is a terrific way to invest in real estate, especially for those who are young or just starting out. Let's look at some of the primary benefits, beginning with those that are most fitting for a chapter on creative finance.

1. **Low-Down-Payment Financing:** For generations now, the U.S. government has offered programs and incentives to encourage home ownership that allow buyers to obtain a mortgage with a very low down payment at highly favorable rates. One of the most popular of these options is the FHA loan, which allows homeowners to buy a one- to four-unit owner-occupied home with just a 3.5 percent down payment. That means if you're looking to buy a $300,000 triplex and plan to live in the property for at least one year, you may need as little as $10,500 for the down payment (plus some money for reserves and closing costs, of course).

    FHA loans are not the only type of financing available for owner-occupied properties. Some banks offer loans with down payments as low as 5 or 10 percent, as well as other creative options for homeowners who plan to buy and live in duplexes, triplexes, and fourplexes.

    For this reason, house hacking can be one of the best strategies for investors who are looking to get started with multifamily investing but lack the traditional 20 to 30 percent in cash needed for a down payment. Of course, lower down payments typically mean higher monthly payments and some extra monthly fees (known as PMI or MIP), so be sure to run your numbers accurately to make sure your low-down-payment house hack is a success.

2. **Lower Living Expenses:** Many finance gurus tout the idea that if you want to be wealthy, you need to save and invest more money. True, of course. But they go on to teach that the best way to save more money is by cutting small expenses like coffee or extra television channels from your budget. However, most people's largest expense is not coffee—it's housing.

   In fact, according to the Investopedia, most Americans spend a whopping 31.5 percent of their income on their rent or mortgage payment and just 3 percent on clothing and about 5.6 percent on eating out.[17] If you want to dramatically decrease your monthly spending, isn't it time to take a look your biggest expense? Enter house hacking. It offers the unique possibility of living in your home for free, or for far less than usual, while also experiencing all the other advantages of owning investment property (such as appreciation, loan paydown, and tax benefits).

   For example, let's say you purchase a triplex for $300,000 and decide to live in one unit. Each of the two remaining units rents for $1,200 per month, for a total of $2,400 per month. The total monthly payment on your $300,000 property, including taxes and insurance, is about $1,700. That leaves you $700 extra for repairs, CapEx reserves, utilities, and other expenses, which should be more than enough to allow you to live for free, and maybe even make money doing so! Of course, not all house hacks allow you to live for free, but even living for significantly *less* than before is a huge win.

3. **Rehab Ready:** One of the best ways to quickly build wealth through real estate is by purchasing a fixer-upper and actually fixing it up. However, most lenders do not want to lend on a distressed property, and even if they would, you'd still have to pay tens of thousands of dollars out of pocket for the rehab. But there is one type of loan that combines the benefits of a low down payment with the financing to fix up a property to build instant equity: the 203(k) loan.

---

[17] "The Spending Habits of Americans," Investopedia, February 2, 2020, https://www.investopedia.com/financial-edge/0512/the-spending-habits-of-americans.aspx

A subset of the FHA loan, the 203(k) allows you to bundle the cost of repairs into your property's loan and pay just a 3.5 percent down payment on the sum total. In other words, you get to fix up your property, enjoy living in a newly rehabbed property, experience gains in appreciation, and attract better tenants due to your improvements to the property—all for just 3.5 percent down.

Perhaps with a little work that $300,000 triplex we've been discussing could be rented for a higher price and be worth a lot more money. Let's say you decide that $50,000 of improvements (replacing flooring, repainting, adding a bedroom) is about right. That brings the total investment to $350,000. Ordinarily, you'd have to come up with 20 to 30 percent down plus the entire $50,000 for the rehab, meaning you'd need more than $100,000 in savings to buy and rehab that triplex. The 203(k) loan, however, allows you to pay just 3.5 percent of the total $350,000, or $12,250, plus closing costs and reserves.

This 203(k) loan is also likely to be a fixed-rate mortgage and have an exceptionally low interest rate. Also, as with the traditional FHA loan, you won't have to pay it back when you move out. You can simply leave after one year and rent your unit to a new tenant, capitalizing on even more cash flow. Because you improved all the units, they now rent for $1,400 per month, so with three fully rented units, you're bringing in $4,200 in gross revenue, and your PITI payment is still less than $2,000 a month. The cherry on top? That $300,000 property you spent $50,000 rehabbing is now worth $400,000, giving you substantial equity as well. Your net worth is growing, your cash flow is bursting at the seams, and you're on your way to financial freedom.

4. **Works in Any Market:** House hacking works in any market, period. You can house hack in Tulsa, Orlando, Maui, New York City, and probably even Antarctica (if you don't mind sharing space with a penguin, which I wouldn't recommend; they are obnoxiously loud tenants). Of course, this isn't to say every duplex, triplex, or fourplex will work as a house hack. As with any investment, you must do your due diligence, seek a deal that meets your criteria, analyze the deal accurately, and manage the property effectively.

5. **Investor Training Wheels:** Right now my daughter, Rosie, is learning how to ride her first "big girl" bike. It's a colorful bike covered with stickers of popular cartoon princesses. It's very cute, and I'm sure you'd love it. Anyway, this bike is set up the same way almost every

child's first bike is—with training wheels. When she tips too far to the left, the left training wheel keeps her from falling over; too far to the right, the same safeguard exists. This gives her the ability to ride her bike for real, but offers significant safety in case things (or she) go sideways. Which brings us to the fifth and final reason why house hacking can be such a powerful tool for new investors: You're given "landlord training wheels."

Because you live at the property, and your mortgage is likely low enough to be affordable even if you weren't renting the other units out, you get real-life experience with some safeguards to keep you from falling over. It's on-the-job landlord training. You'll get to experience firsthand the intricacies of owning rental properties. You'll find what you like, what you don't, what breaks often, what looks good, what looks bad, how you should talk with tenants, what policies you need to put in place, and more. House hacking can help you build the systems, the skills, and most importantly, the confidence needed to build lifelong, generational wealth.

Analyzing a House Hack

As you can imagine, running the numbers on a house hack is slightly different from the process we laid out for other multifamily investments. You'll need to make a few adjustments to determine your maximum purchase price (MaPP) and your expected cash flow. When analyzing a potential house hack, I like to think about it as two completely separate investments.

To start, you'll follow the same steps we outlined earlier. That's because, at least initially, you'll be living in one of the units and not collecting any rent from it while lowering your living expenses. But that situation won't last forever. Someday you'll move out, and the property will need to make sense in that scenario as well.

First, you need to analyze the deal to see how much you, personally, will be required to pay to live in the property or, even better, how much pure cash flow you can expect to make each month. To do this, follow the Four-Square Method for analyzing an investment, leaving out the unit where you'll be living.

For example, let's look at a fourplex where every unit should rent for $1,000 per month. You'd use $3,000, not $4,000, as the total rent. In other words, assume from the start that you'll be living for free. Then move on to the expenses, adding up every charge you might be responsible for as landlord. In a house hack, most expenses will be the same as for other multifamilies, but you may be able to save on (though not eliminate) some items, like property management or repairs, if you plan to perform those tasks yourself.

As with all small multifamily real estate, looking at the difference between total income and total expenses will give you your monthly pure cash flow (or lack thereof). If your cash flow is negative, don't panic! Remember, we did not include any income from the unit you'll be living in, so any negative cash flow is really just the amount of money you'll have to pay to live in the property.

Compare this number to what you would normally have to pay to live somewhere else, and you can determine whether the investment makes sense. For example, maybe you'll find that after all income (not including your unit) and expenses are accounted for, you'll be "losing" $300 per month in cash flow. All that means is that you're paying $300 to live in your unit. But since you'd normally be paying $1,000 to live there, that's a $700 savings—which is way better than trying to save $700 by cutting out your daily coffee ritual. Of course, the ultimate house hack investment would generate positive pure cash flow even without any rent from your unit, meaning you'd be getting paid to live there for free. But don't object to a house hack just because you won't be living rent-free. Compare your new situation to what life would be like without house hacking.

Even if the house hack looks good on paper so far, you're not done—because eventually you'll move. The loan you obtain on a house hack typically requires you to stay in the property for one year; after that you're free to go. As mentioned earlier, one of the key benefits of house hacking is that you are not required to find a new loan just because you move out. Instead, you get to keep that owner-occupied loan in place even though you no longer live in the property!

The second part of analyzing a house hack deal is running the post-move-out numbers. In other words, you'll treat the investment exactly as you would treat a traditional multifamily investment, assuming that all the units are rented out and all the expenses are as they would be for a non-hacked property. If that means adding in property management expenses and increasing your repair budget, then do so. Now take a look at your final pure cash flow number, as well as your cash-on-cash (CoC) return, and determine whether the investment still meets your criteria. Are you making your minimum profitability threshold (part of your CCC, which we looked at in Chapter Eight)? If not, you'll want to strongly consider other options, because a deal that makes sense only as a house hack but turns bad once you move is no deal at all.

House Hacking FAQs

What if I don't want to live with my tenants?

If living near your tenants doesn't sound appealing, remember that there are many different types of house hacking properties available, and not all involve living close to your tenant. We've seen numerous small multifamily properties where the units are so well separated (with individual entrances and different addresses) that residents of one unit would hardly know the others existed. Ultimately, if living at the same location as your tenant for a year doesn't sound like a sacrifice you're willing to make for the betterment of your financial situation, no worries. It's not for everyone. There are still plenty of ways to invest in small multifamily properties that have nothing to do with sharing space! However, for many, if not most, would-be real estate investors, house hacking is *the* critical first step toward achieving financial freedom.

Can I house hack multiple times?

Yes and no. There is no overall restriction that limits you to a certain number of house hacks. However, the most common limitation comes into play when using an FHA loan, which is the most popular method for financing a house hack. As you'll recall, an FHA loan allows you to buy a one- to four-unit property with just a 3.5 percent down payment. Sounds amazing, but here's the catch: You are allowed only *one* FHA loan in your name at a time. Yes, perhaps you could obtain one in your name and your spouse could obtain one in theirs, but that's about it.

This is one of the reasons we recommend buying cosmetic fixers—properties that can be remodeled slightly to increase their value. By increasing the value of your small multifamily property, you may be able to refinance your property with a non-FHA loan after that first year or two, obtaining a more traditional loan and freeing yourself to obtain another FHA loan. While FHA loans generally offer the lowest down payments available for house hackers, many lenders offer non-FHA loans that require just 5 or 10 percent down, so be sure to ask. You may need to put slightly more down, but using one of these loans can give you the ability to house hack several times in a row, quickly building your portfolio with quality assets, significant cash flow, and very little money down.

How do I get my spouse or significant other on board?

Ahhh, the spouse question. It's rare that both people in a couple discover the amazing power of real estate investing simultaneously. The disparity increases when only one of the lovebirds decides that they want to move into a small multifamily property and house hack. If you think house hacking sounds ideal but your partner thinks you're insane, try these two options:

1. **Share Your Vision with Emotion:** Have you ever heard the saying "People buy with emotion and justify with logic"? It's true, and it applies to selling your spouse or significant other on house hacking as well. You can't persuade them with logic alone. You need to make them *feel* the benefits. Sure, you can talk about the cash flow you'll receive, but what does that cash flow do? Does it allow you to work less? Vacation more? Retire early? Share your vision with emotion, then let the math justify it.

2. **Media Changes Mindset:** When I first got into real estate investing, I was hooked. My wife, Heather? Not so much. It was so foreign and strange to her. Heather's only acquaintance with the industry was via late-night TV gurus and warnings from distant relatives who had "lost their shirt" investing in the 1980s. To help change her mindset, I turned to media. I am a firm believer that the shows we watch, the books we read, and the social media we consume change our behavior. Want to become vegan? Start watching vegan documentaries and listening to vegan podcasts. The same applies if you want to run a marathon, improve your marriage, or become a more spiritual person. Media changes mindset—and it does so almost subconsciously!

Therefore, when I needed to convince Heather that I wasn't losing my mind, I asked her to read a few real estate investing books. Specifically, I wanted her to read *Rich Dad Poor Dad* by Robert Kiyosaki, because that book was so powerful in changing my own mindset. Of course, she wasn't too keen on my giving her a book to read, so I made a simple trade: I'd read any book she asked me to if she read that one. A month later, she had finished *Rich Dad Poor Dad* and she got it, just as I had. Me? I finished the entire *Twilight* series. #TeamEdward.

Do I have to manage the tenants myself?

No. You could easily hire a property manager to find and manage tenants. You don't even have to tell the tenant you own the property; you're simply another resident. But if they ever research the legal ownership on the county records, you may have an awkward conversation.

What if I need to move in less than one year?

You'll get hauled off to maximum-security prison to share a cell with a three-fingered man named Bruno or a one-eyed lady named Beatrice.

Just kidding, sort of.

You see, when you obtain an owner-occupied loan, you are telling the mortgage company that you intend to live in the property. Usually, these loans require that you intend to live in the property for at least one year. If you lie and never planned to live in the property at all, hoping to just use the owner-occupied loan to obtain a low-down-payment mortgage on a rental property, that's considered mortgage fraud, which could land you in jail with Beatrice and Bruno. *Do not do that.*

However, what if your circumstances change during that first year? Now, we're not attorneys, so be sure to consult with one, but if caught leaving in less than one year, the assumption is that the government would look at the situation on a case-by-case basis and attempt to decide if there was an "intent to commit fraud" or not. The bottom line: Plan to stay for at least one year and *actually* stay for at least a year unless extenuating circumstances outside your control force you to move. Keep it legal and avoid committing mortgage fraud.

How does management differ on a house hack?

In reality, managing tenants who live next door to you (or above or below you) isn't much different from managing a tenant who lives twenty miles away. At least it *shouldn't* be. It can be tempting to treat your tenant-neighbors as friends, forgoing the official policies and procedures that good property management requires. After all, bumping into your tenant the morning after charging them a late fee on their missed rent can be awkward, so some house hackers have a tendency to let things slide. *Don't do this!*

Keep business business. Follow the same processes and systems you would for any other property and you'll have a much easier time managing your tenants. Sure, they could drop off the rent at your house, but make them follow the same procedures as any other tenant. If nothing else, this degree of formality will help reinforce the business aspect of your relationship and ensure that your relationship stays professional.

What are the first steps if I want to become a house hacker?
The first steps in house hacking are really the same as for any other kind of multifamily investment we've covered so far. First, educate yourself on what you want and establish your CCC. Then talk with lenders to find out what loan options are available based on your income, your credit, and other factors. Next, connect with a real estate agent (or develop an off-market funnel) to begin obtaining leads to fill your deal pipeline. After that, analyze those potential house hacking opportunities to find a deal that makes sense. Finally, make an offer based on your MaPP, and when you get an offer accepted, do your due diligence and buy the property.

KEY TAKEAWAYS

- House hacking means living in a property while using that property as an investment, which has many significant financial benefits.
- There are several different flavors of house hacking, including the traditional small multifamily house hack, the BRRRR house hack, the ADU house hack, and more.
- To analyze a potential house hack, run your numbers using the Four-Square Method, but do it twice. First, assume you'll be living in one of the units and receiving no rent from that unit. Second, analyze for after you move out. Both scenarios should make financial sense.

Chapter 16

CREATIVE FINANCING PART II: PARTNERSHIPS

"Alone we can do so little; together we can do so much."

—HELEN KELLER

Investing in multifamily real estate takes money. Thankfully, it doesn't always have to be *your* money. In fact, one of the reasons we love multifamily real estate so much is because creative financing (the art and science of putting together deals using other people's money) is much more common than with single-family investing.

The larger a deal is, the higher the likelihood you'll find a variety of creative finance tools for the investment. Creative financing (often no- or low-money-down investing) is *not* about having no money; indeed, it is most often used by people with a lot of money. You could even argue (and we do) that most individuals who build massive wealth through real estate investing do so by using no- and low-money-down financing methods. Therefore, whether you have $100 in your checking account or $1 million, this chapter is going to help you turbocharge your results.

The Stack shows how you can build wealth quickly by scaling your investment portfolio *exponentially*. Whenever we teach this topic to investors, the inevitable question arises: "How do I get the money for these big expensive properties?" Stay tuned because the answer is found in this chapter.

In my first book, *The Book on Investing in Real Estate with No (and Low) Money Down*, I compared creative real estate investment strategies to a contractor's tools and I'll repeat the analogy here. If the only tool you have is a large hammer, there are very few projects you can tackle. Perhaps you could pound some nails or do demolition on some cabinets. Add a tape measure, pencil, saw, and drill to the tool belt, and suddenly there are many more projects you can take on, like that swing set your daughter has been begging for or the raised garden your partner requested. Add a jackhammer, air compressor, excavator, and crane, and just like that, you can build a city. You get the point: The more tools you have access to, the bigger the projects you can tackle. The same applies to financing real estate projects. If the only tool in your belt is the traditional bank loan with a 20 percent down payment, you will miss *many* opportunities. Your ability to build wealth and the speed at which you do so will be limited by the need to save up cash for down payments. But as you gain knowledge of creative financing strategies—even just a basic familiarity with how those strategies work—you'll be able to apply them to whatever deal comes your way.

This chapter is designed to help you fill your tool belt, financially speaking, in one particular area: *partnerships*. You'll learn how partnerships can allow you to make great real estate deals with little-to-no money down of your own, as well as the best ways to find partners and get them to say yes.

Financial Partners

"There's no way you're going to be able to buy this one, Brandon. No job, no steady income, and you don't have any savings."

That's what Nancy told me when the triplex lead crossed my desk. The moment I saw the property, I knew I had to have it. Three separate houses on one small lot. Definitely a fixer-upper, but mostly cosmetic. Separate water meters for each unit. Win-win-win. And the entire thing was listed for less than $70,000. Then Nancy began her lecture.

Who's Nancy? No, she's not my wife. Or my mother, or my agent.

Nancy is… me. And sometimes you.

Negative Nancy.

Nancy is the part of our brains that loves to argue for our limitations, to convince ourselves of why things can't be done. And, on the surface, she was right: I didn't have a job, since I was attempting to make it as a full-time house flipper, and equally important, I didn't have any savings, because all my cash was tied up in a house flip. I did the commonsense thing: I listened to Negative Nancy, canceled all my ambitions, and turned on the TV. Just kidding! I wanted to make sure you were still paying attention.

Instead of complaining about my lack of cash, I remind myself of a famous quote I'm paraphrasing here, "You don't lack resources; you lack resourcefulness." Well, I could be resourceful. I could figure this out. Rather than allowing Negative Nancy to control my destiny, I asked the simplest yet most powerful question in the English language: "How?"

How do I buy this triplex, which was going to provide incredible ongoing cash flow, despite not having the money or the ability to obtain a loan? By simply asking the question, I got Negative Nancy to shut up and Resourceful Ron to pipe up. (What? You don't have names for your different personalities?! Am I the only one?)

The answer I (or, rather, Ron) came up with was simple: "Maybe someone else can help fund the down payment you need."

Brilliant! Give that man a raise!

I simply needed to find a partner who would be willing to fund the down payment. After all, I found the deal, and then I would manage the contractors and handle the ongoing property management. I'd put in the work, and they would get a passive return. I just needed someone with some cash—and the willingness to trust me with it.

That epiphany changed everything for me. I suddenly realized that I could do unlimited real estate deals as long as I had other people who were willing to put up the money. And then Nancy realized a basic fact that almost stopped me completely: I didn't know anyone with money.

At the time, I was living in a very low income area of Washington—Grays Harbor County. I didn't hang out with wealthy people. I don't think I knew a single millionaire. *Come on, Ron. Help me out here!*

But then a chance conversation changed everything. I mentioned the pickle I found myself in to a friend from church and asked whether he knew anyone who would be interested in partnering on this property. His response? "I might be interested, actually."

Sure enough, he and his wife became my silent partners on that deal, fronting 100 percent of the down payment, 100 percent of the closing costs, and 100 percent of the rehab budget. In exchange, they received 50 percent of all profits from that investment, including cash flow and future appreciation. This truly became a win-win partnership, because I brought incredible value to the table (a solid deal, experience, knowledge, and the ability to make it all happen), and they brought incredible value to the table (money, and the ability to obtain a mortgage). Together, we formed an alliance that benefited both parties. I was able to invest without a dime of my own money, and they were able to invest without a single hour of work.

Nearly ten years later, we still own this property. Today it's worth around $200,000, yet we owe less than $50,000 on the loan. Each year, usually in January, my partners and I get together at a local Mexican restaurant. Over a plate of the world's best huevos rancheros, I write out two checks: one to my partner and one to myself, each equal to 50 percent of the cash flow profits we made the previous year.

This year, my wife and I spent a stupid amount of money on an outdoor furniture set to go around our pool. It was thousands of dollars, but the amazing thing is that it was kinda *free*. You see, my wife and I agreed to use our last year's profits from that property to remodel our pool area, and I still have several thousand dollars remaining. I think I'll buy a wood pergola next.

This story is not fiction—it's real life. And it's just one example of what's possible with a partnership. Did I have to give 50 percent? Did they have to supply the down payment? Did I have to manage the property? No, no, no—but at the same time, yes, yes, yes! Each partnership is unique, and the perfect partnership is the one that makes both sides feel as if they are using their most valuable attributes and receiving a fair return on their investment. This deal and partnership worked great for us. Since that first official successful venture, I've used partnerships numerous times, as has Brian. In fact, we continue to use partnerships today in our business, buying multimillion-dollar multifamily properties with limited partners, which you'll learn more about in Volume II. In other words, we're still doing today what I did years ago with that first partnership: We're finding great deals and raising the money needed to buy them. The size of the investments have scaled, but the core approach is the same: Work together for mutually beneficial deals.

You might be wondering: Why would a money partner go in on a deal even though they put in most, or all, of the money? Why wouldn't they just pursue the deal themselves? It's a fair question, but the answer is fairly simple: They don't want to. As we're sure you've picked up in the course of reading this book, buying multifamily real estate (or any kind of real estate, for that matter) is not a passive activity. Yes, over time, with the right systems in place, you can make it highly passive, but at the beginning it takes a lot of knowledge, hustle, and money. Not everyone has all three, nor do they want to contribute all three. Some people would rather make half the money without having to do the work. Therefore, the secret to being able to finance real estate deals is simple: Complete the Deal Delta.

The Deal Delta

The Deal Delta is a concept I introduced in *How to Invest in Real Estate: The Ultimate Beginner's Guide to Getting Started*. It is straightforward but powerful:

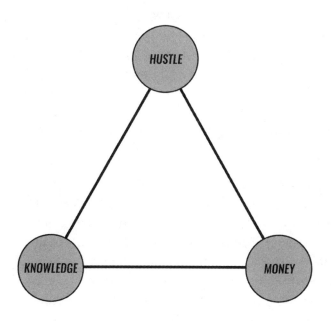

At its core, a real estate investment needs three things to work:

1. Knowledge
2. Hustle
3. Money

Now pick just two.

In other words, someone must have the *knowledge* to put together a real estate deal: They must know why a certain deal works, how to find leads, how to run the numbers, which market works and which doesn't, and so on. But knowledge alone is not enough; after all, how many times have we failed at a diet even though we knew what to do? Therefore, in addition to knowledge, a real estate deal needs someone to take the right action, to *hustle*. This can mean generating leads, answering phone calls, analyzing the leads that come in, making offers, networking, managing contractors, managing the property manager (or the property itself), and more. But even with all the right knowledge and the right hustle, an investment still needs *money* in order to work. Money for the purchase or down payment. Money for closing costs. Money for any necessary rehab. Money for reserves.

Here's where partnerships come in handy. Remember, you, personally, do not need to supply all three components of the Deal Delta. *Just pick two.*

If you're like most beginning real estate investors, the one component you will not be able to bring to the table is money. Therefore, you will need to get really knowledgeable about multifamily investing, do the daily work needed to land some great deals, and get somebody else to supply the money. However, even if you come up with the deal of the century, money partners won't automatically flow to you. You'll also need to learn how to *find* potential partners.

Finding Money Partners: Dig Your Well

Maybe you think you don't know any rich people and, even if you did, they would never give you money. Fine, that might be true (for now). But does someone have to be rich in order to provide you the money for a deal? They would need to have *some* money, yes. But my partners on the triplex deal did not consider themselves rich. They worked administrative jobs for the local county government and had lived in the same small house in a small town for nearly thirty years. What mattered is that they had enough for the down payment, as well as the ability to obtain a loan due to their moderate income and low debt. Therefore, don't assume those around you are not capable of helping you finance your next deal. You never know who might have an extra $20,000, $50,000, or even $100,000 sitting in a bank account earning less than 1 percent, just waiting for an opportunity like the one you could provide.

Now that we've established that potential partners can be found everywhere, let's get into how to connect with them. The entire strategy for finding partners boils down to this tried-and-true networking advice: Dig your well before you're thirsty. In other words, if you wait until you've got a deal to try to build relationships with potential financial partners, you'll struggle and maybe fail. But if you begin building solid relationships with many potential financial partners now, you'll have options to choose from when you land those great deals.

To begin digging your well, you'll have to let the world know what you're doing (or planning to do). Begin talking about real estate with anyone who will listen. Post interesting real estate articles on your social media. Find out who your friends' landlords are and ask for an introduction. Attend local real estate meetups (check the listings at www. biggerpockets.com/events) and talk with everyone. You will need to cast a wide net in your search for potential partners.

"Networking" is often considered a dirty word, but it really just means "making friends." That's it. Make friends. Talk with people. Be interested in them and they'll be interested in you. Even if you're an introvert, you may find that when you ask people questions at a meetup, they'll divulge their life story—with minimal talking on your part.

While getting to know your connections, continue to maintain your well. One of the biggest mistakes people make is engaging only in "need-based" networking, meaning they reach out to their contacts only when they need something from them. Instead, be intentional about keeping track of those in your life who could make great partners and stay in regular contact with them. This could be as simple as sending a quick text message or a short email. In episode 401 of *The BiggerPockets Podcast*, relationship specialist and podcaster Jordan Harbinger shares a strategy he calls "Connect Four." Each day, Jordan spends just a few moments going through his text messages and sends four "rekindling" messages, reaching out to individuals he hasn't spoken with in several months to rekindle the relationship. Brilliant! Although it might sound insincere, it's exactly the opposite. You're creating a system around natural connections to ensure you are not engaging in need-based networking but rather genuine relationship building.

Convincing Money Partners: The KITE Method

Why should someone invest with you? The answer goes beyond the quality of the deal you're offering. Hear me out on this: Of course the deal matters, and without a good deal, you'll struggle. However, people aren't investing in a deal. They are investing in *you* and your ability to make the deal happen. If I gave the world's best real estate deal to a 4-year-old and told them to run it, how would that work out? Probably not well.

In my experience, if you want to raise money, you must be able to demonstrate four basic attributes, which can be expressed in the acronym KITE (because I like acronyms and it just worked out that way). To get other people to trust you with their money, focus on developing and demonstrating these four traits:

1. **Knowledge:** Do you have the knowledge needed to pull off the deal? If you're brand-new to multifamily real estate investing, you might not. There's good news, though: Information is *everywhere*. You're off to a good start by reading this book, but don't stop there. Listen to real estate podcasts. Attend real estate classes. Take investors out to lunch and ask them specific questions. Then ask yourself, "Am I the smartest person on this particular topic in my area?" If not, dig deeper and keep learning. If so, dig deeper still and keep learning. You can never learn too much.

2. **Integrity:** Integrity means doing what you say you're going to do, *no matter what*, even when no one else is looking. When you say you're going to wake up at 6 a.m. and jog, do you lie to yourself and hit the snooze button? When you say you'll finish that project at work but you're not quite done as 5 p.m. rolls around, do you stay late—maybe even all night—just to finish it? Integrity means doing what needs to be done, no matter what, all the time. It means people can trust you with their money because you've been trustworthy in all areas of your life. One of my favorite sayings is "How you do anything is how you do everything." Start living a life of pure integrity.

3. **Tactics:** Real estate investing, while simple, is not always easy. It doesn't just "work" magically; someone has to work it. There are many

things to be done, and many people fail to do them. "Tactics" refers to having a plan and being able to demonstrate exactly how you're going to earn a strong return on an investor's money. Who's going to manage the deal? What kind of legal entity are you going to use? What happens when things go worse than you expected? When will investors make their money? How much can they expect? You should know the answers to all these questions—and be able to communicate them to potential partners.

4. **Experience:** The number one predictor of success is not what someone *says* they'll do but whether they've done it *before*. Experience speaks volumes when trying to find partners and raise money, and for good reason: In the beginning, you don't know what you don't know—and many novice investors don't even know they don't know what they don't know. How do you overcome this when you're just getting started? Well, a few ways.

First, you can gain experience on smaller deals on your own before forming partnerships. Borrow money from banks or hard-money lenders (which we'll discuss in the next chapter) before borrowing from other people.

Second, if you simply must start raising money from partners, begin with friends and family who don't care as much about your real estate investing experience because they know your character from other areas of your life. This was exactly the case in the story of the partnership at the beginning of this chapter.

Third, you can borrow someone else's experience. I'll give you a real-life example. Recently, I started raising money for some large real estate deals, primarily mobile home parks. Because I had never done a large syndication (which we'll talk about in Volume II) or a real estate fund before, I decided I needed someone with more experience on my team. I brought in an investor named Brian Murray (yes, *the* Brian Murray, co-author of this book!), a man who has a ton of experience investing with syndications and large real estate deals. Additionally, because I'm currently trying to buy mobile home parks, I brought in Ryan Murdock, who has more than a decade of experience managing this asset class.

I "borrow" these experts' experience to boost my own, and you can do the same. Sure, you might have to give away some of your profit. But here's what I asked myself: "Let's say I give away half the equity in my own company to bring in people who are way more skilled and experienced than I am. Will I do more deals—or at the very least, will I do a better job with those deals?" The answer was a resounding *yes*. It's worked for me, and it can work for you.

Finally, when it comes time to talk with a partner, presentation matters. You may possess each of the KITE traits in abundance, but unless you can effectively demonstrate your knowledge, integrity, tactics, and experience (not to mention the specifics of the deal), you'll struggle with finding someone to get on board. One of the best ways to demonstrate your abilities is by using either a PowerPoint presentation that outlines your qualifications and the details of the deal (or potential deals) or an "investor packet" that outlines those details in a multi-page PDF.

Debt and/or Equity Money Partners

Earlier, I told the story of the triplex that taught me the value of financial partners. In that situation, my partners received a 50 percent stake in the investment, for better or for worse. If things went extraordinarily well, my partners would make more. But if things went bad, my partners would have to share in future losses. This is known as an equity partnership because the money partners have equity in the deal. It doesn't have to be 50/50, but in an equity partnership, all partners share in the profits and losses.

This, however, is not the only type of money partnership. I own another triplex for which a money partner agreed to put up 80 percent of the purchase price of the property (I put 20 percent down), and I pay him a 5.25 percent interest rate per year on that investment. Yes, this is a loan and not much different from one you might obtain from a bank, but this person could also be seen as a money partner because he has a vested interest in my long-term success. He wants that consistent passive income.

However, when I raise the rent over time, this partner doesn't participate in the upside. At the same time, if the economy takes a nosedive and I experience excessive vacancy, my money partner still gets the same amount of cash deposited into his checking account each month. This is known as a debt partnership and, while less common with individual partnerships, is an option for you to consider and discuss with potential partners. After all, as we said, the ideal partnership is one where both sides are accomplishing their goals. My equity money partners are interested in growing wealthier through their investment and are willing to risk the potential downsides for the opportunity to participate in the long-term upside. My debt partners, on the other hand, are more interested in preserving their capital and receiving consistent checks, regardless of the economy or the performance of the property.

Don't assume your potential partner wants an equity partnership when they might actually prefer debt, and vice versa. Talk with your potential partners to discover their needs, desires, and ambitions. Then put your minds together and make magic.

KEY TAKEAWAYS

- If you don't have the money to invest in real estate, that doesn't mean you can't. Instead, one option is to find a financial partner, someone who can bring all, or some, of the money to the table in exchange for your bringing the deal, the knowledge, and the hustle.
- Potential financial partners should be found by digging your well before you're thirsty. In other words, start intentionally building relationships with people and nurturing those relationships *before* you find a deal.
- It will be hard to find a partner unless you can demonstrate you can fly a KITE: the **K**nowledge to pull off the deal, the **I**ntegrity to uphold your side of the partnership, the **T**actics to make the deal work, and the **E**xperience needed to justify their risk.
- Partners can split equity with you, participating in a deal's profits and losses, or they can simply lend you the cash in exchange for a fixed rate of return. Don't assume you know what your potential partner prefers—talk with them to find out.

Chapter 17
CREATIVE FINANCING
PART III: BRRRR

"Money often costs too much."

—RALPH WALDO EMERSON

Before committing to multifamily real estate, I attempted to be a house flipper, just like the ones on TV. I wanted to buy nasty properties, fix them up, sell them, and make a huge profit. On paper, the house flip seemed like a much better option than law school, which I had been strongly considering. I could make tens of thousands of dollars on a flip and would only have to do some painting and light rehab—or so I thought. I jumped in, attempted to flip my first property, and immediately faced a trifecta of bad things.

First, I decided to do all the work myself, though I had no idea how to fix a leaking pipe. Second, I used a hard-money loan (a short-term loan often used by house flippers that comes with high interest rates and high fees) that cost me an arm and a leg each month. Third, the real estate market had begun to free-fall. This was in 2008 and *no one* wanted to buy a house. Except me, of course, because I had dreams of making millions by flipping. Those home improvement shows never explain that housing markets aren't always great.

After nearly a full year of rehabbing this property and three months of the home sitting on the market without any interest, I was struck with the realization that I might not be able to sell. I felt sick to my stomach, knowing that my short-term loan was coming due soon. I would have to face my wife and explain why I abandoned a prestigious law career to, at best, break even on a failed dream. I would have to accept that all the naysayers were right, and I was just wasting my time flipping houses. All along the way, the monthly payment on the loan was driving my wife and me deeper and deeper into credit card debt. It was a nightmare. But rather than give up, I asked the all-important question: "How?"

How can I get out from under this crushing monthly debt? How can I not lose this property to foreclosure? How can I survive this economic crisis? Should I just fire-sale this and get out, making no money or maybe even losing money? On paper I knew this property was worth what I was asking, but no one was buying. Then a simple answer came to me: "What if I rented this home out? It's totally fixed up. Someone would love to rent this nice property, and I bet I could rent it for more than my current loan payment." And that is exactly what I did. My wife and I advertised the property and found a family to move in that very week. But this, of course, presented me with another problem: the hard-money lender. My loan was almost due, and I had no way to pay them back.

Once more, I asked the all-important question: "How?"

This time, the solution was much simpler. I had a nice property. It was fully rented. It was worth more than what I had invested in it. (I had purchased the home for around $50,000 and spent around $50,000 fixing it up. I believed it would appraise for around $130,000.) I talked to the same bank that had given me a loan on my primary residence and applied for a conventional loan. When the appraisal came in exactly where I hoped it would, they gave me a loan for $100,000, which allowed me to pay off the hard-money loan and my credit cards in full. That's right: I got 100 percent of my money back and obtained a thirty-year conventional loan.

Additionally, because the new loan carried a much lower interest rate, my payment dropped as well, giving me several hundred dollars per month in cash flow from this property. Because I had rehabbed the property, I experienced very few repairs over the following years. Best of all, I had paid off all my debt, so now I could go do the whole thing again, and again, and again.

This is how I stumbled into a powerful strategy that allows a real estate investor to quickly collect nice, cash-flowing rental properties using the same capital over and over (or, in my case, using no money at all). Several years later I wrote a blog post for BiggerPockets.com about this experience, breaking down the process into five parts. I called it "BRRRR," which stands for:

1. **Buy:** You purchase the home using "short-term" money from a hard-money lender, a loan against a retirement account, a private loan, seller financing, a line of credit, or maybe just cold, hard cash. Ideally, you use the same source of short-term money for the rehab, though you could use another source, such as a credit card.

2. **Rehab:** You fix up the property, focusing on repairs that will increase the *value* of the property while also increasing its *durability*. Unlike flippers, you'll actually end up owning this property for years, so using building materials meant to withstand the rigors of tenant life is a must.

3. **Rent:** In most cases, a remodeled home will rent for more than a non-rehabbed property. Because you just fixed up the property, it will require fewer repairs than non-rehabbed properties. This translates to better tenants, better cash flow, and a better landlord experience.

4. **Refinance:** After fixing up the property and renting it out, you now have a property banks will be much more willing to give a loan on. Typically, banks will offer a 70 to 80 percent loan-to-value (LTV) refinance on a rental property. This means the bank will give you between 70 and 80 percent of whatever the property ends up being worth after all the work has been done (its after-repair value, or ARV), which you can use to pay off the short-term loan. Of course, if you've done your math right (more on BRRRR math shortly), you'll have substantially increased the value of your property, which enables you to get a refinance that will entirely pay off your short-term money plus reimburse you for most, if not all, of the money you spent on the rehab. In fact, it's possible to have *no* money invested in a completed BRRRR deal.

5. **Repeat:** Once you have received all your (or your short-term lender's) money back, you can now repeat the process again and again. Essentially, you are recycling your money over and over to build a sizable portfolio fast.

The name BRRRR, though silly and rather annoying to say out loud, took off. I didn't, however, invent the *concept*. People have been BRRRRing as long as there have been real estate investors. What I did was break down this somewhat complicated strategy into a series of steps that people could grasp, get excited about, and actually do. And they are, in fact, doing it often! BRRRR has become one of the most popular strategies in the real estate industry. There are now lenders who specifically aim to help BRRRR investors, and hundreds of podcast episodes, blog posts, and forum posts that address the topic. There are also numerous books on the strategy, including the definitive official guide written by David Greene—*Buy, Rehab, Rent, Refinance, Repeat: The BRRRR Rental Property Investment Strategy Made Simple.* You should definitely read it if you plan to use the BRRRR method.

Although this origin story involved a single-family home, the great thing about the BRRRR strategy is that it works equally well (perhaps *better*) for multifamily, which is the primary way both Brian and I use it today. You see, the BRRRR strategy relies on one vital premise: being able to substantially increase the value of your property via the rehab. Only in that way can you build the equity needed to refinance the loan. Thankfully, increasing the value of a multifamily property is entirely doable. By lowering your expenses, increasing your income, and generally improving your property, you can substantially increase the value of that property. For this and many other reasons, multifamily BRRRRing just works. Don't worry if you don't 100 percent understand the BRRRR strategy yet. It's more complicated than a traditional "put 20 percent down and move on" investment. But sometimes more complications mean more rewards.

Analyzing a BRRRR

To analyze a BRRRR, we are going to run two sets of numbers. First, we will determine how much we can pay for the property—the Maximum Purchase Price (MaPP)—working backward like a house flipper would to determine how much they can pay to make the kind of profit they need. Next, we'll run the numbers like a rental property owner would to find out what kind of pure cash flow and cash-on-cash (CoC) return we can expect.

Determining Your MaPP

Every property has a number that makes it a good deal; that number is the MaPP, the highest amount you can pay to get the profit you desire. Our job, as investors, is not to blindly walk around looking for a good deal, but rather to figure out what number makes a given property a good deal. We do that by working backward, starting with the ARV.

The following formula represents an ideal BRRRR, one in which you recover 100 percent of your capital during the refinance:

$$ARV \times LTV \text{ from Lender} = \text{Total All-in Costs}$$

$$\text{Total All-in Costs} - \text{Refinance Closing Costs} - \text{Rehab Costs} - \text{Initial Closing Costs} = \text{MaPP}$$

For clarification, "rehab costs" include any holding costs paid out during the rehab phase, such as hard-money interest payments and utility costs. Example: One day while driving for deals, you find a fourplex in severe need of a paint job and a new roof. The property is located in a Class B neighborhood in your city, but the property's condition screams Class D. You reach out to the seller and learn she would love to get rid of the property—a headache she inherited from her mother almost a decade ago.

To figure out what refinance value a future lender might allow, we're going to start with the end in mind: What's the property going to be worth when it's all fixed up? Remember, residential properties are typically valued based on what other, similar properties have sold for (comps). In this case, you talk with a real estate agent friend of yours, and although this is an off-market property, they offer you some free advice and show you comps that would justify a $400,000 value once the property is entirely rehabbed.

Next, you speak with your favorite local lender and find that they will offer a refinance for 75 percent of whatever the final valuation is. This tells you that in order to leave no money in this deal after all is said and done, you'll need to be all-in for less than $300,000 (which is 75 percent of $400,000).

Then you'll subtract the refinance costs you'll eventually have to pay (we'll call it $5,000, as it typically ranges between $3,000 and $8,000 depending on your lender and your location) and the rehab costs on the property, which your contractor estimates to be $80,000. Finally, we'll subtract the closing costs we'll be responsible for when we initially purchase the property, including any lender fees. In this case, we'll add $5,000 for title closing costs and another $10,000 for lender closing costs (for a total of $15,000 in initial closing costs). Here's where we are at:

$400,000	ARV
× .75	Lender's LTV
$300,000	Total All-In Costs
−$5,000	Refinance Closing Costs
−$80,000	Rehab Costs
−$15,000	Initial Closing Costs
$200,000	MaPP

Now you have the number you can offer the seller. After some discussion and negotiation, you realize the seller will go to $210,000, but no lower. Even though $210,000 is higher than your MaPP, this does not spell the end of the deal. Remember, anything above your MaPP on a BRRRR calculation is simply money you'll likely need to leave in the deal after the final refinance. You weigh your options, decide you really like the property, and that $10,000 left in the deal is something you are comfortable with, assuming the property will still make sense financially from a cash-flow standpoint. The next step is to analyze the property using the Four-Square Method to calculate your pure cash flow.

Analyzing for Pure Cash Flow

Running the Four-Square Method on a BRRRR investment is not much different from running the numbers on a typical multifamily investment. You will, however, need to do this *three* different ways to accommodate the three distinct phases of the BRRRR investment:

1. **Rehab:** The first phase is when you are rehabbing the property. During this phase, you may have tenants in some of the units, or maybe all the units were cleared and you are 100 percent vacant. During this time, you'll want to know how much cash flow you're earning, or losing, each month.
2. **Post-Rehab/Pre-Refinance:** The second phase is when you've rented the property out but are still using the short-term money. Remember, short-term money, like hard money, is often much more expensive than traditional long-term money, so your cash flow may be significantly less than it will be after the refinance. Ideally, during the pre-refinance period, you'll still be able to achieve some cash flow, but even if a property ends up breaking even or slightly losing money, that doesn't mean it's a terrible deal. This period of time, known as the seasoning period (more on this below), should last twelve months at most, so don't panic if the returns don't look promising right away: They are just temporary! But it's still good to know what you can expect during this period and make sure you're prepared.
3. **Post-Refinance:** Finally, the math we are most interested in comes after the refinance into long-term money. How is this property going to perform in the long run? Specifically, we pay close attention to CoC return, pure cash flow, and annualized total return for each year following the rehab.

Next, run the numbers using the Four-Square Method we learned in Chapter Eight to determine just how much pure cash flow and cash-on-cash return you can expect. Ideally, since we're BRRRRing a multifamily property, we can keep several of the units occupied while renovating the exterior and the interior of vacant units. This means that unlike with a single-family house, we may be able to break even or even make money during the rehab and pre-refinance phases. After the refinance is complete, we should be cash flowing like an ATM, if we bought right.

Let's revisit the fourplex analysis we just did, with an initial purchase price of $210,000 but an all-in refinance for $300,000. In other words, after purchasing the property for $210,000, you paid $15,000 in initial closing costs, put in the $80,000 needed for rehab costs, and paid $5,000 in closing costs on the refinance, obtaining a new loan for $300,000 (which was 75 percent of the ARV), leaving $10,000 of your own cash in the deal.

To save time here, we're going to walk through only the post-refinance analysis—how much cash flow we can expect in the long run after we refinance. Here's how that looks on the Four-Square Method, as we begin in Box 1, move down to Box 2, then up to Box 3, and finish with our CoC return in Box 4.

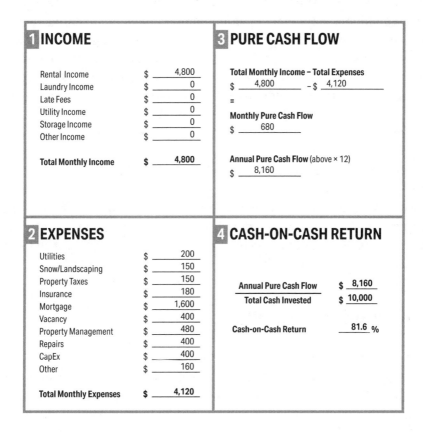

To quickly summarize what we see in the four boxes:
- Our total monthly income comes out to $4,800, assuming we can rent each unit for $1,200 per month after the rehab has been completed.
- Our total monthly expenses come to $4,120, after including everything from utilities to CapEx and more.
- This leaves us with a monthly pure cash flow of $680, which works out to $170 monthly cash flow per unit (MCFPU). And, of course, multiplying that $680 by twelve, we get $8,160 per year in pure cash flow.

- Finally, if we're making $8,160 per year and we only have $10,000 left in the investment, that works out to an 81.6 percent CoC return.

Wait a second... 81.6 percent CoC return?! Didn't we say a good metric to aim for would be 5 to 20 percent, depending on the Class of the property? Yes, and now you see the immense power of the BRRRR strategy. By finding a fixer-upper, fixing it up, and pulling most or all of your capital out, you turbocharge your return because you're making great cash flow while having almost nothing invested in the deal. Just for fun, imagine if you had purchased the recent example for $180,000 instead of $210,000. Rather than leaving $10,000 in the deal at the end of the day, you'd have *made* $20,000 after the refinance. When you're making cash flow without any money invested, you're experiencing an *infinite return*. We sure love the BRRRR strategy!

One final note on BRRRR analysis: If the above process seemed a bit long and cumbersome, it is. That's why BiggerPockets invented the BRRRR Calculator, an easy-to-use analysis tool designed to help you do everything we just did—in under five minutes. It also allows you to print out beautiful PDF reports that can showcase the strength of your deal. Check it out—it's pretty awesome—at www.biggerpockets.com/brrrr-calculator.

Six Benefits to BRRRRing

1. Requires Little to No Money Down

This benefit may already be clear, but if not, let's make it even more explicit: One of the primary benefits of using the BRRRR method for acquiring rental properties is the ability to build your portfolio using no or low money down.

A typical multifamily rental property requires anywhere from 20 to 30 percent down, and then you'll need to pay out of pocket for any rehab, closing costs, and unexpected expenses. With the BRRRR strategy, you are able to wrap many, if not all, of these costs into the short-term loan at the beginning. Then, if you've done your math right and accurately estimated the ARV of the property, you can refinance that short-term loan into a long-term loan and still have little or no money in the deal.

Even if your short-term loan won't fund the rehab of your property and you're forced to pay for it out of pocket, all is not lost. You can potentially get back *more* in the refinance than what you owed the short-term lender, thereby paying yourself back for the money you spent on repairs. In other words, even if you have to invest some of your own money at the beginning, you may be able to get much of this money back out again so that it's not left in the investment.

2. Reduces Risk

We've heard people complain that the BRRRR strategy is risky because you're not putting a lot of money into the investment. We're happy to show you that is not accurate. Yes, there are risks associated with the BRRRR strategy, and we'll cover those in a moment. But risk because of your down payment is actually the *opposite* of what you're getting . To explain this, let's look at two investments side by side.

Option 1: Traditional Already Fixed-Up Fourplex Rental

> Purchase Price: $300,000
> Bank Down Payment Requirement: 20%
> Down Payment Amount: $60,000
> Total Loan: $240,000
> Closing Costs: $5,000
> Rehab Needed: $0
> **Total Capital Needed Up Front: $65,000**

Option 2: Fixer-Upper Fourplex Using the BRRRR Strategy

> Purchase Price: $200,000
> Rehab Needed: $35,000
> Closing Costs: $8,000
> Short-Term Loan: $240,000
> **Total Capital Needed Up Front: $3,000**

> ARV: $300,000
> Bank Refinance Requirement: 20% LTV
> Refinance Closing Costs: $4,000
> New Long-Term Loan Amount: $240,000
> **Total Capital Left in Deal: $7,000**

The first deal, the traditional rental investment, has a total loan amount of $240,000. The second deal, after the final refinance, has a total loan amount of $240,000. In other words, the loan is for the same amount, because what both deals have in common is the same equity. The difference is that the equity on the first was *bought*, while the equity on the second was *earned*. Now, we're not saying you should never put a down payment on a property, because, of course, there are times when that would be appropriate.

Here's the point: Which investment is *riskier*? Both deals have the same final loan amount and loan terms. Therefore, all things being equal, the pure cash flow would be exactly the same on both. But the traditional investment has $65,000 of your cold, hard cash invested in the deal, while the BRRRR deal has just $7,000. If the worst happens and you lose the investment, would you rather lose $65,000 or $7,000? Plus, it would take a lot longer to earn $65,000 back in cash flow than $7,000, making your CoC return much lower.

When people complain about low- and no-money-down strategies being risky, what they are really complaining about is people who buy that traditional $300,000 property with a no-money-down $300,000 loan (which is hard to do, but stay with us as we make this point). If you owe $300,000 on a $300,000 property, *that* is risky, because if you're forced to sell, you'll lose a lot of money due to closing costs and sales commissions. If the market drops, as it does from time to time, you could find yourself upside down, with negative equity. *That* is risky. We love the BRRRR strategy because it allows us to have the safety of significant equity in a property and experience the higher cash flow benefits of a lower LTV loan, all without needing to put a lot of money down.

3. Scales Faster With Recycled Capital

When you use the BRRRR strategy to build your portfolio, you are continually able to reuse the same capital to invest in properties, allowing you to scale the growth of your portfolio much faster. Let's say you're starting with $30,000 in savings. You decide to buy a nice triplex with the BRRRR strategy, using that $30,000 to help obtain the short-term loan and pay for some of your rehab costs. After you've rehabbed the property and rented it out, it appraises for significantly more than what you owe (of course), so you refinance the property and get your entire $30,000 back.

Now you can use that same $30,000 again to buy another property. In the meantime, you've probably saved up even more money, so perhaps you have another $20,000 to add to your war chest, giving you $50,000 to invest in the next deal. You use that $50,000 to BRRRR a six-unit property, which you soon refinance to get back your $50,000. You repeat this process again and again and again, using the same recycled capital to quickly scale your business all the way to financial freedom.

4. Reduces the Pain of CapEx and Repairs

As you know, stuff breaks in rental properties. Refrigerators go out, carpet gets wine stains, and water heaters fail. These breakdowns generally spread out over time, so every month or two (or, in some cases, every week or two) you need a handyman to replace or repair something. However, with the BRRRR strategy, you are front-loading many of those repairs and replacements. The carpet is new (or, better yet, you replace it with quality vinyl plank flooring); you replace the fridges and install a new water heater. As a result, once your tenants move in, you should experience significantly fewer repairs, which boosts your cash flow while minimizing your involvement in the property.

5. Rapidly Increases Your Net Worth

As you know, equity is the difference between what your property is worth and what you currently owe on the property. And while cash flow is wonderful for helping you pay your bills and achieve financial freedom, it's equity that transforms your personal net worth. In other words, the more equity you have, the richer you are (at least on paper!). When you use the BRRRR strategy correctly, you end up with a significant amount of equity, even though you didn't have to put that money down. You are effectively jump-starting your equity and adding significantly to your net worth with each property you acquire. You're not starting from nothing and saving up for the next forty years to become a millionaire. You are jumping from, perhaps, a zero-dollar net worth to tens of thousands in equity/net worth, then jumping again with your next purchase.

Going back to the earlier example, if you turn $7,000 into $60,000 of equity, that's a whole lot better than starting with $7,000 and growing that by 8 percent per year in the stock market or even 12 to 15 percent with a traditional real estate investment. Now you can do it again and perhaps add another $60,000 of equity. And then another. With each property you add, you increase your net worth by leaps and bounds.

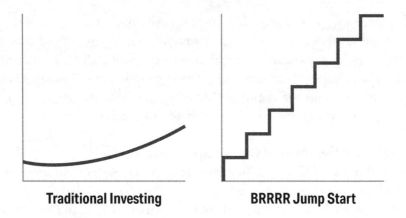

| Traditional Investing | BRRRR Jump Start |

6. Works on All Property Types and Sizes

The BRRRR strategy works for single-family homes, small multifamily real estate, large apartment complexes, and even mobile home parks (we are using it right now with this asset class). It works with self-storage, senior housing, and low-income housing. Heck, it even works in most businesses that have nothing to do with real estate.

Because the BRRRR strategy works at all different levels, it will allow you to scale your business using The Stack method. You can BRRRR a duplex, then use that to BRRRR a fourplex, and soon BRRRR a ten-unit, then a twenty-five unit, and then maybe you'll BRRRR a shopping mall. The possibilities are endless, and you'll be limited by nothing more than your ambition and creativity. Master the BRRRR strategy and it will serve you for the rest of your life, making you a fortune and leading you to financial freedom.

Risks and Rewards: Four Keys to a Successful BRRRR

BRRRRing is riskier than many other types of investing—we won't deny it. The success of your BRRRR strategy hinges primarily on your ability to refinance later on, get your money back out, and pay off your short-term lender. Of course, risk is not something to run from, but you need to arm yourself with knowledge of the potential dangers as well as the solutions to any problems you may encounter. In this section, we're going to provide four keys to a successful BRRRR so you can correctly buy, rehab, rent, refinance, and repeat your process, accelerating your journey toward becoming a multifamily millionaire.

Rule No. 1: Line Up Your Lender First

One of the biggest risks to BRRRR investing is being unable to refinance the property after the rehab. This risk can be substantially reduced, however, by simply lining up your refinance lender before you even purchase a property. You can have a good degree of confidence in your ability to obtain that refinance if you speak with and get preapproved by a lender before you begin a BRRRR.

Specifically, be sure to get answers to all the questions from your Lender Call Sheet, which we mentioned in Chapter Fourteen and you can find at www.biggerpockets.com/multifamilybonus. You'll especially need to know the LTV they offer on a refinance and their seasoning requirements (the period of time between when you buy the property and when you can refinance the property). Also take into account any changes to your personal life (such as job changes) that you might experience in the coming year as you wait for your refinance.

Furthermore, ask whether this lender can accomplish a cash-out refinance or only a rate-and-term refinance. The difference? A rate-and-term refinance limits your new loan to the same amount (or less) as your previous loan. However, a cash-out refinance will give you up to a specific percentage of the property's value (the LTV), no matter the amount of the previous loan.

Let's look at a simple example to illustrate this. You buy a property for $50,000 and finance the purchase with a $50,000 hard-money loan. You spend $20,000 on a credit card fixing it up, and now the property is worth $100,000. Because your lender has agreed to a cash-out refinance for up to 75 percent of the property's value, or $75,000, this sounds like a great BRRRR deal. You should be able fully pay back the hard-money loan, pay off the credit card, and even have a little left over for closing costs. But if you got a rate-and-term refinance instead, the new loan would be limited to $50,000, not the full $75,000, despite the increased value of the property.

Call around to different lenders and know your options before starting your BRRRR. You don't want a nasty surprise at the end. And once you settle on a lender, keep an open line of communication with them throughout your rehab process so you can navigate any changes in the lending environment as they occur.

Rule No. 2: Stay on Budget and on Time

It's *really* easy to overspend on a rehab. We've both done it, and you'll probably do it too. Just be aware that if you blow your rehab budget, it will affect the amount of money you personally need to invest in the deal. Spending more doesn't necessarily mean you'll increase the value of a property proportionally. Therefore, if your BRRRR was budgeted to allow you to leave zero dollars in the deal after the refinance but you have to put an extra $20,000 into the rehab, you may have to cover the overage with your own money.

To stay on budget, follow these four steps:

1. Fully understand the work needed to achieve the final result (getting an inspection before buying the property should be very helpful) and create a detailed scope of work that covers everything. For more on this, be sure to read *The Book on Estimating Rehab Costs* by J Scott.

2. Always include a "whoops/overages" line item in your budget. No matter how good you are at the first step, there are always unknowns that won't be revealed until you get into a project. We like to include 10 to 15 percent of the total budget for unknowns.

3. Get quality contractors to do the work, or if you plan to do the work yourself, *be* a quality worker! One of the surest ways to blow your budget is to hire someone to do the work, then need to hire someone else to fix the first contractor's mistakes.

4. Hold your contractor accountable to their bids, timeline, and quality of work. An entire book could be written about that one sentence, as there is an art and a science to managing contractors effectively. If you go in blind, you'll be robbed. For a great discussion on how to manage contractors, be sure to listen to episode 314 *of The BiggerPockets Podcast* in which Andresa Guidelli explains how to choose and manage contractors.

Rule No. 3: Nail Your ARV

The after-repair value (ARV) is one of the most important metrics to get right when you're embarking on a BRRRR investment. After all, the refinance amount is based on the ARV, as most banks will lend between 70 and 80 percent of the new value. If the appraisal on your BRRRR comes in low, your new loan will be low. In extreme cases, your new loan may not even be enough to pay off the initial short-term loan, putting you in a position where you'll need to bring money to the closing table just to refinance. That's about as fun as trying to bathe a cat, so be sure you accurately predict the ARV of your property.

How do you nail your ARV? By basing your estimate on good data (talk to a local real estate agent for comps); doing the right rehab work at a quality level that will deliver the highest ARV; getting broker price opinions, or BPOs, from experienced agents in the area; and being conservative in your estimates. While you can't know with 100 percent confidence what value an appraiser will give your property, you can usually get pretty darn close.

What if the appraisal on the refinance comes in low? First, consider challenging the appraisal. Examine the appraisal, including the comps the appraiser used, to determine whether the value is fair and reasonable. After all, an appraisal is just an opinion. Oftentimes, appraisers are in a rush and/or don't fully understand the market they are evaluating in, which could lead to their inaccurately appraising a property's true value. Although the lender would probably require you to pay for a second appraisal, it might be worth the cost. For more on dealing with appraisers, don't miss episode 382 of *The BiggerPockets Podcast*, in which investor and appraiser Josiah Smelser shares how to encourage your appraiser to give you the highest valuation, as well as tips on how to challenge their data to improve your property's value.

What if you can't get the appraisal increased? Or worse, what if the market truly did drop? After all, the value of properties goes up and down regularly. One large risk of the BRRRR strategy is the market dropping after you make the initial purchase. If that happens, your property will not be worth what you thought it would be when you're ready to refinance. What then?

First, you could suck it up and refinance for whatever the bank offers, knowing that you'll have to leave more money in the deal. This is still a better scenario than if you had just put the normal 20 percent or more down on an investment. Your CoC return is still likely through the roof. But if these options don't work, you may have one final option, which actually might not be that bad: selling. Since you ideally have 20 to 30 percent equity in the property, the market would have to drop those same percentages before you'd be "underwater" and lack the ability to sell. As long as you stayed on budget, you have enough equity so that even if the market dropped significantly, you should be able to sell the property for more than you invested in the deal.

This is another benefit of using the BRRRR strategy on small multifamily properties. You can list and sell the property while tenants are paying rent, because you're probably selling to another investor. You have just totally remodeled a property and rented it out at top dollar. There are many investors who would love to purchase a "turnkey" rental property from you. True, you may not make much, or any, profit from the transaction, especially if you have to do a fire sale in a hurry. But the bottom line is that you can still get out.

Rule No. 4: Understand Seasoning
Let's say you find an amazing duplex to BRRRR. You use short-term financing to buy the property, rehab it beautifully, and rent it out to some great tenants at high rates. This whole process took just six weeks to accomplish, from the time you signed the closing documents to the time you signed the rental agreement with your new tenants. You're ready to refinance so you can stop paying the more expensive short-term-money rates and get all your cash back out. But when you apply for the loan, the lender says, "Nope!" Why? Because of seasoning.

When you BRRRR a small multifamily property, traditional residential lenders typically require a period of time between when you buy the property and when you refinance it. This period of time is known as seasoning and can affect your math, so it's important to understand how seasoning works and factor it into your plans. Seasoning is typically six months long but can be as long as twelve months for some lenders. This means you may have to continue paying the higher rates on whatever short-term financing you used for the first six to twelve months, which can affect cash flow in the first year.

To avoid this scenario, before you even purchase your BRRRR, talk with several lenders in your market, explain what you are trying to do, and ask them what their seasoning requirements are. Second, when running the math on your BRRRR, be sure to account for this seasoning period.

A final note: Seasoning is typically only applicable to traditional financing of *residential* properties that are backed by either Fannie Mae or Freddie Mac, government-sponsored entities that buy mortgages from banks so those banks can reloan their capital. Commercial loans typically do not have a seasoning requirement. Additionally, portfolio lenders, which are those banks or credit unions that make loans that are not ultimately repurchased by Fannie or Freddie, often do not have seasoning requirements. Definitely check around to see your options!

KEY TAKEAWAYS

- The BRRRR strategy means you **B**uy a fixer-upper with short-term money, **R**ehab that property, **R**ent that newly renovated property out to great high-paying tenants, **R**efinance that property into a long-term (low-interest) mortgage—getting most or all of your cash back out—and **R**epeat the process as you build your portfolio.
- To analyze a BRRRR, work backward from the after-repair value (ARV) to find the exact amount you could pay. Then use the Four-Square Method to ensure that the property produces the right amount of profit at that price.
- BRRRR is powerful, but it can be risky. Reduce this risk by lining up your refinance loan before you purchase a property, staying on budget and on time for your rehab, getting an accurate assessment of your ARV, and understanding how seasoning works so you can time your BRRRR correctly.

Chapter 18
MAKING AN OFFER THAT STICKS

"I'm going to make him an offer he can't refuse."

—MARLON BRANDO IN *THE GODFATHER*

You'll never get a deal without first making an offer. However, not all offers are created equal—even if the price of competing offers is the same. That's right, offering on a piece of real estate is about more than just price. In the pages that follow, we'll break down exactly how to make an offer and, more importantly, how to get that offer accepted. Finally, we'll close with some of the most powerful negotiating strategies we've encountered and show you how to implement them.

How Offers Work
When a perfect deal crosses your desk and you've run the numbers to find

exactly how much you can pay (your MaPP), it's time to pop the question to the seller. If you're new to real estate, this can feel scary, but making an offer is no more difficult than tying your shoes or cooking—once you know the process.

At its core, an offer conveys to the seller several vital pieces of information about how you would like to buy their property. Let's walk through several of these key elements.

- **Name(s):** You'll need to decide who is going to officially buy the property. Is it you? You and your spouse? An LLC? A trust? If you're not sure, that's okay. We'll cover this in Chapter Twenty-One.
- **Purchase Price:** Obviously, a big part of the offer is the price you are willing to pay.
- **Earnest Money:** Earnest money is a deposit you put down immediately after your offer is accepted, and your offer should specify the exact amount. This deposit is typically held by a third party (like the title company) and ensures that you don't waste the seller's time by walking away from the deal. Earnest money is typically 1 to 3 percent of the purchase price but could be higher or lower depending on the situation.
- **Financing Method:** A seller needs to know how you plan to obtain the funds to pay for the purchase. Therefore, in the offer, you will specify whether you plan to pay cash or use a loan.
- **Closing Date:** Your offer will also specify the date you will close the deal and officially take ownership of the property. Many offers include verbiage that allows for automatic extensions if either party needs more time to close, sometimes for an added fee or increased earnest money.
- **Closing Costs:** The offer should list who will be paying the various closing costs associated with the transaction.
- **Contingencies:** Your offer should also include stipulations that clearly define the reasons you can back out of the deal and have your earnest money refunded without penalty. Most of these contingencies have timelines attached, after which the contingency expires. For example, many offers include a ten-day inspection contingency or a twenty-day document inspection contingency. The five most common contingencies are:
  1. **The financing contingency,** giving you the ability to back out if you can't obtain financing.
  2. **The inspection contingency,** giving you the ability to back out if you find something in the inspection that concerns you.

3. **The document inspection contingency,** giving you the ability to review the seller's documents and back out if you find discrepancies between how the property was marketed and what is true.
4. **The appraisal contingency,** giving you the ability to back out of the deal if the appraisal comes in lower than what your financing requires.
5. **The title contingency,** giving you the ability to back out if the seller cannot give a clear title (prove that they have full legal ownership and the right to sell the property).

Of course, an offer contains much more than the seven elements we just discussed. (A purchase and sale agreement can run dozens of pages.) But the items above are typically the most important and the most likely to be negotiated later in the process.

Now let's talk about the exact process for making an offer. This can differ depending on several factors, most notably, whether you are buying an on-market or off-market property. We'll explore each separately; then we'll bring them back together and talk about how to make sure your offer is accepted.

How to Make an On-Market Offer

A small multifamily property that has been listed for sale by a real estate agent and is currently on the MLS is an on-market property. To make an offer, you will use a real estate agent and they'll handle most of the paperwork and details. Remember, a real estate agent is paid by the seller of the property (usually a commission of 5 to 6 percent of the purchase price) so, as a buyer, it's free for you to have an agent. Your agent will help you fill out a document known as a purchase and sale agreement (PSA), which outlines the specifics of what you're offering, including the price and a few million other details. (Okay, maybe less than a few million, but you'll be shocked at how long some PSAs can be.)

While you *can* use the same agent or brokerage as the seller (known as "dual agency"), we advise this only if you have ample experience investing in real estate. The seller's agent is legally and ethically bound to get the highest price possible for the seller (who is, after all, the one paying their fee), and that is not necessarily in your best interest. That said, the reason some experienced investors use the seller's agent is to increase that agent's motivation to convince the seller to accept your offer. If they represent both sides of the deal, they get both sides of the commission, effectively doubling their income while doing little extra work. When you get to the point where you know more than the average real estate agent and don't need their help with negotiation, you can consider using the seller's agent. Until then, you should use your own.

How to Make an Off-Market Offer

A great real estate agent can be immensely helpful in making sure all the i's are dotted and the t's are crossed and helping you negotiate the best price. But what if the property is not listed for sale by a real estate agent— in other words, it's off-market? Maybe you found the deal by driving for deals, through direct-mail marketing, or on Craigslist. What then? Can an agent still help?

As we just mentioned, an agent is typically paid by the seller of a property. The seller will sign a listing agreement with the agent that spells out how much they will sell the property for and how much the agent will make for doing so. With an off-market deal, no such arrangement exists, and you'll have a tough time convincing an off-market seller to fork over tens of thousands of dollars to an agent. Typically, if the deal is off-market, you will *not* be using a real estate agent. Instead, you'll need to dot the i's and scribble those t's on your own PSA. This, however, is not as hard as it might seem. Here are a few options for getting this essential form into your hands so you can begin making offers.

- **Online:** You can find PSAs online through websites like LawDepot. com and USLegalForms.com or as part of your BiggerPockets Pro Membership. However, using a canned online form could present problems down the road if the form is incomplete, filled out incorrectly, or contains provisions not applicable to your state or local laws. Rarely does a canned form cover all the nuances of a deal, and if things were to go bad, how confident are you that your PSA will protect you? If you do plan to obtain your PSA online, just be sure it is designed for the state you plan to purchase real estate in.
- **Title Companies:** Many title companies (which we'll discuss in a moment) also offer PSAs for free to potential customers. Call a few local title companies to see what they might have.
- **Attorney:** Of course, you could go to the opposite end of the spec-

trum and hire an attorney to prepare a full PSA for you, but this could cost hundreds or even thousands of dollars. However, this might be money well spent, especially if you're buying larger properties. (The bigger you go, the more important attorneys are at this step.) You can also take a hybrid approach by getting a PSA online or from a title company and having an attorney review it. Once your attorney either draws up a PSA or signs off on a PSA template, you can then recycle the document for future deals in that market.

Eleven Tips for Making a Compelling Offer

There is a good chance that when you make your offer, you'll be competing with many others who are pursuing that same deal—even if you're offering on an off-market property. Therefore, you'll want to do everything in your power to make your offer stand out.

1. **Put Your Best Foot Forward:** If you know you have competition, don't play games. Submit your best offer right away—your MaPP. Many investors love to talk about the "deal" they got by paying, say, $200,000 for a property listed at $300,000, but if the property makes sense at $300,000 and you'll be competing with others, make the best offer you can to get the deal.

2. **Offer Fast:** Sometimes the offer that gets accepted is the first one to come in. This is why we stress building up a deal pipeline and being proactive in working your LAPS funnel daily. We aim to make our offers before anyone else has even had a chance to look at the property. We want to talk with the seller and begin building our relationship with them quickly—and you can do the same.

3. **Close Faster (or Slower):** As part of your offer, you'll define the target closing date. Typically, bank loans take thirty to sixty days to close, so you may not be able to shorten that timeline. But if you're using another form of financing, perhaps you can close faster, maybe even within a week. On the other hand, some sellers would prefer to delay their closing, for personal or tax reasons. Aim to understand the motivation of the seller and work as fast, or as slow, as they would like.

4. **Reduce or Waive Your Inspection:** Inspections are important because you need to know what you're buying. However, to improve your chances of landing a deal in a competitive environment, you could consider waiving your inspection contingency. You'll still do an inspection,

of course, but you are waiving the right to get your earnest money back if you do find something negative in the condition of the property. More risk, for sure. But worth it? Maybe, under the right circumstances. You can also mitigate the risk by bringing a contractor or inspector with you on your walk-through prior to extending the offer.

5. **Shorten or Waive Your Financing Contingency:** Most real estate offers include a financing contingency that allows the seller to get their earnest money back if their financing falls through. However, a financing contingency can be shortened (meaning, it might not last till closing, but you might have a certain number of weeks to back out due to financing) or waived entirely. As when waiving your inspection, you risk losing your earnest money if your financing falls through, but this might be a risk you feel comfortable taking to sweeten your offer.

6. **Include Proof of Funds:** No one wants to waste time, especially sellers who are ready to unload a property. They don't want to tie up the property with a pending contract only to have the buyer be unable to afford the property at the finish line. Therefore, get your financing lined up ahead of time and have your lender give you a "proof of funds" or preapproval letter. If you'll be paying cash, print out a copy of your online bank statement showing the money is ready and waiting to be deployed.

7. **Make It Personal:** Remember this one simple fact in real estate and you'll go far: People like to sell to people they like. It's true! In *The Book on Rental Property Investing*, I shared of one of my favorite tactics for getting someone to like you: Submit a personal letter with your offer. This letter, which we've also included at www.biggerpockets.com/multifamilybonus, shows the seller that you aren't some faceless investor but a real, live person. I even include a photo of myself and my family. It might be easy to say no to XYZ Corporation, but it's harder to say no to my 4-year-old daughter, Rosie!

8. **Increase Your Earnest Money:** Earnest money tells the seller, "I'm going to close on this property or else you can keep this money." Therefore, the more money you put on the table, the more confident the seller will be that you can close. If you can put down $30,000 instead of $10,000, your offer will look better to the seller.

9. **Give Them Options:** Rather than giving the seller one option to approve or deny, why not give them several options to choose from?

This technique shifts their perspective from thinking "yes or no" to deciding "which one?" For example, we often offer an all-cash price and another price with financing attached. Or we'll offer a price with normal bank financing and another, higher price if the seller is willing to do seller financing. (Similar to the debt partnership described in Chapter Sixteen, this is when the seller becomes the bank.) Use your imagination and give the seller choices rather than an ultimatum.

10. **Include an Escalation Clause:** Although this isn't necessarily going to make your offer more compelling, an escalation clause could help you land a deal even when you are initially outbid. An escalation clause is a legal clause, put into your offer, that tells the seller you will increase your offer up to a certain level if someone else submits a higher offer than you. For example, you might bid $500,000 for a property and include an escalation clause that says you'll pay $5,000 more than any other offer up to $540,000. If someone else submits an offer for $520,000, your offer immediately becomes $525,000 and you'll have the highest offer. Without such a clause, the seller would probably take the other offer, leaving you in the dust.

11. **Re-Offer:** You will get rejected—it's part of the game. In fact, we typically lose 90 percent of the offers we make. You never know when someone is going to finally accept that their property isn't worth what they listed it for and come around. However, when they finally reach that point, they aren't going to seek you out. They'll wait for someone else to offer a higher amount and grab a great deal.

Therefore, whenever your offer is rejected, don't think of it as a no, but rather as a no-for-now. Then re-offer later. We usually set a reminder to re-offer on deals two to three weeks later. Usually we don't change a thing in the second offer; we just resubmit the old offer with an updated date. Each time you offer on a property, the seller experiences two things: Their internal projection of what their property is worth decreases, and their confidence that you are a legitimate buyer increases. Therefore, don't take no for an answer. Stop re-offering only after someone else lands the deal. Until then, it's still in play!

There is no surefire way to get your offer accepted. Sometimes you simply can't pay what someone else is willing to pay. That's how it goes. However, the eleven tips we just outlined should help you increase the percentage of offers that do get accepted. In a competitive market, every trick that can give you an edge over the competition is worth pursuing, and when you're consistent over the long haul, you will eventually land an incredible deal.

After Submitting Your Offer

Whether you're submitting an on-market or off-market offer, you will get one of the following responses:

1. **Yes:** If your offer is accepted, congratulations! It's time to get that PSA over to a title company or attorney, depending on your state.

2. **No:** Sometimes (okay, most of the time) your offers will be rejected. Maybe you were outbid, or maybe the seller just didn't like your price. It's not a bad thing. Every no is just one step closer to a yes. More importantly, every no could turn into a yes down the road. If the seller accepted an offer from someone else, that doesn't mean it's a done deal. Many deals fall apart, so ask whether you can put in a "backup offer" if the first offer falls through. Should that happen, your offer will be accepted next. However, if the no is simply because the seller didn't like your price, consider raising your offer (if the deal still makes sense) or simply re-offer a few weeks down the road. You never know when their motivation to sell will increase—your "low" offer might look pretty darn appealing by next month.

3. **Highest and Best:** In a competitive market, many sellers receive numerous offers on their property. In this situation, most sellers (or, more accurately, their agents) will put out a call for highest-and-best offers. In other words, the agent is starting a bidding war and wants to see who will pay the most. Unlike a typical auction, however, you don't get to see what the other offers are. You simply have the option to raise your bid or sweeten your offer in other ways and hope it's better than everyone else's. If you find yourself in a highest-and-best situation, don't get caught up in the hype and overpay. In addition to (or in place of) raising your price, consider making your offer better by closing faster, offering cash, increasing your earnest money, passing on a contingency, or making your offer stand out in some other way.

4. **Counter:** When a seller decides that your offer was not good enough but wants to continue the negotiation, they will counter with their own offer. For an on-market deal, this is typically done formally

with an official counter document, but if the deal is off-market, you might discuss this counteroffer over the phone or at a seller's kitchen table. Perhaps you offered $250,000 on a triplex. The seller, who really wanted $300,000, might counter at $275,000. Then you have the option of countering again, accepting, or walking away. There are a lot of psychological games to be played at this stage, and you never know what the other party is thinking. It's real-life poker, and it's just as fun.

5. **Silence:** Finally, sometimes a seller will simply refuse to respond to your offer. This is most common when you've offered significantly less than what the seller is looking for. Consider this a no, but follow the same guidelines outlined above. A no is not always forever.

KEY TAKEAWAYS

- Whether you're making an on-market or off-market offer, you'll be filling out a purchase and sale agreement (PSA), which includes the names of all parties involved, the address of the property, the purchase price, contingencies, and more.
- Simply firing off an offer works, but you can dramatically improve your odds of getting an offer accepted by following some simple tips and strategies.
- After submitting your offer, you'll encounter one of five responses: yes, no, highest-and-best, a counteroffer, or silence. Don't get discouraged when a deal doesn't work out. Motivations change, so keep following up and re-offer regularly until the property is sold.

Chapter 19
DUE DILIGENCE

"Research is formalized curiosity. It is poking and prying with a purpose."

—ZORA NEALE HURSTON

Congratulations! If you've reached this point, you've successfully found a multifamily property, analyzed it, made an offer, and had your offer accepted. However, the deal isn't done yet, and now we enter one of the most crucial phases in the acquisition process: due diligence.

Due diligence entails diving into the specifics of the property to make sure there are no skeletons in the closet and the property is as you believe it should be. In residential real estate, most investors also refer to the entire period between the offer being accepted and the deal closing as the due diligence period. In this chapter, we're going to walk you through several things you should be doing during the due diligence period to ensure you are prepared and ready to close on your multifamily property.

Lining Up Your Title Company or Attorney

Every state is unique with respect to the exact manner in which a real estate deal is closed. The biggest difference is typically found in the use of an attorney versus a title company. Some states (mostly in the West) rely on title companies to handle the closing transaction process, while other states (mostly in the East) rely on attorneys for this. If you're unsure about the customs in your area, talk to any local investor or agent to find out the norm.

If you are using a real estate agent and purchasing on-market deals, your agent will help you choose a title company or attorney after your offer has been accepted. If you are pursuing a deal without an agent, you might need to find an attorney or title company yourself. We recommend asking a real estate investor or agent in your area (you can find them, of course, on BiggerPockets.com) for recommendations. Then you'll take the signed contract to the title company or attorney and open up escrow, which means you've hired them to begin handling the transaction. They will likely have some additional paperwork for you to fill out, but at this point, the process is fairly straightforward. They'll guide you through the specific legal process of closing. The title company or attorney will get to work on verifying that the seller has the legal ability to sell and will prepare the documents and get all parties to sign at the end.

The rest of the due diligence, however, is on you. Let's dive in.

Property Inspection

In the previous chapter, we mentioned the inspection contingency, which gives you a certain number of days to inspect the property and keep your earnest money if you must back out due to some unforeseen problem with the property. The clock typically starts ticking on your contingency the moment both parties sign the PSA (which is referred to as acceptance), so you'll need to embark on getting your inspector scheduled to look at the property right away. Even if you waived this contingency, it's still important that you conduct a thorough inspection of the property as soon as possible to make sure you know what you're getting into. In addition, if you plan to do a large rehab, now would be a good time to bring in your contractor(s) as well.

You might feel you have a pretty good grasp on the condition of the property and be tempted to save some money and skip the inspection. We highly recommend *not* doing that. Inspectors are trained to see things you can't or won't. They'll crawl under the property, check out the attic, and climb onto the roof. They'll inspect the plumbing, the electrical, the foundation, the appliances. They'll see signs of trouble that your untrained eye would glance right over.

Then they'll put all their findings into a nice, neat, easy-to-read document for you. And the entire thing is not that expensive: Inspectors typically charge around $600 for a small multifamily duplex or up to a few thousand dollars for a larger complex. But this easily pays for itself if they find just one problem you didn't expect. To locate an inspector, simply ask for referrals from local real estate agents or investors.

A word of warning: Inspectors are paid to find bad things—and they will. Many new investors (and even experienced ones) get that sick feeling in the pit of their stomach when they begin thumbing through the inspection report, as they witness page after page of language that convinces them they're buying a property that's being held up by toothpicks and bubblegum. The truth is that no property is perfect. Don't panic if your inspection report looks like an encyclopedia of bad news. *It's supposed to!* You will need to decide what you can live with, what you can ignore, what you can put on your list to fix later, what is definitely a deal breaker, and what you will renegotiate with the seller (more on that in a moment).

If you are new to investing, we recommend you accompany the inspector on their entire inspection and ask questions. A lot of them. Inspectors are typically more than willing to show you what they are seeing and even offer their opinion on how critical any issue is. For example, on an inspection report, you might see a photo of a rotted beam and the words "foundational support post under the house failing, which could lead to the collapse of this section of the house." Your mind might scream, "Aghhhhh! Run!" But if you were with the inspector when they discovered this, they might turn to you and say, "See this post here? You'll want to get this replaced. Should be a simple job for a contractor, maybe an hour of work." The report is designed to give *facts*. The inspector can give you *commentary*.

What if Something Is Truly Wrong with the Property?

Sometimes an inspector will turn up a serious problem. In that case, as mentioned earlier, you have four options: live with it, deal with it after closing, walk away from the deal entirely, or go back to the negotiating table with the seller. It's this last option we want to spend some time on now. The practice of renegotiating a deal after discovering something during the due diligence process is known as retrading and is somewhat of a dirty word in real estate investment circles.

Retrading is the practice of renegotiating the price of a property due to additional research done by the buyer after the initial offer has been accepted. The reason retrading is typically looked down on is because some investors engage in a terrible practice: They lock up a property at a higher price knowing full well that they will retrade later after the property has been taken off the market and the seller has lost all other potential buyers. We *never* recommend this deceptive retrading strategy, and if you engage in it, you will earn a bad reputation in your local market. In fact, when you buy larger deals (as you'll learn in Volume II of *The Multifamily Millionaire*), sellers will require you to list any instances in which you have retraded a deal and your reasons for doing so.

Of course, retrading is sometimes necessary. The inspection might turn up serious issues you were simply unaware of, leaving you no choice but to either back out of the deal or renegotiate. For example, you might get an eight-unit apartment building under contract for $1 million. Your inspector discovers that the material used on the flooring was asbestos and it will cost $100,000 to remove. You could always abandon the deal, but why not bring the issue to the seller and attempt to get them to either (a) fix the problem before closing, (b) reduce their price by $100,000, or (c) offer you a financial credit at closing so that you can remedy the problem yourself? After all, the seller is now aware of this issue and it will probably turn up again with future buyers, so accommodating your request may be in their best interest.

During this renegotiation phase, the seller may agree to one of the above options, so you'll amend the PSA (or add addendums to cover this change), or they may refuse you. If they refuse, you have a choice: You can move forward anyway and buy the property, adjusting your projected returns to account for the problems you discovered, or you can back out of the deal, assuming you are within the time frame of your inspection contingency (or risk losing your earnest money).

Five Seller Documents to Inspect

While it's your property inspector's job to look over the physical condition of the property, it's your job to review the documents supplied by the seller. Typically, your offer will include a certain number of days for the seller to supply documentation supporting the financial situation of the property. You'll want to take a close look at the following five types of documents:

1. **Leases:** If the property is currently rented, you will need to get a copy of all leases for existing tenants. This is to ensure that the amount of income the seller is claiming to receive is actually the amount on the leases. This is also to verify the tenants *have a lease* and when their lease expires. Since the lease goes with the property and you'll be held to whatever was agreed upon in the lease, read each lease carefully to make sure there is nothing weird.

   For example, you'd hate to find out after closing that the lease contained a provision allowing the tenant to park their mobile home on the front lawn. Also keep in mind that the rent listed on the lease may be different from the rent reported by the seller because rent may have been raised without a new lease being signed. If this is the case, as it often is, you'll want to get the tenant to sign a document known as an estoppel agreement before closing. More on that in a moment.

2. **Rent Roll:** The rent roll is a list of all current tenants, their addresses, their monthly rent, and their current security deposits being held. This number should line up with the rent reported by the seller in their marketing of the property (or in previous conversations). If not, you need to investigate to discover where the discrepancy is. Additionally, take note of the security deposits being held by the seller. Security deposits transfer with the property, so it's important to know how much security deposit money the landlord currently holds. Note that this is not technically your money; it's the tenants' and will need to go back to them someday.

3. **Income and Expense Reports:** Often referred to as a profit and loss statement (or P&L), an income and expense report shows the entire financial picture of the property, ideally on a month-by-month basis. You'll want to get at least two years' worth of reports so you can see the history of the property. It's not uncommon for a seller to mislead (i.e., lie to) a buyer about their expenses, but the income and expense report should show a breakdown of the numbers. For example, say the seller tells you the water bill for the property is $200 per month. However, you realize that although it was only $200 last month, the average was $300 a month over the past few years. That's an important metric

to adjust in your numbers. Maybe it was $200 that month because several units were vacant—and the seller was hoping you wouldn't notice.

4. **Tax Return:** No, you don't need to see the seller's entire tax return, but you will want to see the part of their tax return most relevant to this particular property. With small multifamily real estate, in most cases the seller will report their income and expenses on IRS Form 1040, but if the property is held in a partnership or another unique kind of entity, they may have an entirely separate business tax return (Form 1065) specifically for that property.

   Again, you'll want to see at least two years of returns to make sure the income and expenses being reported to you are the same as the ones being reported to the IRS. Although a seller may mislead the "market" about how much it costs to run their property, they are not likely to mislead the government because the more expenses they claim on their tax return, the less taxes they'll pay.

   For example, a dishonest seller may conveniently "forget" to tell a buyer about the $500 a month they pay for landscaping and may even leave it off the income and expense report, but you can bet they'll include this $500 per month expense in their taxes! Checking the seller's tax return keeps them honest and ensures you are getting exactly what you intend to.

5. **Contracts with Third-Party Services:** Finally, you'll need to review any contracts with third-party service providers, such as those covering laundry machines, cable TV, internet, security systems, landscaping, snow removal, and more. These services are typically tied directly to the property and will be *your* responsibility after the sale, so it's important to know what you're agreeing to. Many of these contracts renew automatically, so you should be familiar with the terms of each contract.

Other Due Diligence Considerations

Estoppel Certificates

Imagine purchasing a fourplex where each unit rents for $1,000 per month. Your math has shown your property is going to be a home run, and you're excited when you finally close the deal. Then you wait for the first of the month to roll around so you can collect that first rent check and… each tenant pays just $750. Shocked, you call up each tenant and they tell you, "Yeah, I only pay $750. It's all I've ever paid." Or maybe the rent does come in at $1,000, but when a tenant moves out, they inform you they would like their $5,000 security deposit back. You, however, received only $1,000 from the seller when you closed. Is the tenant lying? Was the seller lying? What's going on?

If the above scenario makes you nervous, it should. Part of due diligence is making sure you don't get caught in a situation like this. People lie, people forget, people try to steal. That's why the real estate industry, especially the multifamily sector, uses a simple tool known as an estoppel certificate to make sure any discrepancies are sorted out ahead of time.

The estoppel certificate is a form that the tenant, not the landlord, completes to document the details of their tenancy. A few weeks before closing, you will typically supply the seller with your estoppel certificates, and they can get them signed and returned to you. The certificate, at a minimum, should have the tenant specify:

- The names of all individuals living in the unit
- Whether they have a signed lease
- Their monthly rent
- Their security deposit
- Whether they paid for last month's rent
- What utilities they currently pay
- Any appliances they own in the property
- Any pets living in the unit and any pet deposits they've paid
- Any problems with the unit
- And more

The tenant will sign this document, which will serve as proof—in the tenant's own words—of the details of their tenancy. You should receive all signed, completed estoppel certificates prior to closing, and you will be responsible for verifying that the information supplied by the tenant lines up with the reporting supplied by the seller. When the two don't align, it's time to find out why and make sure all parties agree before you close. To assist you, we've included a sample estoppel certificate at www.biggerpockets.com/multifamilybonus.

Permits

I once bought a house with a nice existing unit above the garage (for a total of two units). This ADU had been built nearly twenty years ago and been used as a rental ever since. The property was projected to produce significant cash flow, which I was excited to get. After closing, I began renovating the property. Toward the end of the process, the local building department stopped by to inform me that the ADU was illegal. Although the previous seller had obtained permits when they constructed it, they never had a final inspection done. The county informed me that several items, including the exterior staircase going up to that second unit, were not to code and would need to be altered. After $10,000 and nearly a year, I got the final permits signed off—twenty years after the ADU had been built.

Don't let this happen to you. Before closing on a property, make sure there are no open permit issues with the local government. You can do this by visiting the local building department and explaining to them that you plan to buy the property and want to see what outstanding permits or infractions may cause you issues.

Zoning

The same types of concerns apply to zoning. If you are purchasing a multifamily, be sure that the area is either zoned for multifamily use or the property has been grandfathered in to allow for this use. You'd hate to buy a triplex only to find out the third unit was illegal. (Ask me how I know...)

Insurance

During your due diligence period, you'll be lining up the insurance needed for the property. Insurance for multifamily properties works about the same as for single-family homes with some minor exceptions, such as loss of rent coverage. You should get bids from several insurance companies and, once you decide on a plan, work with the agent to ensure the policy is paid for and goes into effect before the closing of the property.

If you are obtaining a loan on the property, your lender will want to be listed as "additionally insured." If your lender is going to escrow your insurance payments along with the property taxes (as is common with conventional residential loans), the title company will likely handle most of the paperwork needed to accomplish this.

Automatic Mortgage Payments

Amid the jumble of tasks that must be completed after closing on a property, your mortgage payment can easily slip through the cracks, especially if you're accustomed to all your payments being automated. To avoid this, set up your automatic mortgage payments during the due diligence period. Last year I refinanced a small multifamily property that I'd had set up on automatic payments for years. After the refinance I forgot to set up the new automatic payment. Since I was used to not paying that bill manually, it didn't get paid until the lender called me. My credit score dropped one hundred points due to that single oversight, and it took almost a year for my credit score to fully recover. Don't make the same mistake: Set up your automated mortgage payments ahead of time or, at the latest, on the day of closing.

Management

If you plan to hire a property manager, the due diligence period is when you'll do so. Your property manager will need some time to prepare to take over, draft a letter to the tenants, and make sure the rent is paid to the right location. (We'll talk more about hiring a property manager in Chapter Twenty.)

If you plan to manage the property yourself, you'll need to prepare a letter to the tenants introducing yourself and informing them of how they can pay their rent. I typically send this letter a day or two before closing so that it arrives on the day of closing.

Signing the Documents

At last, the day has come. You've double-checked all the numbers, lined up your financing, verified the documents, and you're ready to close! Closings typically take place at the office of the title company or the attorney who has been working through the title and escrow process. However, in a post-COVID-19 world, many more closings are handled by mobile notaries at the buyer's and seller's respective kitchen tables. (Honestly, this is much more convenient and much less awkward!)

To save time at the actual closing, we recommend reading all your documents beforehand. (The title company or attorney can typically email you a copy a day prior to closing.) Pay special attention to the so-called settlement statement (formally, the HUD-1), which lays out the financial details of the transaction and accounts for every penny spent, including the earnest money, the loan amount, various closing costs, and the down payment. Make sure nothing looks out of the ordinary. Mistakes do happen and no one cares about these expenses more than you, so care enough to take your time.

Just like that, you've successfully closed on your multifamily property. (Okay, maybe it'll be a few days after signing, depending on your location, but it's *happening*.) While bells may not peal to mark the occasion, once you're handed those keys and get word that all the paperwork has been recorded with the county government, you're going to feel like you climbed a mountain.

KEY TAKEAWAYS

- Depending on your location, the closing transaction process will be handled by either a title company or an attorney. Talk to any local investor or agent to find out what's customary in your state.
- During due diligence, you'll be getting a professional inspection of the entire property and examining several key documents to verify the seller's claims about the property's financial history.
- You will also need to obtain estoppel certificates from current tenants, verify there are no issues with zoning or permits, order insurance for the property, and set up your automatic mortgage payments and property management systems. Finally, you'll sign the necessary documents and close on the property. Congratulations!

Chapter 20

MANAGING SMALL MULTIFAMILY PROPERTIES

"Perfection is not attainable. But if we chase perfection, we can catch excellence."

—VINCE LOMBARDI

The year was 1184, and a number of feuding nobles from across the Holy Roman Empire had gathered together in an effort to negotiate terms for peace. The nobles chose to hold this assembly in a large room at the Church of St. Peter in the city of Erfurt, in modern-day Germany.

Suddenly, as the hundreds of nobles bickered and bartered, the floor began to shift and shake. Before anyone knew what was happening, the entire floor collapsed, sending the guests down into the latrine pit below, and more than sixty nobles died that day, drowning in... well, you get the idea.

Now, I'm not going to lie. I first read that story several years ago and have been itching to include it in a book or video or blog post since that day—so I'm pretty darn proud of its inclusion here. You, however, might be wondering, "What the hell does this have to do with managing rental properties?"

No, managing tenants isn't going to land you in a pile of human excrement. However, what the horrendous story of the Erfurt latrine pit disaster of 1184 can teach us is this: No matter the intentions of the group that gathered in that church, the foundation was not solid enough to hold up, leading to the nauseating death of many. In the same way, no matter how excited and proud and motivated you might feel about acquiring your multifamily rental properties, your journey is not over—you *must* have a solid foundation below your feet. (Pretty good anecdote, right? Now go tell your friends that story!)

When it comes to small multifamily properties, good management is not just an option—it's a requirement. Bad management can destroy even the best of deals. But excellent management is the foundation that will ensure your cash flow is secure and set you on the path to financial freedom. This chapter will explain how to lay this solid foundation at your small multifamily properties.

Self-Management versus Professional Management

When I first got started with multifamily properties, way back when I was house hacking that first duplex, I managed the property myself (alongside my beautiful wife, Heather). After all, we lived at the property, so we knew we could handle it. And in a way, I enjoyed managing tenants.

Today I don't manage anything myself. Most of my portfolio is managed by professionals, and while I think I could still do a pretty good job at managing tenants, self-management no longer serves my goals. You'll need to decide what is best for you. To help you make the best choice for your specific goals and circumstances, we've laid out some factors to consider when deciding whether to manage your multifamily yourself or hire a pro.

Cost

Hiring a professional property manager costs money. Small local property managers typically charge between 8 and 12 percent of the rent each month to do their job, with some fees often added in. Management for an eight-unit property where each unit rents for $1,000 a month could cost you more than $800 a month, which is likely a significant portion of your cash flow. Spread out over a small portfolio, self-management *could* lead to earlier financial independence because you wouldn't be losing all that extra cash flow to a manager.

However, self-management has a cost as well: *opportunity* cost. In other words, if you're busy taking phone calls and scheduling maintenance on broken appliances, who's out there looking for deals? The more time you spend on the $20/hour tasks (like managing properties), the less time you can spend on the $2,000/hour tasks of finding deals, negotiating, creating systems, or playing with your children in the backyard.

Skill

Managing tenants is not something to be treated lightly. It takes considerable skill to know how to find the right tenant, screen them to ensure they will be a good fit, stay within the law, and balance the need for good customer service with the hammer of justice when a tenant gets out of line. Far too many landlords have been walked over, become confused and dismayed, and ultimately failed in their role because of their lack of skill. They think they can wing it, but they end up hating every moment of their landlording life.

But landlording can be learned—and it's not PhD-level stuff. This chapter is a good starting point, although if you're truly interested, you should not stop here. Lengthy books have been written on the topic of tenant management. (I should know. My wife, Heather, and I wrote *The Book on Managing Rental Properties*, with more than 400 pages of detailed, step-by-step instructions for being a successful landlord.) If you're willing to learn the necessary skills, great. If not, don't even think about it.

That said, not all professional property managers have the skills to be effective managers either! Yes, you read that right. Many property managers are terrible. There is no universal certification process for property managers. Some states do require that a property manager have a real estate license, but all that means is they can define the difference between a lien and an encumbrance—not too helpful when it comes to managing tenants.

Therefore, if you're going to hire a property manager, it's vital that you hire the *right* one. Just as when looking for a real estate agent or a lender, you shouldn't simply rely on the company you drive by each day on your commute or the company your brother's friend's fiancé uses. A great property manager will keep your cash flow machine on the tracks, while a bad property manager will send your property careening into the bottomless pit of despair, so it's worth taking the time to find the right one.

Time and Difficulty

Some think landlording is going to be the hardest, most time-intensive task they could ever take on and, as a result, refuse to self-manage. However, it's not that tough or time-intensive, at least when you have only a few units. Managing a small multifamily rental property probably takes a few hours per month once it's "stabilized," meaning the property is fixed up and a tenant has moved in. You may need to call a plumber when there's a leak or fix a cabinet door when it falls off. At the end of the month, you'll have to record the income and expenses in a spreadsheet or using some management software. It's not rocket science.

On the other hand, some people think that landlording is going to be easy and headache-free. They don't realize that it's a *business* and that it's *work*. When the tenant doesn't pay their rent, these unprepared landlords cry out in shock, "What?! No one said this was going to take effort!" A door knob falls off and the unprepared landlord shrieks, "This building is a money pit!!"

Laughable, but true. Managing rentals is not terribly difficult, but it's not something you can do in your sleep. It requires a certain time investment as well as some occasional *stress*. After all, these tenants are renting *your property*, something you put a lot of your hard-earned money into, as well as your blood, sweat, and tears (literally) to make it a great place to live. And they are now *refusing* to pay rent? Or they are calling and complaining about their upstairs neighbor's nighttime activities? Or they decided to change their oil on the brand-new concrete driveway and permanently stain it?

These problems do occur, and when you're on the front lines dealing with them, they hit closer to home. It's one thing to see the problem on a monthly financial report from a property manager, and another thing altogether to get the call yourself. That said, should you refuse to self-manage because it seems stressful? Definitely not! It might add *some* stress to your life, but with the right systems in place, landlording doesn't have to be stressful. "Stressful" is just another word for "lack of systems." If you know how to handle problems, they become increasingly less stressful.

The Bottom Line

Self-managing rental properties doesn't have to be complicated, time-consuming, or difficult. However, it can be all those things if you don't commit to learning how to be a great landlord. If you're still unsure whether you should self-manage, answer the following questions:

1. Are you willing to learn how to be a great landlord? Will you build systems, learn the landlord-tenant laws, follow systems and processes, and continually seek to improve? Will you put in the time? If you said no to any of these, don't self-manage.

2. Is your time better spent finding additional deals to grow your portfolio? If so, then consider hiring a professional. But if self-management gets you into the game sooner, helps you better understand and control your investment, and ultimately helps you accomplish your goals, don't be afraid to roll up your sleeves and become a hands-on landlord.

Regardless of what you choose, keep reading this chapter to gain additional perspective on both self-management and professional management. First, we'll look at how to find a great property manager, and then we'll look at how to succeed if you plan to self-manage.

Hiring a Property Manager

Hiring a good property manager is similar to hiring a great real estate agent, contractor, or other vendor, which we've covered in previous chapters. It begins by getting referrals from experienced landlords in your area, compiling a list of several property management companies that come highly recommended, and interviewing those managers.

Ideally, you want a property manager with many years of experience that offers great customer service, handles repairs quickly and correctly, responds quickly to your calls or emails, and provides professional reporting monthly. We've put together a list of questions to ask a property manager that will help you compare your candidates so you can the choose one that's right for you. You'll find our free Property Manager

Interview Form at www.biggerpockets.com/multifamilybonus.

Once you select a property manager, you'll sign a contract with them to manage your property for a set amount of time, usually one year. If the property is occupied, you'll want to line up the manager before closing so they can handle the transitioning of the tenants, including making sure the tenants are notified about the change of ownership and the procedure for paying rent. Your property manager will likely need copies of all existing leases and may ask to hold the security deposits as well.

Finally, even when you hand over your property to professional management, your job is not done. Management companies control hundreds, sometimes thousands, of units. You are simply not a big deal to them, and they will never care about your property the same way you do. Therefore, you'll still need to keep your finger on the pulse of your investment to ensure you are receiving the income you expect and that your expenses are reasonable. The best way to do this is to review the financial statements provided by your property manager each month. Look for anomalies in the statements, such as units that are not generating rent or expenses that are higher than expected.

Managers are people too, and they make mistakes, so it's your job to make sure they are doing their job correctly. Don't fall into the trap of lazy ownership just because you hired someone else to manage your investment. An hour or two a month and the occasional email or phone call to your management company can ensure problems are discovered and dealt with quickly, maximizing your returns and minimizing your involvement.

Self-Management

If you choose not to use a professional property manager, you will, by default, need to self-manage. I'm not going to lie to you and say every moment of self-managing rentals is fun. It's sometimes annoying, stressful, and frustrating. But if you've done even a little homework on how to manage tenants, it's not that hard and you *can* do it.

To be a successful landlord you'll have to master certain skills. The good news is that those skills are well documented and can be learned. In this section, we'll cover one of the most important of those skills—how to pick the right tenant. Then we'll detail the essential knowledge you'll need to become a five-star landlord to your five-star tenants.

Finding a Five-Star Tenant

Pick the right tenant and landlording will be a breeze. Pick the wrong tenant and landlording will be a nightmare. The right tenant will make or break your experience, and not all tenants are created equal, so let's talk about how to identify the perfect tenant.

Just as when hiring employees, you cannot predict with absolute certainty how a tenant will ultimately work out. Any reader of this book who has hired employees for their business knows that someone can *seem* great at first but then fail to live up to expectations. However, in the business world, interviews, background checks, and skills tests can weed out the least qualified applicants and improve your chances of hiring a good employee.

The same applies to finding a good tenant. There are a series of steps you can take to weed out the obvious bad apples and identify those who are mostly likely to be great tenants. We call these people "five-star tenants" because they meet or exceed expectations in five key categories:

1. **Income:** A tenant who doesn't earn enough money obviously is not going to be able to pay the rent. Most landlords (including us) use the simple 3x rule when setting their income criteria: The tenant must earn three times what the rent is. If the rent is $1,000, the tenant should earn $3,000 gross. Tenants can supply pay stubs, but because those are so easy to fake, we always call the current employer to verify income.

2. **Job Stability:** Just because a tenant has a job *today* doesn't mean they'll have a job *tomorrow*. For this reason we always look at job stability to determine whether to accept a tenant. We like to see at least six months in the same job or at least two years in the same profession. In other words, if your prospective tenant just started a new job, that wouldn't automatically disqualify them, but you'd like to see that their previous job was in the same line of work.

   As with income, be sure to verify an applicant's employment situation. Confirm with the current employer how long the tenant has worked there and whether the job is likely to continue in the near-term future. Some jobs are seasonal or temporary, so you'll want to make sure their job is going to last.

3. **Rent History:** When hiring an employee, one of the best indicators of future performance is past performance, specifically, how their previous employers talk about the applicant. This goes for tenants as well. We always talk with previous landlords to find out what kind of tenant

an applicant was. We recommend you ask the following five questions:

- Did they pay on time?
- Did they leave their unit in good condition?
- Did they give proper notice before moving out?
- Were they respectful toward other tenants?
- Would you rent to them again?

How someone has been is a great indicator of how someone will be. Personally, we'll let other landlords be like Mother Teresa and offer second chances. As for us, if a prospective tenant gets negative reviews from past landlords, that means a hard no. Also, be sure to check with all previous landlords (at least within the last five years) instead of just the current one. If the landlord is having a problem with your prospective tenant, they could lie in hopes of passing their bad tenant on to you.

4. **Good Credit:** Good credit doesn't guarantee a good tenant, but terrible credit often indicates a pattern of financial irresponsibility. Any failure to meet financial obligations is not a good sign for someone who you will be relying on to meet a financial obligation. Personally, we like to see a minimum credit rating of 600.

5. **Criminal History:** The last thing you want in your property is violence. Therefore, you'll want to minimize the chances of renting to someone who may harm others or engage in behavior that could hurt your property or finances. That said, having a blanket "no criminal history" policy can lead to discrimination—even though it may be unintended—and put you at risk of not abiding by fair housing laws. Minorities in the United States are arrested and convicted at much higher rates than others. Therefore, the U.S. Department of Housing and Urban Development (HUD) has issued guidelines for reasons you can and cannot reject a potential tenant.

For example, you may not reject an applicant based on *arrests*, as arrests are not the same as convictions. But even when a conviction is present, the landlord must "show that its policy accurately distinguishes between criminal conduct that indicates a demonstrable risk to resident safety and/or property and criminal conduct that does not."[18] In other words, a landlord must be able to show that

---

[18] "Office of General Counsel Guidance on Application of Fair Housing Act Standards to the Use of Criminal Records by Providers of Housing and Real Estate-Related Transactions," U.S. Department of Housing and Urban Development, April 4, 2016, accessed at https://www.hud.gov/sites/documents/HUD_OGCGUIDAPPFHASTANDCR.PDF

the criminal conviction could lead to property damage or violence. Speeding tickets or marijuana use convictions shouldn't count. Our policy currently states "no recent violent criminal convictions," which we believe covers our bases.

Finding a five-star tenant is not an option for us; it's a requirement. We want tenants who have the highest likelihood of paying rent, paying it on time, taking care of their unit (our property), and staying for the long term, so we don't have to repeatedly re-rent the unit.

We've included additional details on the step-by-step process for finding, screening, and leasing to great tenants in a bonus supplement that you can find at www.biggerpockets.com/multifamilybonus. Please, please, please read this bonus content, and also read through *The Book on Managing Rental Properties* by my wife, Heather Turner, and me.

Becoming a Five-Star Landlord

About 200 years ago, Thomas Jefferson wrote, "The government you elect is the government you deserve." What was true then is still true now: Our government is a reflection of the nation as a whole because it is elected by the people. The same principle applies to landlords and tenants: Terrible tenants are a reflection of terrible landlording skills, while great tenants are a reflection of great landlording skills. This isn't to say a great landlord will never have a bad tenant—they do slip through the cracks occasionally. But your experience will be much more pleasant and the overwhelming majority of your tenants will be great when you improve your skills enough to become a five-star landlord. To be a five-star landlord, you must:

1. Know and Follow the Law

Landlords play a crucial role by satisfying a basic necessity: the need for housing. As such, landlords have a great deal of influence on and responsibility for their tenants' quality of life. Therefore, a five-star landlord must be well-versed in the local laws that govern the landlord-tenant relationship and follow those laws in all aspects of their business. Specifically, there are four areas of the law you'll need to consider.

First, you must follow state and local laws. For example, if a tenant doesn't pay on time, some states allow you to issue a three-day notice, while others require a ten-day notice. Each state has its own laws, and many cities have their own laws that build upon the state's laws, so be sure to familiarize yourself with both. To see your state's landlord-tenant laws, search online for your state or city and "landlord tenant laws." You'll find more than enough information to get you going.

Second, you must follow local zoning ordinances and laws. For example, you should not add another unit to your multifamily property without ensuring that it complies with the laws laid out by the local government. These zoning ordinances are typically handled at the county level.

Third, you must comply with tax laws. This will require accurately accounting for all the income you receive and all the expenses you incur. You must have proper bookkeeping and be able to prove, if ever audited, that you followed applicable tax law.

In addition to simply paying their taxes, five-star landlords aim to *understand* the tax laws regarding owning rental properties so they can employ strategies to minimize their tax liability while maximizing profits. For more information about tax strategies, we recommend Amanda Han and Matthew MacFarland's two books, *The Book on Tax Strategies for the Savvy Real Estate Investor* and *The Book on Advanced Tax Strategies*. They will tell you everything you need to know to be a five-star landlord when it comes to taxes.

Finally, you must follow the laws regarding discrimination. There are many good reasons to reject prospective tenants: They don't make enough money; they don't have a job; they murdered nine people last week. The legal (and moral) trouble, however, comes when you discriminate against someone for a reason that the government defines as *protected*. The U.S. government has defined several "protected classes" that cannot be used as grounds for discrimination. Currently, at the federal level, these protected classes are:

- Race
- Color
- National origin
- Religion
- Sex
- Familial status
- Age

In addition to the seven protected classes above, many states have added other protected classes, such as gender identity, sexual orientation, and criminal history.

What does this all mean? Obviously, that you can't refuse to rent a property to someone because they are of a certain race, religion, sex, and so on. However, some of the finer points might not be as obvious. For example:

- "Familial status" means you can't say "no kids" in your marketing or discussions with tenants.
- "Disability" discrimination would include not allowing a handicapped tenant to build a ramp.
- "Sex" discrimination would mean not saying to a tenant, "There are a lot of men in this property, so you might feel more comfortable at another property."

To be a five-star landlord, you must know the laws and follow them. Breaking the law can land you in court and even prison, so follow the rules, stay legal, and stay out of trouble.

2. Be Firm but Fair

Every morning, I start my day reading on a large reclining chair in my living room. At some point, Rosie will sleepily emerge from her bedroom, stumble down the hallway, and climb onto this large chair with me. Then she'll lovingly look up at me and with a sweet little voice ask the same question she has asked every single morning for more than a year: "Dad, can I have some chocolate ice cream?"

Now, to be clear, my wife and I have never given our daughter chocolate ice cream for breakfast. We have no idea how she got the idea that chocolate ice cream is on the breakfast menu, nor do we understand why she has insisted on asking every single morning for more than a year, without a single victory. (That's persistence!) I always reply the same way: "No honey, we don't have chocolate ice cream for breakfast." She grumbles a bit, usually asks why a few times, and eventually accepts the reality that I'm not going to give in today. She'll try again tomorrow.

As a fellow chocolate lover, I know it would thrill my daughter to have chocolate ice cream each morning for breakfast. Maybe I could toss on some chocolate fudge, mix in some chocolate chip cookies, and top it off with a dollop of whipped cream and a cherry. But as a parent, I know that what she *wants* and what is best for her are not the same. As a parent, you have to choose to do what's right for the well-being of all involved—even when your child doesn't understand. The same principle applies to landlording.

A landlord who gives in to every whim and whine from a tenant will quickly find themselves with an out-of-control situation that ends poorly for everyone. Therefore, a five-star landlord understands that they must be firm but fair. This is our guiding principle when dealing with tenants. It means enforcing rules and guidelines fairly and not deviating from them based on momentary desires or emotions. In other words, you should run your business as a business.

The best example of this involves late rent. To be honest, I don't *like* charging late fees. It's not something landlords look forward to. Then why charge a late fee? Because if you're not firm in enforcing your policies, your tenant will be trained to not follow them. If I allowed my child to eat chocolate ice cream each day, she, and her health, would suffer. If I allow tenants to pay rent whenever they feel like it, that increases the chance that the rent will never get paid, which could eventually lead to a costly eviction. If you recall the famous children's book *If You Give a Mouse a Cookie*, giving a little bit opens you up to giving up more later, and it always turns out bad in the end.

Maybe you want to be a "nice" landlord, so when your tenant is late on the rent, you call and ask about it. They offer a reasonable excuse about their paycheck being delayed or needing the money for a medical bill, and your heart goes out to them. You say it's no problem and tell them to pay when they can. Two weeks later, they pay the rent and you think, "Great! I just did a good deed!" But now rent is due again in two weeks, and the tenant doesn't have enough because they are used to taking the rent out of every other paycheck, but they're using that paycheck to pay for their other bills. The following month they don't pay again, and they know that you'll be fine with it. You've already set the precedent. Eventually they pay, but the trend continues. Their car breaks down and they need to use the rent money to repair it. Their dog needs to be neutered. Their tenth anniversary is right around the corner and they need to buy a special vacation for their significant other. All good causes, of course.

Before you know it, the tenant is four months behind on rent. You've established a pattern of being nice, and you've trained them to be irresponsible. It's *your* fault! You finally get wise and decide to make them pay up, and they get upset with you when you file a legal notice demanding the rent. They end up getting evicted and it stays on their record for a decade, making it harder for them to rent anywhere else in the future. And it's all because you wanted to be nice. You decide that landlording isn't right for you and get out of real estate entirely, telling everyone around you that real estate investing doesn't work and only leads to ruin.

This is *not* fiction. This is real life for millions of failed landlords. Not only does bending the rules hurt you financially, it also hurts the tenant. You are feeding your tenant chocolate ice cream for breakfast every time you choose appeasement over following the rules. You are setting yourself and your tenant up for failure by your actions. And you get the landlord-tenant relationship that you deserve.

Oher issues will arise that force you to be the bad guy by enforcing the rules, for example:

- The tenant moves a dog into their unit, despite your "no pet" policy.
- The tenant decides that piling up garbage outside their house is easier than taking it down the driveway and placing it into the garbage can.
- The tenant decides to repaint the bedrooms neon green because they like the look better.
- The tenant plays loud music each night, annoying all your other tenants.

These are real-life challenges that only get worse when you choose to be passive.

Of course, this doesn't mean you have to be a jerk. You are a professional running a professional business. Be kind, courteous, and empathetic. Listen, don't judge. Say "please" and "thank you." Don't burden your tenants with unnecessary rules or regulations. Keep it fair and do the right thing. But don't allow tenants to break the rules simply because you want to avoid conflict. If you can't do this, hire a property manager who will.

3. Treat Your Rentals Like a Business

My wife and I spent a few months living on the island of Oahu as we prepared to make the move to being full-time Hawaii residents. While living there, we discovered a cute little shaved-ice shop that we quickly fell in love with. From the moment we walked in the door, we were greeted by the line of high-school employees behind the counter. They asked about our day and engaged in earnest conversation with genuineness, acting as if we were the only customers all day. The store was clean and fun. Hawaiian music played out of speakers at just the right level. Videos of epic surf rides looped on the televisions around the room. And the flavors they offered were perfect, ranging from classics like strawberry and grape to local favorites like lilikoi and kula berry. The personal experience and the shaved ice were perfect every time.

The only downside was the line that stretched out the door and around the corner, day and night, but even that didn't bother us because of how quickly and efficiently they moved customers through. There is a reason this local-shaved ice business was so popular, and why they've expanded to several locations around the island: They run a solid business. The owner of this establishment isn't just selling ice and artificial flavoring. He's running a business that happens to sell ice and artificial flavoring. It's a minor difference on paper, but a tremendous difference in practice. Anyone can sell ice. It takes a savvy business owner to do it profitably and sustainably.

Good business owners are hard to find. The skills needed to run an efficient and profitable business are not innate; they must be developed. Clearly, the owner of the shaved-ice shop my wife and I fell in love with had mastered the art of running a business—yet most landlords don't. Many don't even realize they are running a business!

To be a five-star landlord, you must run your rentals as a business, not as a hobby. It's essential if you want to work less. It's essential if you want to earn more. It's essential if you want to grow a portfolio that will build generational wealth. How do you transition from merely owning rentals to owning a business? Although entire books could be written on this topic (and many have been), let's nail down six specific ways you can begin organizing your rentals into an efficient and profitable business.

1. **Systems and Processes**: Although the casual conversation, great music, and perfect flavors at the shaved ice shop appeared so off-the-cuff, they were anything but. The business operated like a well-oiled machine because of the many systems and processes followed by the staff. A system is a standardized way of doing something that can be used over and over to maintain stability, consistency, and profitability. A process goes into more detail by defining the actual steps needed to make the system work. In the shaved-ice shop, the entire flow of customers through the line was a system consisting of steps in a process,

including greeting customers at the door, engaging in conversation, asking about flavors, measuring the exact amount of flavoring, and more. Think of a process as the cumulative items on a checklist, and your various checklists become your system for doing things.

Great businesses have systems and processes that guide every moment of their operation. There is a standardized way tasks are done, decisions are made, customers are served, and profit is generated. Good systems and processes are continually refined and perfected, allowing a business to grow without constant input from the business owner, relying on habits rather than emotions or spur-of-the-moment decision making to govern the actions of the company.

A five-star landlord relies on systems and processes to operate a profitable business. For example, a five-star landlord will have systems for:

- Receiving rent
- Taking phone calls
- Bookkeeping
- Addressing maintenance concerns

Additionally, a five-star landlord will have processes for:

- Advertising their unit for rent and following the same steps each time to ensure consistency, beginning with cleaning the unit, taking pictures, posting them to Zillow and Facebook, handling inquiries, and so on.
- Screening tenants, including collecting an application and an application fee, running a background check, and more.

In other words, a five-star landlord doesn't run their business based on intuition. They have a set way of doing business that is repeatable and scalable because they have systems and processes in place. In the beginning, of course, you'll need to develop these systems and processes, but hopefully this chapter will give you many to start with. Then seek to continually refine them. Create checklists. Ask yourself, "How can I put this into a manual that my company will always follow?" Stick to your systems and processes and you'll turn your business into a well-oiled machine.

2. **Office Hours:** A five-star landlord knows they do not work 24/7, and they train their tenants to know the same. Having set office hours

helps transform landlording from a hobby to a business, in both your tenant's view and your own mind. This begins with establishing a second phone number that's dedicated solely to your business. (We typically don't give our tenants our personal cell phone number.) You can get a free Google Voice number, at voice.google.com, that allows you to receive calls at specific times on your cellphone and have those calls transferred automatically to voicemail at other times.

Let your tenants know that they can call anytime between whatever hours you set (we say 10 a.m. to 4 p.m.) and after-hour calls will be answered the following day. If you like, give your tenants an alternative "emergency number" on the after-hours voicemail recording, but don't worry too much: Late-night emergencies are extremely rare. (Personally, we have had fewer than two each in fifteen years of landlording.)

3. **Professionalism:** Good businesses exemplify professionalism in every way, and a five-star landlord does the same. Sure, you could sign a lease on the hood of a car in your pajamas, but what are you telling your tenant about your management style? Instead, aim for professionalism in everything related to your rentals and how you conduct every single interaction with your tenant. Yes, you may be a small-time landlord with only a few units, but your tenants don't have to know that. Be professional and act as if you have 1,000 units. Your tenants will respect your policies.

4. **Online Rent Payment:** Have a solid system in place for collecting rent—either online or via automatic withdrawal from your tenant's checking account. Never collect rent in cash or in person. (You'd never see the owner of the shaved-ice business driving to someone's house to pick up payment for their evening dessert, so why should you?) Make it easy on your tenants and yourself. There are many online tools available that allow landlords to collect rent online; we've compiled a list that you can find at www.biggerpockets.com/property-management-tools.

5. **Inspect What You Expect:** A smart business owner doesn't simply create systems and processes and then run away to the beach, hoping everyone does what they've outlined. Instead, business owners must inspect what they expect. In other words, you must keep regular tabs on how your landlording business is carrying out your systems and processes. For example, if you expect your tenants to keep their decks

clear of debris, you'll need to have a system for regularly inspecting those decks, such as an annual property inspection. If you expect tenants to pay rent on time, you must inspect the process each month to ensure late fees are applied and paid.

6. **Preventive Maintenance:** A friend of mine recently became a fire-fighter, a dream he'd had for nearly four decades. One afternoon he told me a secret about firefighting that had never occurred to me. "The interesting thing about fighting fires," he said, "is that 99 percent of my job actually consists of *fire prevention*. We spend most of our time making sure fires don't happen in the first place."

My friend didn't know it at the time, but he was actually offering some incredibly insightful advice that could benefit all business owners, especially landlords. Many landlords live entirely in reaction to the world around them, responding to issues and continually putting out fires. The roof leaks, so they call a roofer. The water heater dies, so they replace it. A handrail breaks, so they hire a handyman to build a new one. While there is nothing wrong with this, a five-star landlord knows that many repairs can be avoided in the first place by having a system for preventive maintenance. Each quarter or each year, the property should undergo a routine maintenance check of all the major systems. (We've included a full checklist at www.biggerpockets.com/multifamilybonus.)

Managing multifamily properties doesn't have to be hard as long as you operate your business like a business, which is a matter of implementing professional practices as well as cultivating a professional mindset. Do this and eventually you'll reach a point where your business operates itself, giving you the freedom and flexibility to live the life you imagined when you first became interested in real estate.

4. Be Responsive

Years ago, a tenant who was also a friend (always a bad idea) texted me about his toilet not working correctly. Because he didn't go through the normal channels of calling my business line and talking with my wife, I simply forgot about the problem... until several weeks later, when he informed me it was *still* broken, yet his four college-student roommates had continued to use the toilet anyway. I'll spare you the details, but let's just say it was messy.

In that case, I had failed at one of the key attributes of a successful landlord: being responsive to a tenant's needs. No matter how nice your property is or what year it was built, you will deal with the occasional water leak or pest problem or appliance malfunction or crack in the wall. A five-star landlord doesn't let these problems fester; they respond to issues quickly and quickly remedy them. When it comes to repairs, speed matters—and not just for the tenant. The longer you let a problem go, the worse it becomes and the greater the impact it will have on your bank account.

Whether to do your own repair work is a matter of personal choice, but regardless, you need to have several reliable contractors or handymen you can call when needed. Therefore, always be on the lookout for these service providers, adding them to your contacts so can access them when you need them. Also, being responsive applies to more than just maintenance concerns. It means calling tenants back if you miss their call as well as keeping potential tenants informed on the progress of their application and on your move-in process. Ask yourself, "If I were in the tenant's shoes, would I feel cared for?" If not, consider finding ways to make yourself more responsive to the needs of your tenant.

Of course, being responsive doesn't mean doing whatever the tenant asks. It means responding in a reasonable amount of time in a way that makes the tenant feel heard and understood. If a tenant calls and asks whether they can move their boyfriend in, don't leave them in limbo. If you need to think about it or review your policies, simply tell the tenant you'll call them back by 5 p.m. with an answer—and actually do that! Being responsive to your tenant is not only good for the tenant, it's good for you. A tenant who feels you are responsive to their needs will stay longer, cause less drama, and help keep your multifamily property operating at peak efficiency.

Responsiveness applies not just to your tenants but to your market. As a five-star landlord, you should be able to answer the following: Are you charging the right amount for rent? Can you get more? Should you charge less if you're having trouble filling vacant units? Are there concessions or bonuses you should be handing out to be more competitive in your market? A great landlord understands their local market and can adapt to changing conditions quickly to maximize their income.

5. Exhibit Resiliency
Finally, a five-star landlord knows that they are not in this business for

a week or a month or a year. They are playing the long game, which means they must have the resiliency to fight through challenges, big and small. You will be stressed. You might even want to give up. But a five-star landlord doesn't surrender. They look at challenges as lessons in improving their business. They have a habit of asking, "How do I make sure this doesn't happen again?"

Resiliency isn't something we're born with; it's something we cultivate. You can as well—and it begins with a choice. Will you allow yourself to give up? Or, like the famed conquistador Hernán Cortés, who supposedly burned his ships upon landing in the New World, will you remove the possibility of retreat from your mind?

Five-star landlords understand that although they can't change what others do, they have 100 percent control over their own response. They don't dwell on the present; they focus on the future. They are resilient—because they have to be.

KEY TAKEAWAYS

- Professional property managers can be a great addition to your team, but they do come with a cost. When deciding whether to hire one or self-manage, choose carefully so that you can best meet your goals.
- A five-star tenant is one who earns enough income to cover the rent, has a stable job, has great references from previous landlords, has a good credit score, and won't cause harm to others or engage in behavior that could hurt your property or finances.
- A five-star landlord is one who knows and follows the law, is firm but fair in their dealings with tenants, treats their business like a business, is responsive to their tenants, and exhibits resiliency when things get tough.

Chapter 21
ACCOUNTING, TAXES, LEGAL ENTITIES, AND TERRIBLE PUNS

"The best way to teach your kids about taxes is by eating 30 percent of their ice cream."

—BILL MURRAY

We know it's tempting to skip this chapter. But we beg you, don't! This chapter could save you *so* many frustrations and headaches—and even plenty of money—down the road. We promise we'll keep it light and maybe even toss in a joke or two along the way.

Speaking of light, one time somebody stole all the lamps and light-bulbs in Brandon's house. We guess you could say he was... *delighted!* (Okay, we didn't say the jokes would be *good.*)

Here's pretty much everything you need to know about accounting and taxes when it comes to real estate in four simple sentences:

1. Track your income.
2. Track your expenses.
3. Deduct actual expenses and phantom expenses from the income to know your profit.
4. Pay taxes on the profit.

That's about it. Well, that's *almost* it. These four steps are really what accounting and taxes are all about, but as you can imagine, the devil is in the details. In this chapter, we're going to spend just a few short paragraphs discussing numbers 1 and 2. After all, we've covered how to accurately keep track of the money that comes in and the money that comes out of your multifamily investment.

However, we want to spend a bit longer on the third item, deductions. We're sure you've already heard (and if not, we'll tell you right now) about how favorably real estate is treated in the U.S. tax code. Mostly that has to do with deductions and, more specifically, something known as depreciation, a "phantom" expense that helps real estate investors pay lower taxes than almost anyone else.

Speaking of bank accounts, you'll definitely want to set up separate business checking and savings accounts for your property. These accounts should be used solely for placing all income from the property into and paying all bills out of. You should never pay property bills from your personal checking account, and you should never pay personal bills from your business checking account. Keep the business separate, not only for legal reasons but also to simplify your accounting.

Bookkeeping Basics

The key to good accounting is to track every single dollar that goes into your rental and every single dollar that you spend caring for your rental. Of course, there are numerous software options to assist you with this, from robust accounting programs like QuickBooks and Xero, to landlord-specific management software that you can find on www.biggerpockets.com/tools/landlord-resources. Or, as I did for the first decade of my rental property business, you can use a spreadsheet to track your numbers. (We've included a spreadsheet that you can use to track your income and expenses at www.biggerpockets.com/multifamilybonus.)

How to Track Your Income and Expenses

The exact method you use to track your income and expenses is less important than making sure you actually *do it*. So many real estate investors simply ignore or are haphazard in addressing this essential aspect of their business and find themselves in legal trouble down the road. Good accounting leads to good decision making, so make the decision now to track your income and expenses carefully. For the rest of this section, we're going to show you how to track these in a spreadsheet, but even if you use software, the same principles apply.

When using a spreadsheet, at the start of a new month you'll want to download your entire transaction history from your bank. Then you'll need to place each and every item into a *category*. (If you use software, it should pull this information directly from your bank account, but you'll still need to make sure each item is placed in its correct category.) For income, we would suggest specifying each income source, such as "rent," "late fees," or "laundry income." For expenses, you may want to simply use the categories that the U.S. government has already supplied for real estate owners on IRS Form Schedule E, which are:

- Advertising
- Auto and travel
- Cleaning and maintenance
- Commissions
- Insurance
- Legal and other professional fees
- Placement fees
- Mortgage principal
- Mortgage interest
- Other interest
- Repairs
- Supplies
- Taxes
- Utilities
- Depreciation expense or depletion
- Other (list)

Using the government-supplied categories makes tax time a breeze. You'll simply add up your year-end total and place it in the same spot on your IRS Schedule E.

BASIC RENTAL PROPERTY INCOME & EXPENSE TRACKER

	Jan	Feb	Mar	Apr	May	Jun	Jul	Aug	Sep	Oct	Nov	Dec	Year-End Summary
Income													
Unit 1													
Unit 2													
Unit 3													
Unit 4													
Unit 5													
Late fees													
Storage income													
Parking income													
Laundry income													
Other income													
Sum of income													
Expenses													
Advertising													
Auto and travel													
Cleaning and maintenance													
Commissions													
Insurance													
Legal and other professional fees													
Placement fees													
Mortgage principal													
Mortgage interest													
Other interest													
Repairs													
Supplies													
Taxes													
Utilities													
Depreciation expense or depletion													
Other (list)													
Total expenses													
Total income													
Sum of profit													

The "Weird" Expense: Capital Expenditures (CapEx)

Back in Chapter Eight, we looked at capital expenditures, commonly known as CapEx, in some detail. If you'll recall, those are higher-cost improvements or replacements to the property that don't happen regularly but do happen. We've covered how to account for them when analyzing a property. Well, now it's time to look at how CapEx is treated from a tax standpoint. Although it's a little weird, it's important to understand.

When a business makes money, the owner has to pay taxes. Thankfully, these are usually due only on the profit. For example, let's say you have a business selling T-shirts and you sell a shirt for $20. Chances are you paid some money for your office rent, ink for the printer, and the shirt itself. Let's just say that means you made only $5 in profit on the shirt, and so you'll pay taxes on that $5. Make sense? The cost of the shirt, the rent, and the ink were all deductible expenses.

CapEx is different in that the IRS requires all CapEx, such as adding a new appliance or replacing the flooring in a rental, be deducted over multiple years, since that item is going to last for many years. Unlike the ink, which is used up right away after purchasing it, CapEx items have a longer life span. Therefore, the IRS requires that you spread out your deductions over the life span they've decided upon for any given item. This process is known as depreciation, and it's exceptionally important for real estate investors to grasp. Stick with us, get a drink of water (or something stronger), and let's make sure you fully understand this!

Depreciation

To better illustrate the concept of depreciation, we'll use an example. The stove in the upstairs unit of your fourplex goes kaput. You head to the local appliance store and pick up a $500 stove. The IRS knows that the stove will last many years. Five years, to be specific. (Okay, it will probably last much longer, but the IRS says five years for appliances, so we are required to use their number. Maybe they are cooking with *really* high heat.) Rather than deducting that entire $500 in the year we bought this stove, we are going to evenly spread out that deduction over the time the IRS has allowed: five years. Therefore, we'll deduct just one-fifth of the cost of that stove each year for five years: $100 this year, $100 next year, $100 the year after, and so on.

When tracking your monthly income and expenses, it's okay to list the whole $500 on your document (in the row labeled "Depreciation expense or depletion"), but be sure to leave a note about exactly what it was you bought. That way, come tax time, you'll remember that you (or, hopefully, your CPA) will have to treat the item differently.

Now let's complicate things by introducing a concept that will make you more money right now: bonus depreciation. Bonus depreciation is sometimes included in legislation designed to encourage business owners to make large capital improvements to stimulate the economy. In essence, bonus depreciation allows a business owner (including real estate investors), under certain rules, to depreciate a higher percentage of the *cost* of their CapEx in the first year—sometimes 100 percent. Everything we just told you about spreading out the cost of that $500 stove over five years? You may have the option to toss it out the window and deduct the entire $500 right away.[19] Why does this matter? We'll give you four reasons.

- First, because depreciation is not optional for capital expenditures—it's required by U.S. law. You should understand how it works, even if you'll be hiring a CPA. Tracking your CapEx over the course of a year will make year-end tax preparation much easier.
- Second, depreciation itself might not be optional, but *bonus* depreciation is an option, and a really great one for most business owners because it allows them to pay less taxes in the near term. Any flooring you buy, paint you purchase, and appliances you install can significantly offset the amount of money that has to leave your bank account and flow into the loving arms of the IRS.
- Third, understanding the tax consequences associated with different property improvements can help you make better decisions.
- Fourth, we're spending so much time on this because depreciation can potentially help you pay *no* taxes at all.

Speaking of depreciation, we were going to tell you a good tax joke right here... but we doubt you *depreciate* it. Hah!

The Amazing Tax Benefits of Depreciation

At this point, you probably have a pretty good understanding of why the IRS requires you to spread out the deduction for a stove, flooring, a roof,

---

[19] As of the time of publication, bonus depreciation is slated to exist in full effect until 2022, when it will begin to be phased out until the ability is removed entirely by 2027.

and so on. Well, here's where this concept of depreciation gets really interesting: Not only can you write off a portion of the cost of that stove or flooring each year, you can actually write off a portion of the cost of the *entire building* each year. Wait, what?

Yes. Specifically, if you own a rental property that derives more than 80 percent of its revenue from people (as opposed to businesses), you'll be able to spread out the cost of the building (just the building, not the land) over 27.5 years. Why 27.5 years? No one seems to know. If the value of the building (again, not the land—the IRS doesn't let us depreciate that) is $500,000, then we can take $500,000 divided by 27.5 to get an annual deduction of $18,181 per year. If your property made only $18,000 in profit throughout the year, that means you would be able to, legally, show on paper that you made *no* money and thus pay no income taxes on that money.

A few important notes:

- **Mortgages:** Yes, you can still depreciate a building even if you have a mortgage on the property. In other words, even though you didn't actually *spend*, let's say, $500,000 on a property (because you bought it with a loan), you still get to depreciate the full $500,000. *Awesome.*

- **Commercial versus Residential:** As mentioned above, if your property derives 80 percent or more of its income from people, as opposed to businesses, the government considers this a residential property and requires that you depreciate the building over 27.5 years. On the other hand, if you own a commercial property, such as a retail shop, warehouse, or office building, you'll spread out that deduction over 39 years. Why 39 years? Again, who knows. I'm sure the government has its reasons, but it all seems arbitrary to us. The only time this might apply to you as a multifamily investor is if you own a mixed-use property (part commercial, part residential, such as an apartment that has retail shops on the ground floor). Otherwise, you'll be using 27.5 years.

- **Building versus Land:** Again, the government knows that land isn't going to break down over time, so they allow a deduction only on the building's value. Not sure what your property is worth versus the land? Although you could pay for an appraiser, there is an easier way to find out: Check with your local assessor. Each assessor in the United States will give a value to the land and the improvements on the land, such as buildings. Although the value itself could be wildly off, it's the *ratio* we can use. For example, if the local assessor believes your property to be worth $400,000 in total and $100,000 of that is land while $300,000 is "improvements," we know that one-fourth of the value of the property is being allocated to the land and three-fourths to the improvements. We can apply those percentages to the purchase price of the property, regardless of its appraised value. If you paid $800,000 for the property, you would simply take three-fourths of that $800,000 and, for tax purposes, you should be able to deduct $600,000 over 27.5 years.

- **Pay It Back:** If this deduction seems too good to be true, it just might be. You see, depreciation can be a wonderful thing when it comes to helping investors make money without having to pay taxes on that income. Some investors are making six- and seven-figure incomes each year and not paying a dime on that income! But here's the catch: When you sell that property, the IRS requires you to pay back the taxes you had skipped out on. This is known as the recapture of depreciation, is based on your ordinary income tax rate, and is currently capped at 25 percent. Let's say you depreciated $10,000 per year for ten years, for $100,000 in total deductions. If your ordinary income tax rate is 25 percent, you might owe the government $25,000 when you sell. Unless, of course, you use a 1031 exchange, which we'll talk about next.

We apologize if you find this material *taxing*, but we think it's important stuff.

The 1031 Exchange

It's our hope that when selling a property, you make a lot of money. That, after all, is why we're in this business. And if you've held the property long enough, you should. Over time, that property has likely increased in value (hopefully a lot) and you've been paying down that mortgage for years as well. Now you go to sell your property and you clear $200,000. Congratulations! But...

Enter: Uncle Sam.

You see, Uncle Sam (the IRS) has been waiting. He's been kind to you for years, giving you that nice depreciation benefit and helping you get richer. Now, however, he wants his cut, a tax known as the long-term capital gains tax, which is currently up to 20 percent, based on your income. To go back to our example, you could end up owing Uncle Sam $40,000 on that $200,000 profit *plus* the recapture of depreciation we just talked about. Let's assume the recapture of depreciation was going to be another $20,000, making your total tax bill $60,000.

Making $200,000 and giving the government $60,000 of that is not my idea of a good day. (That said, it's *still* a lower percentage than many W-2 job earners pay.) But you have another option: a 1031 exchange.

The 1031 exchange is a section of the tax code that allows investors who follow certain rules (such as buying a more-expensive property and doing it within a specified and short time frame) to defer paying taxes if they reinvest their money in another "like-kind" purchase, such as another rental property. It also defers that recapture of depreciation.

That $200,000 in profit you owe $60,000 on? Reinvest your $200,000 and—*poof!*—no taxes owed to Uncle Sam, yet. You see, at some point, Uncle Sam is going to want to be paid. However, the current U.S. tax code allows you to do as many 1031 exchanges as you want. In other words, maybe you'll use that $200,000 to buy a $1 million property, which you increase to $500,000 in profit later on. You do another 1031 exchange and take that $500,000 and turn it into $1 million. You turn that $1 million into $2 million and so on. Each time you sell your property, you do another 1031 exchange into a more expensive property. Of course, the cash flow on these future deals is mostly yours to keep (you'll be depreciating each subsequent property over that 27.5 years, helping you pay little tax on the cash flow) and then, someday...

BAM!

You get hit by a bus. And you die.

Sorry. As Ben Franklin said, there are only two guarantees in life: death and taxes.

But here's the cool thing: All the taxes you've been deferring (and the amount gets bigger and bigger each time) essentially get wiped out when you die. Your heirs inherit your properties by what's known as a stepped-up basis. This means that the cost basis is "stepped-up" from its original level (when you bought it) to today's fair market value, and your heirs will pay taxes only on any increase in value from that day forward.

Hopefully you avoid getting hit by a bus and instead die peacefully in your bed at a ripe old age. Regardless, 1031 exchanges *could* help you avoid capital gains tax for the rest of your life, and also not burden your heirs with the tax. Win-win.

What if you don't want to own rentals until you die? You must first understand that there are mechanisms by which investors may elect to do a 1031 exchange into completely passive real estate. For example, they may do a final exchange into a huge property that they own a very small percentage of. Therefore, they make a nice return for years without needing to do any work. An experienced CPA can help you identify these types of options. If you eventually decide to settle up with the IRS and pay all the deferred taxes, you will likely have significant net worth to cover this tax bill. The neat thing is that you'll probably still have significantly more money at the end than you would have had if you had paid the government each time.

This section on the 1031 exchange is meant simply to whet your appetite. There are *many* rules and guidelines that must be followed to do an exchange properly and legally. You'll learn plenty more about the specifics by reading Volume II of *The Multifamily Millionaire*.

One final note on 1031 exchanges: Although tax-deferred exchanges date all the way back to the Revenue Act of 1921, at each election cycle the provision is revisited and candidates threaten to do away with it. It's impossible to know what the future holds, but our advice is to take full advantage of 1031 exchanges while you can.

Hiring a CPA

Sherlock Holmes paid almost no income taxes. He was a *master of deduction*. You can be one too, but the great news is you don't have to be. Instead, you should hire a qualified CPA to help with your taxes *and* offer ongoing proper and legal financial help. We're often asked, "When is the right time to hire a CPA to do my taxes? How many properties should I own before hiring someone?" Our answer: Hire one *now*. A *good* CPA will pay for him- or herself, and a *great* CPA will make you wealthier. Get that great CPA on your team now, even if you're just getting started. They will not only help you with taxes but also assist you with making decisions as you build your portfolio.

However, you will need to find a CPA who specializes in helping real estate investors (unless you also happen to also be a farmer—in that case you should look for an *accowntant*. Get it?). The CPA doesn't necessarily have to be "local" to you, as most of the applicable tax laws will be at the federal level, but they do have to understand the intricacies of real estate investor tax law and be familiar with your state and local tax requirements. (Your brother-in-law who worked for three months at the local supermarket pop-up-tax-tent each spring is not going to cut it.)

As with most other professionals you'll need to hire for your business, get recommendations from other real estate investors. Interview several CPAs and pick the one you feel has the best experience working with real estate investors and is someone you can see yourself working with long term.

LLCs and Entity Issues

Have you ever wondered why superheroes typically wear masks and spandex? I mean, besides the fact that it looks *really freaking cool.* It's because they want to protect their personal life and the lives of those around them. Imagine if the Joker knew exactly who Batman was. He'd quickly take Batman's girlfriend hostage and threaten to toss her off a building. Okay, that's exactly what happened, and it's a common story in almost every superhero's life. The bad guy finds out who the superhero really is and goes after the hero's friends or family.

And while you might not feel like a superhero, this same logic applies to why real estate investors focus on investing within a separate legal entity. No, not because someone is going to toss your significant other off a building. But a separate legal entity, like an LLC, is a "mask" that separates you from your business. The business, like Batman, can take some punches, but your personal life (your home, your car, your savings account) is ideally kept safe if something goes wrong with the business.

Consider this example: Your twelve-unit apartment building has been making you money for years. Then one day your maintenance man leaves a small broom handle out on the sidewalk after cleaning up. A tenant, of course, slips and falls and... dies. (It was a rough fall.) The family of the tenant sues you and wins a judgment for $5 million. Of course, you have an insurance policy on the property, so it's okay, right? Maybe not. Your insurance policy *might* offer only $1 million in liability coverage. Where will the other $4 million come from? That's right: your pocket. You probably don't have $4 million just sitting around, so instead, the courts force you to sell your rental property and every other property you own, which includes the cute home you've lived in for ten years and raised your kids in. They even force you to sell your wife's diamond earrings and empty all your bank accounts, and in the end you still have to declare bankruptcy. Now your earring-less wife has left you and you're eating a steady diet of government cheese and living in a van down by the river.

All because you decided to invest in real estate. *Maybe Mom was right. You should have sold insurance.*

Okay, this example might be a *bit* dramatic, but it could happen. It's very possible that your insurance may not cover you if you get sued. This is why investors want to wear a superhero mask, also known as putting the property in a legal entity. No, a legal entity isn't necessarily going to completely "hide" you from those looking for you (though it definitely makes finding the owner a bit more complicated). But the legal entity, when properly set up, makes sure that if you get sued, only the assets (money, property) that are owned *by that entity* are going to be lost. In other words, Batman could die, but Bruce Wayne would be okay.

One quick caveat: Although the LLC is designed to separate *you* from the LLC, most small multifamily loans will require a personal guarantee. In other words, you (not the LLC) are responsible for paying the loan back. Even if you put a property into an LLC and the worst-case scenario happens, meaning you get sued and they take the property, you may *still* be personally liable for the loan. An LLC is not a "get out of jail free" card, and there are risks—even with an LLC. Risk is part of the business, but not a reason to avoid it. Therefore, if you think putting a property into a legal entity is a good idea, good job. It is (usually) a good idea. However, it's slightly more complicated than that. (Because of course it is!)

Types of Legal Entities

There are several types of legal entities an investor could consider: an LLC, a C corporation, an S corporation, a family trust, a limited partnership, and more. Rather than spend time explaining the details of each, let's just say that most investors use LLCs. Of course, for some investors, other options are much better, usually due to personal tax considerations. The only way you are truly going to know the best option for yourself is to get on a conference call with your real estate attorney and your CPA. In thirty minutes or less you can explain to them what you are attempting to do and ask for their feedback.

Furthermore, although you *could* set up your LLC yourself or through one of many online legal providers, we do *not* recommend that. You're a multifamily real estate investor—you're in the big leagues now. Pay the right people to do this for you so you can make sure it's done right. There are places to skimp and save as an investor. Getting sound legal advice and protecting your personal assets is not one of them. This is an example of why good lawyers never lose their appeal. (That joke didn't go over your head, right? *Lose their appeal?* Okay, we're starting to stretch here. Fortunately for you, this chapter is almost over.)

Properly Using Your Entity

Earlier in this book we briefly discussed the tax differences between residential multifamily properties (those with two to four units) and commercial multifamily properties (those with five or more). This distinction comes back into play when talking about legal entities. If you obtain a traditional residential mortgage on a residential property, usually your lender will allow you to purchase the property *only* in your own name, not in the name of an LLC or another entity.

Many investors choose to buy the property in their own name and then, post-closing, will transfer the ownership to an LLC they own. While this is common, many lenders specifically prohibit this practice through a "due on sale" clause in the mortgage, which gives the lender the right to foreclose if you sell the property. You might say, "But I didn't sell the property. I transferred it to an LLC that I own." True, but legally this could still be considered a sale for zero dollars, and thus trigger the clause. Will a lender follow through with this clause? In our experience, we've never seen it done. (Chances are you could transfer the property back into your personal name if they did have an issue.) However, since it's a possibility, it's something you need to factor into your risk tolerance and discuss with your attorney.

On the other hand, if you obtain a commercial loan, you will almost certainly purchase the property in some sort of legal entity (as suggested by your attorney). Unlike residential lenders, commercial lenders are accustomed to working with LLCs. In fact, they will likely require that you use one.

Once you open the entity, it's important that you keep all entity transactions and all personal transitions separate. You'll open up a separate bank account, get a separate debit/credit card for that entity, and so on. Never mix personal and entity expenses, or you could risk a judge declaring your entity invalid. Getting a legal entity for your investments is a good way to protect yourself against loss, but even if you can't use an entity to purchase your multifamily property, that doesn't mean you have to scout your spot to live down by the river. By carrying good insurance with adequate liability coverage, you'll be able to protect yourself in case of a lawsuit. For additional coverage and peace of mind (and for a relatively low cost), you can obtain an umbrella insurance policy, which gives you significant extra coverage in the event that you get sued and your property's policy doesn't fully cover the judgment.

Legal entities can be powerful tools in the investor's tool belt, one more way to reduce your risk as you build your business. But as any superhero will tell you, with great power comes great responsibility, so obey the rules and guidelines. Don't wing it when it comes to entities. Get a real-estate-focused attorney and CPA together and set up a legal entity that will carry you through the *Dark Night*.

KEY TAKEAWAYS

- Bookkeeping is essential to owning multifamily real estate—and fairly simple once you have a solid system that documents your monthly income and expenses.
- The U.S. tax code offers several key benefits for real estate investors, including depreciation and the 1031 exchange. Be sure to regularly consult with a qualified CPA to ensure you are properly taking advantage of these benefits.
- Legal entities are designed to separate you from your investment property in case of problems like lawsuits. Definitely consult with a qualified real estate attorney to ensure you have the right entity for your situation.

Chapter 22

GETTING TO THE NEXT LEVEL

"All our dreams can come true, if we have the
courage to pursue them."

—WALT DISNEY

The world changed in 1985.

No, not because that happens to be the year I was born. That was also
the year the greatest video game of all time—Super Mario Bros.—was
born.

In this game, the main character, a short mustachioed plumber named
Mario, navigates a series of levels of increasing difficulty, moving mostly
horizontally across the Mushroom Kingdom in an attempt to reach, and
save, the entrapped Princess Peach. The game consists of eight worlds
and each world contains four sub-levels, for a total of thirty-two stages.

Mario journeys across the land, through dark castle dungeons, deep underwater, and even bounces over clouds to reach the final stage, where he encounters the sinister Bowser guarding the princess over a pool of hot lava. At an average time of five minutes per mission, the game would take the average player more than two hours to reach the end and rescue the princess—that is, if they didn't lose all their lives in the process.

I, however, could beat Super Mario Bros. in eight minutes. No, I wasn't all that good at video games. I hardly played Super Mario Bros. I simply knew a few shortcuts. (If you're a child of the '80s and '90s, you probably know where I'm going with this.)

After finishing level 1-1 (meaning the first stage of the four stages in the first world) and proceeding on to level 1-2 (the second stage of the first world), there is a hidden switch that gives you the ability to immediately "warp" to level 4-1, completely bypassing the second half of the first world, all of world two, and all of world three. Zipping quickly through world 4-1 and entering 4-2, there is another warp pipe that allows you to skip all the way to level 8-1. A hectic nonstop sprint through all four levels of world eight brought me face-to-face with evil himself, Bowser. But a quick jump over his head opened up the suspension bridge he stood on, and he fell to his doom while I received a kiss from Princess Peach. Victory never tasted so sweet.

As you can see, I didn't have to go through every single level in order to achieve victory. The warp pipes were put there by the game makers as a reward for those worthy enough to seek out an alternate path (or those lucky enough to have an older cousin who shared the secret to success).

When I think of building wealth through real estate, I think about Super Mario Bros. You see, most people, in their attempts to build a solid financial future for themselves and their families, progress through life stage by stage. They have fun in their teens, more fun in their twenties, begin to settle down in their thirties, begin saving money in their forties, and by the time they are sixty or seventy years old, they might have enough to retire on and enjoy the final years of their life.

But many individuals' lives are tragically cut short before they reach the end, because unlike Mario, we only get *one* life. Most financial pundits would like you to stay at your job for forty years, socking away a little money each month.

However, the number one reason why I love multifamily real estate is that it allows you to skip levels on your path to an incredible life. It allows you to live an unscripted journey, one that doesn't require forty years of making someone else wealthy to potentially accomplish success. Multifamily real estate allows you to *warp* to greater and greater levels of success. You are held back by nothing more than your own ambition. It is truly an amazing way to spend the one life we've been given.

Here we are, at the last chapter in this book, but your journey is not over. After all, if you're following the advice in this book and growing your wealth exponentially using The Stack method, you will quickly outgrow the lessons in this volume. You will need to get to a whole new level. *Volume II will show you how to get there.*

Like my cousin who showed me exactly how to beat Super Mario Bros. in eight minutes by using warp pipes, The Stack and the Multifamily Millionaire Model will show you how to use the real-life warp pipes that can help you become a multifamily millionaire.

But it won't happen by accident. It begins by putting into practice the lessons you learned in this book. Start with finding small multifamily properties and learn from these small deals. Then warp to the next level: large multifamily real estate. Like Mario running through the Mushroom Kingdom, there's only one way for you to win: by moving forward—and doing so with speed, confidence, and the occasional shortcut. We know you can do it, and we know you *will.*

The game is yours to play, so get moving. After all, the clock is ticking, and you only have one life—make it count.

We'll see you in Volume II.

Appendix A

MULTIFAMILY REPAIR BUDGET ALGORITHM (MRBA)

We developed the Multifamily Repair Budget Algorithm, or MRBA, because we couldn't find another tool like it. In fact, looking back at our own real estate journey, we can both say that this tool would have made the difference between success and failure on many deals.

The MRBA is an easy-to-use algorithm designed to help you estimate the repairs you can expect on any given property. However, before we walk you through the MRBA, two quick disclaimers:

1. An algorithm is only as good as the data you input. Be honest with yourself and be sure to apply the right adjustments to your measurements.

2. Although we believe this tool to be incredibly helpful in estimating the costs of repairs, each property is unique. In other words, when we look at data over a large number of properties, we can predict certain trends and averages. But when looking at individual components, it's impossible to know the future for one particular unit. So how does this apply to our discussion of repairs? Take these estimates as estimates, but understand that your individual property could perform better or worse. Maybe you'll go the next three years without a single maintenance concern (knock on wood). But it's also possible that a pipe might burst in the ceiling of your duplex, causing $10,000 in damage next week. (We really hope not!) Therefore, look at this tool as a long-term estimating solution. Ideally, over a long time span, we believe these estimates will be correct.

Also, to make this easier, we built a free online tool, the Multifamily Repair Budget Algorithm Online Edition, to help you perform this calculation, which you can access at www.biggerpockets.com/mrba. You can also do this manually with a simple pen and paper if you'd like.

When a real estate appraiser wants to determine how much a property is worth, they look at what similar properties (comparables or "comps") have sold for recently, and then add or subtract based on how a given property stacks up against the comps. We are going to do the exact same thing with MRBA.

We want you to start with a simple number: $100. (That is going to be $100 per unit per month. But for now, let's just leave it at $100 and we'll multiply by the number of units at the end.)

We'll call this your "moving baseline number" (MBN), because we're going to add or subtract certain amounts from it based on your specific property's details. As we work through the following six adjustment factors, we'll move that baseline around until we have a final figure to use for our monthly repair budget. Let's examine the importance of each factor and show you how much to add or subtract from the $100.

1. Property Age

A property built a century ago will typically require substantially more repairs than one built twenty years ago. The materials used in the past are very different from the materials used today, and even if quality materials were used, they simply wear out over time. This is perhaps most apparent in the plumbing and electrical systems.

- Built prior to 1950: Add $30
- Built between 1951 and 1978: Add $20
- Built between 1979 and 1999: Add $0
- Built since 1999: Subtract $20

To walk you through completing an MRBA, we'll assume the following: You are estimating the repairs on a fourplex you would like to purchase. This property was built in 1970. Therefore, you will add $20. MBN: $100 + $20 = $120.

2. Property Condition

When a property has recently been rehabbed, many of the old systems will have been replaced with brand-new systems. Therefore, a property that has been completely remodeled will likely require fewer repairs than a property that hasn't been touched in twenty years. Of course, if the rehab was simply cosmetic, it won't affect the need for repairs on the home's outdated systems (like plumbing or electrical). Spending a little more time and money on a rehab to address outdated systems in the home can save significant repair and maintenance costs over the long term.

Also, if you plan to purchase and fix up a property, be sure to base your calculation on its after-repair condition. In other words, if you are buying a property in Class D condition but plan to fix it up to Class B condition, use the Class B option below.

- Class D condition: Add $30
- Class C condition: Add $0
- Class B condition: Subtract $10
- Class A condition: Subtract $40

Continuing with our fourplex example, you know that although the property needs some work, you'll be doing a full rehab when you buy it, bringing it up to Class B condition. Therefore, you'll subtract $10. MBN: $120 − $10 = $110.

3. Tenant Quality

Additionally, the quality of tenant who will be living in the property will affect the amount you spend on repairs on an ongoing basis. Some tenants are simply more destructive than others. If your tenant base is a rougher-than-average crowd, you will want to compensate for this in your numbers. The quality of tenant you attract will largely depend on the condition of the property, the location, and your marketing efforts. But good tenant screening will hopefully keep out the worst. For the purposes of our algorithm, aim to discover what type of tenant you'll attract and be honest with yourself. Many of our properties, due to location and property type, simply won't attract a Class A or even a Class B tenant. The same might be true for you.

- Class D tenant: Add $20
- Class C tenant: Add $10
- Class B tenant: Add $0
- Class A tenant: Subtract $20

Your fourplex is actually in a pretty great area, and once you fix it up before renting, it should attract some pretty great Class B tenants. MBN: $110 + $0 = $110.

4. Bedroom Count

The more people who reside in your property, the more potential damage. This is especially true with children. I have a 4-year-old daughter, and in just the past month, she has drawn on the walls, peeled off paint/drywall, and dumped sand on the hardwood floor, then pulled the chair across it, gouging the floor. (Keep in mind that landlords cannot discriminate against "family status," such as the number of children, but they can follow state and local laws to limit the number of people per bedroom.) Even if all residents are adults, more people still equals more opportunity for wear and tear as well as accidents. Therefore, the more bedrooms you're renting, the more likely you'll have frequent repairs.

If your multifamily property contains a mixed unit count (meaning that not all units have the same number of bedrooms), find the average, round to the nearest whole number, and use that for your equation.

- Studio units: Subtract $30
- One-bedroom units: Subtract $20
- Two-bedroom units: Subtract $0
- Three-plus-bedroom units: Add $20

Your fourplex contains three one-bedroom units and one two-bedroom. That's a total of five bedrooms in four units, which is an average of 1.25 bedrooms per unit, so we'll round down to one and, therefore, subtract $20. MBN: $110 − $20 = $90.

5. Property Unit Count

The more units you have, the more repair and maintenance costs will be shared among all tenants. For example, if you own a property with two units and the water line entering the property breaks, costing $1,000 to repair, that's $500 per unit. But if you incurred that same expense at a ten-unit property, that would come to only $100 per unit. Therefore, the more units you own, the less we'll allocate on a per-unit basis.

- Two to four units: Add $10
- Five to ten units: Add $0
- Eleven to fifty units: Subtract $20
- More than fifty units: Subtract $30

Because your fourplex has four units, we are going to add $10. MBN: $90 + $10 = $100, ironically, our starting number.

6. Expensive Market Multiplier

Finally, if you've lived in many different cities in your adult life, you'll have noticed that the cost of repairs on a property differs depending on where you are. For example, the cost of hiring a plumber in Cincinnati is probably lower than in New York City.

To compensate for this difference, we created a very simple multiplier to arrive at our final per-unit number. We're going to base this multiplier on the median price of a single-family home in your market. Why a single-family home? Because there is a strong correlation between the cost of labor and the cost of a single-family home! Google the median home price in your neighborhood for this calculation.

All we're doing in this final step is applying the following rule of thumb: If you live in an extremely low-priced market, your repair costs should run about 20 percent less than normal. If you live in an extremely high-priced market, your repair costs should run about 20 percent more than normal.

- If the average price is less than $200,000: Multiply by 0.8
- If the average price is $200,001–$400,000: Do not adjust
- If the average price is greater than $400,000: Multiply by 1.2

The MBN on your fourplex has moved around a bit, but after factor five, we were back at $100 per unit per month. Now let's assume you're buying this property in Denver. A quick Google search shows that the median cost of a single-family home there is $460,000. Therefore, we're going to multiply $100 by 1.2 to get our final MBN of $120.

At this point, all you need to do is multiply the final MBN by the number of units in your property. Therefore: $120 × 4 = $480. That's the metric we want to use when estimating the average cost of repairs on your example property.

Does that seem high? It might, and many real estate investors (especially in the multifamily world) fail to accurately understand just how much repairs cost them over the long term. It's not insignificant! Maybe you'll go twelve months without a single repair on your fourplex and you're feeling really good about yourself. But then suddenly your tenant moves out, leaving a trashed unit and costing you $6,000 in repairs. If you had been setting aside $480 per month for repairs, that $6,000 would be available. Nothing to be too concerned with. But if you didn't set aside that $480, this one repair could destroy your savings account and turn you off from real estate investing.

The amount you save for repairs can truly make or break your investment, so estimate this number accurately. Plan for repairs. Save for repairs. Spend on repairs. That's how a multifamily millionaire operates.

MRBA FAQs

Why not use a percentage?

Although many real estate investors use a flat percentage of the rent collected when allocating their repair budget, using a percentage can be misleading because properties have different rental rates. For example, let's say you want to use 10 percent of the rent collected as your metric for allocating repairs. If you owned a fourplex in a higher-priced market where total rent was $2,000 per unit (for a total of $8,000 per month in gross rent), your repair allocation would be $800 per month. However, if your fourplex was located in a lower-priced market, where rent was $500 per unit for a total of $2,000 per month in gross rent, then your allocation would be just $200 per month. These properties could be *identical* in terms of the age, condition, bedroom count, unit count, and quality of tenant they attract, yet the repair budget for the more expensive property would be four times greater. This might make sense if the cost of repairs at the expensive market were four times greater, but the fact is, replacing a leaky toilet in Cleveland and replacing a leaky toilet in Malibu costs about the same. (You might pay a bit more for labor in expensive markets, but not 400 percent more! We estimated 20 percent more in the final stage of the MRBA.)

Therefore, using a flat percentage to calculate small multifamily repair allocations can be shortsighted. As you get into larger multifamily real estate, you'll tend to use percentages, as you'll be able to look at historical trends at the property to see what actual repair expenses have been over the previous years. But for small multifamily real estate and single-family houses, using an actual dollar figure will likely be far more accurate.

What's included in repairs?

One of the difficulties in estimating repairs is one of semantics. Some might include lawn care as maintenance, while others designate lawn care as its own line item. This also applies to landscaping, cleaning, snow removal, pest control, and other regularly performed work. Sometimes you'll even see certain "contract services" on their own line item in a seller's expense sheet. This could refer to work done by a plumber or a handyman that clearly involves repairs even though it is not included in the repair expense line item. This is not necessarily wrong; people can organize their books however they like (within reason, of course). But when reviewing someone else's repair estimates, you'll want to make sure you are comparing apples to apples, not forgetting an expense or double counting one.

Our recommendation, and the way the MRBA is set up to work, is to *not* include landscaping, lawn care, snow removal, or similar work in the repair items, unless they involve damage to the property (for example, a vehicle drives over flower boxes and your handyman needs to make repairs to the boxes and replace flowers). However, we *do* include contract services, such as those provided by plumbers or handymen who make repairs to the property. Basically, if work involves repairing something, it's a repair expense. If it involves maintaining something, we'll include it elsewhere.

Can't I just use what the seller is claiming as repairs?

When you're buying a small multifamily apartment building, the seller will likely offer some "helpful guidance" as to the amount you'll spend on repairs. Sellers of small multifamily real estate are notorious for falsifying and underplaying their repair budgets, seeking to show the smallest possible projected repair expenses so you, the buyer, will believe you are getting a better deal. This is especially true when the owner knows they will be selling the property in the near future. They'll do everything they can to minimize repairs, even forgoing some much-needed maintenance on the property so their net operating income looks stronger.

Additionally, remember that when it comes to small multifamily real estate, you could go years with hardly any repairs, then suddenly get hit with ten expensive maintenance requests at once. When a seller tries to convince you that their repairs have been very low for several years, assume that there may be significant *deferred* maintenance that needs to be done. Low repair reports from the seller often mean higher repair expenses for you!

Should I actually set aside the money budgeted for repairs each month, even if I don't use it in that month? Or is this just for theoretical budgeting reasons?

This is a personal choice, but we recommend, at least in the beginning, that you set aside the money each month in its own separate account. Human nature is to spend whatever money comes in, so you may not have the money needed for repairs when you require it if you haven't been saving up all along. Establishing a "repair bank account" is a great way to ensure that you are stockpiling money each month to handle the occasional repair when it happens. Furthermore, it just hurts much less to hire that plumber at $200 an hour when you know you have $6,000 sitting in a bank account for this very purpose. It hurts a lot more when you have to take money from your personal bank account to fill your empty business bank account because you already took all the "profit." Of course, a big expense could hit before you've had enough time to save up the cash to cover it, which is why stocking the account with reserves immediately upon purchase is important.

How much should I have in reserves for repairs when I first buy a multifamily property?

Banks typically require that you set aside six months of PITI (principal, interest, taxes, and insurance) payments for both reserves and CapEx when you buy a property. We think this is a pretty good place to start. If your mortgage (principal and interest) is $1,000 per month, your taxes are $3,000 per year, and your insurance is $1,200 per year, then:

P&I: $1,000 per month × 6 = $6,000 for six months

Taxes: $3,000 per year ÷ 2 = $1,500 for six months

Insurance: $1,200 per year ÷ 2 = $600 for six months

$6,000 + $1,500 + $600 = $8,100 in reserves needed at purchase

Finally, understand that some lenders can require up to twelve months of reserves, so be sure to check with your lender for their requirements and follow their guidance. Even though you might require more money up front, remember that these reserves can keep you afloat in a tight spot. You can bet all those owners who didn't get rent for several months during the COVID-19 pandemic were glad they had those reserves!

Appendix B
MULTIFAMILY CAPITAL EXPENDITURE BUDGET ALGORITHM (MCEBA)

Note: The MCEBA process applies only to small multifamily properties, as defined back in Chapter One. For larger multifamily properties, we use different methods to calculate CapEx. You'll learn about those methods in Volume II.

Since you just walked through the algorithm for repairs in Appendix A, we can go more quickly through the algorithm for CapEx, as you should have a pretty good idea of how this works. Remember that we also built a free online tool, the Multifamily Capital Expenditure Budget Algorithm Online Edition to help you perform this calculation, which you can find at www.biggerpockets.com/mceba.

Once again, we'll begin with a $100 moving baseline number (MBN) and subject it to four adjustments:

1. Age of Property
Older properties break down much more than newer properties. This is especially true of CapEx items. For example, a property with a boiler built in 1940 will need to have it replaced at some point, which could cost as much as $10,000.
- Built prior to 1950: Add $30
- Built between 1951 and 1978: Add $20
- Built between 1979 and 1999: Add $0
- Built since 1999: Subtract $20

To walk you through completing an MCEBA, we'll assume the following: You are estimating the CapEx repairs on an eight-unit apartment building in Orlando that you would like to purchase. This property was built in 1940. Therefore, you would add $30. MBN: $100 + $30 = $130.

2. Average Age of Major Systems

Major systems include items like the roof, foundation, windows, plumbing, heating, and pretty much anything else that would cost thousands or even tens of thousands of dollars to replace. Sometimes you'll buy a property where everything has recently been remodeled and most of those systems have been replaced. Other times you'll buy a property and do the repairs yourself. And sometimes you'll buy a property where the major systems are just old and outdated. Because the general age of these major systems as a whole make such a difference in the amount you'll have to spend to maintain or replace them, let's make some adjustments based on their average age.

- Completely remodeled and all systems updated: Subtract $40
- Good condition, but some major systems are getting older: Subtract $0
- Poor condition and barely rentable, with many old major systems: Add $30

You plan to completely remodel the eight-unit apartment building to look and feel brand-new, and you have money set aside to do this. You'll be installing a new roof, updating the plumbing, replacing cabinets and counters, repainting, installing new flooring, and more. Therefore, you would subtract $40. MBN: $130 − $40 = $90.

3. Number of Units

Although larger properties will require more CapEx over time, many CapEx items, such as the roof and parking spaces, are shared across all units. As result, the actual CapEx budget per unit generally decreases as the number of units increases.

- One to two units: Subtract $0
- Three to four units: Subtract $20
- Five to ten units: Subtract $40
- More than ten units: Subtract $50

Your prospective property has eight units. Therefore, you would subtract $40. MBN: $90 – $40 = $50.

4. Median Single-Family Home Price

Finally, you'll need to account for your location, just as we did with repairs, since a water heater replacement is going to be more expensive in Maui than in Cleveland. To do this, we're going to once again look up the median price of a single-family home in your market, since this number correlates well with the cost of labor.

- If the average price is less than $200,000: Multiply your number by 0.8
- If the average price is $200,001–$400,000: Do not adjust
- If the average price is more than $400,000: Multiply your number by 1.2

A quick Google search shows us that the median single-family home price in Orlando, where our prospective eight-unit property is located, is $231,000. Therefore, we're going to do nothing to our MBN. That leaves us at $50.

At this point, all you need to do is multiply the final MBN by the number of units in your property. Therefore: $50 × 8 = $400. This is your estimated CapEx budget, per month, for your property.

As you may have noticed, the factors with the greatest impact on CapEx are the age of the property and the relative condition of the major systems in the property. So many landlords miss this—prepare for CapEx and set aside money each month for this expense.

MCEBA FAQs

If a property is going to be totally rehabbed, why have any CapEx at all?
Because even a full rehab rarely covers *all* CapEx items. For example, it's unlikely that you'll be updating all the plumbing in a property during a rehab, nor will you likely replace all the windows, and you might even be leaving the roof alone because it's in pretty good shape. Now, if you truly are doing a full-gut rehab and basically creating a brand-new house (or if you are buying a brand-new property that was just built yesterday), you *still* should be setting aside money for replacing items.

True, you will likely not have to deal with replacing the roof again for at least another twenty-five years, and maybe you'll sell the property by then, but you may have to change out that water heater five years from now. You may have to change out the appliances in seven years. You may need to replace the flooring in five. Although fully rehabbed or new properties will require significantly less CapEx in the near future, you should still account for some.

By the way, this is also why we *love* to do rehabs when we buy an investment property. By tackling all the CapEx up front, you'll significantly lower the amount of money you lose to CapEx each month. Essentially, you are just prepaying your CapEx rather than waiting for it to pop up.

What if I'm going to be doing all my own work on the property?

The MCEBA assumes you'll be hiring contractors or handymen to repair things when they break. We assume you won't be installing a roof yourself or laying carpet. But maybe you will, in which case, don't change a thing! Although you might save money over paying someone else, materials aren't free. And who knows? Life changes, and five years down the road you may find you no longer want to handle this kind of work.

However if you purchase properties with significantly lower repair and CapEx allocations because you plan to do the work yourself, you may find those deals were not actually deals. An investment should make sense as an investment, not just because you're doing the work. In fact, if you plan to do the work yourself, we have no issue with that—just as long as you pay yourself for the work the same way you would a contractor. This way, when the day comes that you decide to stop doing the work, the expense amount doesn't change, just to whom the check is written.

Won't CapEx Increase Over Time?

Yes! The MCEBA is meant to give you an estimate as to the immediate amount of money you should be setting aside for your CapEx reserve budget. We'd recommend calculating and increasing this number each year.

At this point, we've covered all the major expenses you're likely to encounter, but remember, each area and property is unique. You might find a property with other unique expenses to account for and should incorporate those into your estimates as well.

ACKNOWLEDGMENTS

The Multifamily Millionaire, Volumes I and II reflect an accumulation of knowledge and experience that would not have been possible without the support and contributions of countless friends, colleagues, partners, contractors, tenants, and others. There are just too many people to name here, but please know that we're grateful to everyone who has helped us along the way.

The production and promotion of books like *The Multifamily Millionaire* takes a ton of work, and there were a lot more people involved other than just the authors. We would like to take this opportunity to thank everyone who took the time to proofread the draft manuscript, and Katie Pelton for completing an editorial assessment. We would also like to extend our gratitude to the entire editorial and marketing team at BiggerPockets, including Katie Miller, Kaylee Walterbach, Savannah Wood, Katie Golownia, Wendy Dunning, Laurie Brantley, and Louise Collazo. Thank you for helping to make these books the best they could be and for getting them into the hands of as many aspiring investors as possible.

On a professional level, over the past couple of years, we've had the opportunity to take our investing to the next level through our partnership at Open Door Capital. Our shared experience and journey at Open Door Capital helped prepare us to write these books. As such, we would be remiss if we didn't thank the entire Open Door Capital team, and also all the limited partners who have invested in our projects. We are grateful for your trust and look forward to growing your wealth through our multifamily investments.

Finally, we would like to acknowledge you, the reader. We were inspired to write *The Multifamily Millionaire* to help all the good, hard-working people who have committed to bettering their lives through real estate. We hope these books can play a small part in helping you to achieve your dreams.

The Multifamily Millionaire, Volume II
Create Generational Wealth by Investing in
Large Multifamily Real Estate
By Brian Murray and Brandon Turner

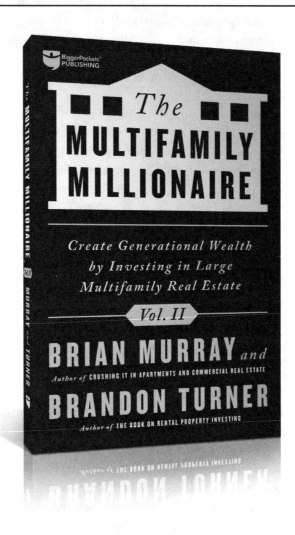

Are you ready to go big with your multifamily strategy and create generational wealth? Turn the page for a sneak peek from the second book in *The Multifamily Millionaire* series!

Volume II is the definitive guide to investing in large multifamily properties—all based on the authors' experience of starting with nothing and building their real estate portfolios to thousands of units. Brian Murray and Brandon Turner share the secrets to their success in large multifamily investing with proven methods and practical advice that will help take your investment strategies to the next level.

Inside, you will learn to:
- Acquire large multifamily rental properties without using your own cash
- Find, underwrite, and negotiate great deals in any market
- Get commercial loans and secure the best terms
- Build a team of rock stars who can help take you to the next level
- Boost property values by using dozens of proven strategies
- Make sure your properties thrive even during a recession
- *And much more!*

Chapter Two
STRUCTURING MULTIFAMILY DEALS

Empty pockets never held anyone back. Only empty heads and empty hearts can do that.

—NORMAN VINCENT PEALE

The first time I heard somebody use the term "capital stack," all I could think of was a big pile of cash. I was pretty sure "first position" had something to do with dance—and when I heard someone reference "mezzanine debt," I thought it was somehow related to stadium seating options. Maybe "mezzanine debt" was a season-ticket financing plan? Eventually I educated myself on such things, but I probably should have made the effort to know the lingo a little sooner.

As you start to do bigger multifamily deals, it's helpful to understand how larger investors look at projects and get a better grasp of the terminology, some of which isn't widely used for smaller properties. An important part of that perspective is understanding deal structure, which is often no more complicated than for a duplex, but on occasion, it can get much more so.

At a high level, there are two types of capital that are used to fund a deal: debt and equity. The capital can come from different sources, and the sources are layered on top of one another to cover the cost of the project. Combined, these layers make up what is referred to as the capital stack (not to be confused with the real estate strategy known as The Stack, which we outlined in Volume I).

The capital stack reflects not only the sources but where each source falls relative to the others in terms of first rights of repayment should the property not perform. Capital stacks are often depicted graphically in the shape of a pyramid. At the bottom are the people or entities who would get paid first if everything falls apart, which means this is the place on the pyramid where capital is the least at risk. In most deals, the lenders are at the bottom of the capital stack.

The equity you contribute out of pocket is almost always going to be at the top of the pyramid. You are not going to get paid until the debt obligations are fulfilled, so your funds are at the greatest risk, but you also have the greatest exposure to the upside. In general, the risk declines as you go lower in the capital stack, but so do the returns.

Debt

Debt is the cornerstone of most deals. In most large multifamily transactions, debt covers anywhere from 65 to 80 percent of the purchase price. That said, Brandon and I have both done all-cash deals for which we didn't borrow any funds as well as deals for which we've financed 100 percent of the purchase price.

Many investors with limited cash resources dream of purchasing a multifamily property with all debt and no equity. While buying a multifamily property with no cash out of pocket is possible, finding these opportunities is exceptionally challenging. Over the past decade I have been involved in hundreds of deals, but I've funded only two properties with 100 percent debt, and both were facilitated through strong lender relationships.

The reality is that you'll need at least some cash to close most deals, although it doesn't necessarily have to be your own cash. While closing without much cash or even walking out of closing with a check in your pocket might seem exciting, you should be cautious about structuring deals this way. Just because you come across a situation that allows you to put in less cash doesn't mean it's the right thing to do. Taking on debt involves risk, so you must be careful not to overextend yourself.

Both Brandon and I have employed creative financing techniques when we knew properties would generate more than enough cash flow to safely cover our debt service. On other occasions we have each walked away from opportunities to use high leverage because we weren't able to identify enough opportunities to add value or didn't want to take on the higher risk associated with the debt.

How much debt you can secure typically depends on the specifics of the property and the deal you negotiate. We'll cover debt and the entire lending process in detail in upcoming chapters, but the amount of debt most lenders are willing to extend is in large part dependent on how much cash a property is generating and its ability to cover the mortgage payments.

In terms of the capital stack, the largest debt is most commonly found at the bottom of the stack in the first position, which is secured by the property. The debt in first position is also called the senior debt. What is the significance of being in the first position? Basically, if you were to default on this loan, this note holder can foreclose and would be paid before anyone else in the capital stack.

Sometimes there will be a lender in a second position that extends mezzanine debt, which is subordinate to the senior debt. This second position in the capital stack fills the gap between senior debt and equity. For River Apartments, the mezzanine debt was extended by the seller. Another example of mezzanine debt is when developers get landowners to partner with them or finance the land portion of the deal through construction.

If there is ever a foreclosure sale, the lender in the second position would get paid only if there are proceeds left over after the first lender is made whole. Banks are not generally comfortable with the risk of being in the second position, so this debt is more likely to be secured from the seller or a private lender. There are some lenders out there, usually debt funds, who do only mezzanine debt and charge a higher interest rate to offset the higher risk.

Below is an example of a potential capital stack:

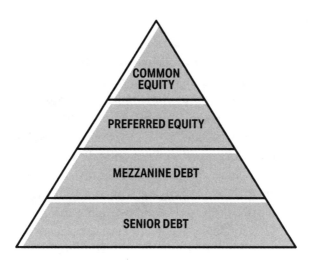

Equity

Equity is the cash portion that sits at the top of the capital stack. In most situations, you will either put this cash in yourself or secure it from partners or investors. For development projects and major restorations, however, equity will often come from a variety of creative sources such as federal and state historic preservation tax credit programs, low-income housing tax credits, state and local development grants, and in some limited cases even the EB-5 Immigrant Investor Program.[1]

A savvy entrepreneur with expertise in these programs can sometimes put a development deal together with very little of their own cash, though the devil is in the details. Most of these types of programs can get complicated and will involve long and arduous slogs through bureaucracy, politics, and paperwork. In many cases, you may find yourself looking at multiple years of development efforts before a project will actually cash flow, and most grant programs require you to front the cash and apply for reimbursement after the work is complete.

For more traditional multifamily acquisitions, the three most common ways to cover the equity portion of a deal are to contribute all the

1 https://www.uscis.gov/working-in-the-united-states/permanent-workers/eb-5-immigrant-investor-program

cash yourself, do a joint venture with other investors, or syndicate the deal. Each of these options comes with its own advantages and disadvantages.

Going Solo

The first option is to cover all the cash requirements of a deal by using your own capital. The legal entity of choice for going solo on a multifamily deal is the single-member limited liability company (SMLLC). (We cover other options in Chapter Twenty.) The biggest advantage to funding a deal yourself is that you can have 100 percent ownership and control of the property. The downside is that you have to come up with the funds. They might come from your personal savings, the sale of other investments, a line of credit, or anywhere else you can drum up some cash.

For my first deal, I drained my retirement account, which I don't recommend. After that, I tried to avoid using my meager personal savings. For most of my deals I was able to secure the necessary cash from adding value to properties in my portfolio and doing cash-out refinances. Using this approach, I was able to accumulate a portfolio of more than 500 units, plus a handful of office and retail properties. I did a couple of joint ventures along the way, pooling my resources with partners. Later, after more than a decade of going it alone, growing organically, and being perpetually cash poor from reinvesting all my profits into more deals, I decided to partner and start syndicating. This allowed me to take my portfolio to the next level, accumulating units in the thousands.

Joint Venture

A joint venture basically entails teaming up with other active investors to do a deal together. The most common way to structure a real estate joint venture is by forming a multi-member LLC, but there are many other potential legal entities you could use. (Again, see Chapter Twenty for more on this topic.) The advantages of a joint venture include the ability to leverage the skill sets and connections of multiple people, as well as the ability to share the workload. Perhaps more importantly, you can pool resources and acquire properties that are larger than you could manage by yourself.

The downside of joint ventures is that you're taking on all the potential perils and pitfalls of investing with partners. You won't be able to keep all the equity either, and depending on how the operating agreement is written, you may not have full control. That said, you are getting a smaller ownership stake in what is likely to be a much larger deal, so you could consider it a wash from an equity standpoint.

A joint venture requires a lot of up-front communication to make sure everyone is on the same page. Responsibilities and ownership should be defined in the operating agreement and can be divided in any way that is agreeable to the parties involved.

How much each partner contributes toward the cash required for closing is also flexible. Cash contributions can be split equally among the partners, or they can be divided to reflect the relative amount of responsibility each partner assumes for, say, the acquisition or day-to-day operations. It's not uncommon, especially in smaller multifamily properties, for one party to put in all the cash and one to put in most of the work, or "sweat equity."

That said, all partners in a joint venture must have some active role in the investment, even if it's minor. If any of the owners are 100 percent passive, then the investment could technically be considered a security and subject to securities law. If you want to accept money from 100 per-cent passive investors, the deal should be structured as a syndication.

Syndication

A syndication is a limited partnership that involves the pooling of money from passive investors to fund a deal. In return for contributing cash, these passive investors, who are limited partners, get part ownership and a preferred share in the profits. By preferred, we mean that the people who invest in your syndication would be the first ones to receive a defined portion of the returns after debt obligations are met. This means you will have two types of equity—common and preferred.

As shown in the earlier illustration of a sample capital stack, preferred equity sits above debt but below common equity. As the one who pulls the deal together, you would be a general partner and hold common equity (sometimes called sponsor equity), which sits at the top of the capital stack and is subordinate to all other debt and equity holders. As a general partner and common equity holder, you are paid last.

On the downside, syndications are significantly more complicated than joint ventures from a legal standpoint, and they usually involve giving up a lot of equity. Depending on how much of the capital you are raising from the limited partners, your ownership stake can end up being severely diluted compared to going solo.

That said, giving up a hefty chunk of equity to passive investors can be fulfilling because it provides you with the opportunity to create wealth for others. However, the real beauty of syndicating a deal is that it allows you to buy properties far larger than you would otherwise be able to afford.

Some syndicators contribute cash of their own alongside the passive investors, but many syndicators raise all the necessary capital from others. That's the big attraction of syndication for a number of investors: *You can buy large multifamily properties with no cash!*

Syndication has become popular because it enables investors to successfully scale to large levels relatively quickly. We've met syndicators who have amassed thousands of units in just a few short years by raising capital to fund their deals. In fact, the fund we own grew from zero to more than 1,000 units in eighteen months thanks to syndication. It's a great strategy but also a complex one, so in the next two chapters we're going to dig deeper into syndication and raising private capital.

KEY TAKEAWAYS

- The two types of capital used to fund a deal are debt and equity, both of which can come from different sources. They are layered on top of one another to make up the capital stack. Where each source falls relative to the others in the capital stack reflects the order of repayment if the project fails.
- Debt is the cornerstone of most deals and is usually in the first position at the bottom of the capital stack. Equity/cash is at the top and is last in line for repayment.
- The most common ways to come up with equity are to contribute the cash yourself, form a joint venture, or do a syndication. Each option has its own advantages and disadvantages.

River Apartments: Part III

While some investors may have been deterred by all the theft going on at River Apartments, I was pretty excited about it. Firing the thieves and replacing them with competent, law-abiding people seemed like a surefire way to reduce expenses. However, even though my heart was warmed by the glowing potential for value-add, I still had to get the property at a fair price and figure out how to structure the deal in a way that would work well for me. I knew this could pose a challenge because I didn't have a lot of equity to invest.

Fortunately, the seller was highly motivated, and the sorry state of affairs at River Apartments gave me some pretty good leverage. After some back-and -forth, we agreed on a purchase price. During negotiations, I also got the seller to agree that they would extend owner financing in the amount of $500,000. This mezzanine debt would be subordinate to the first mortgage and security interest lien held by the bank and was extended at favorable terms. The historical cash flows were sufficient to service the combined bank and seller debt, which gave me a high level of confidence in light of my plans to dramatically improve the property's financials right out of the gate.

The $500,000 in owner financing was extremely helpful to me as the buyer while still being palatable to the seller. The seller's debt was fairly low, and since I would be using bank financing to cover 75 percent of the purchase price, the seller would still receive enough proceeds at closing to pay off their debt and pull out a significant amount of cash.

This is an approach I have used for numerous commercial transactions and continue to use today. During negotiations, I will often wait until later in the process to introduce owner financing in exchange for offering a higher price. I will also negotiate other credits that will allow me to reduce the amount of cash I need to close. Sellers will sometimes agree to these kinds of concessions if doing so will allow them to secure a better price.

For this particular deal, the primary concession I sought (in addition to owner financing) was a closing credit for the massive amount of deferred maintenance at River Apartments. In exchange for accepting the property "as is," I received a deferred-maintenance credit from the seller at closing.

While a deferred-maintenance credit can be for any amount, I decided not to define a specific dollar amount so it wouldn't affect my bank financing. Instead, I included a clause in the purchase agreement for a credit equal to the balance of the seller's reserve escrow accounts on the day we closed.

In cases where a seller has owned a property for a long period of time, as this one had, their reserve account balances tend to grow rather large. Accordingly, I included the following clause in the purchase agreement, even though I had no idea what the existing reserve balance might be:

> Buyer accepts Property "as-is" and Seller agrees to provide Buyer with a credit at closing for deferred maintenance in an amount equal to the balance of the Seller's reserve for replacements account that was established in accordance with the terms of the Seller's mortgage. Seller shall continue to make required reserve deposits and shall not withdraw funds from the reserve for replacements account prior to closing without approval of the Buyer.

I figured I had nothing to lose. There were surely at least some funds in there, and since the seller's mortgage was taken out a long time ago, I surmised it could pay sizable dividends. The seller didn't object to the clause, and I hoped for the best.

I felt good about the terms of the deal I had negotiated, and the seller was happy to have found a buyer who was willing to ignore the hideous financials—but a signed contract is just the beginning. I felt as if the safety bar had dropped down and locked me in place at the beginning of a scary roller-coaster ride. Turns out that was an accurate premonition—it was going to be quite a thriller.

To be continued...

Scan to leave a review or access bonus content

Leave a review on Amazon

Access the free bonus content

More from
BiggerPockets Publishing

The Book on Flipping Houses

Written by active real estate investor and fix-and-flipper J Scott, this book contains more than 300 pages of step-by-step training, perfect for both the complete newbie and the seasoned pro looking to build a house-flipping business. Whatever your skill level, this book will teach you everything you need to know to build a profitable business and start living the life of your dreams.

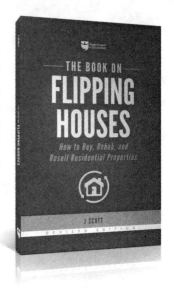

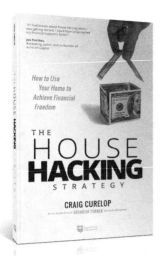

The House Hacking Strategy

Don't pay for your home. Hack it and live for free! When mastered, house hacking can save you thousands of dollars in monthly expenses, build tens of thousands of dollars in equity each year, and provide the financial means to retire early. Discover why so many successful investors support their investment careers with house hacking—and learn from a frugality expert who has "hacked" his way toward financial freedom.

If you enjoyed this book, we hope you'll take a moment to check out some of the other great material BiggerPockets offers. BiggerPockets is the real estate investing social network, marketplace, and information hub, designed to help make you a smarter real estate investor through podcasts, books, blog posts, videos, forums, and more. Sign up today—it's free! **Visit www.BiggerPockets.com.**

Buy, Rehab, Rent, Refinance, Repeat

Invest in real estate and never run out of money! In *Buy, Rehab, Rent, Refinance, Repeat*, you'll discover the incredible strategy known as BRRRR—a long-hidden secret of the ultra-rich and those with decades of experience. Author and investor David Greene holds nothing back, sharing the exact systems and processes he used to scale his business from buying two houses per year to buying two houses per *month* using the BRRRR strategy.

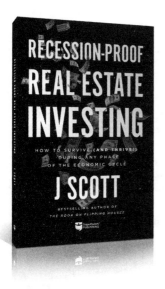

Recession-Proof Real Estate Investing

Take any recession in stride, and never be intimidated by a market shift again. In this book, accomplished investor J Scott dives into the theory of economic cycles and the real-world strategies for harnessing them to your advantage. With clear instructions for every type of investor, this easy-to-follow guide will show you how to make money during all of the market's twists and turns—whether during an economic recession or at any other point in the economic cycle. You'll never look at your real estate business the same way again!

More from
BiggerPockets Publishing

Profit Like the Pros: The Best Real Estate Deals Made by Expert Investors

Remarkable real estate deals are happening all around us. Take a look behind the curtain to see exactly how investors have profited from their best deals ever! With twenty-five real-world stories from seasoned investors across the country, this book uncovers the secrets behind unbelievable real estate deals, from sourcing and funding to profiting. Author Ken Corsini—star of HGTV's *Flip or Flop Atlanta*—has distilled his best investor interviews to educate, entertain, and get your wheels spinning.

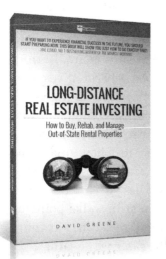

Long-Distance Real Estate Investing

Don't let your location dictate your financial freedom: Live where you want, and invest anywhere it makes sense! The rules, technology, and markets have changed: No longer are you forced to invest only in your backyard. In *Long-Distance Real Estate Investing*, learn an in-depth strategy to build profitable rental portfolios through buying, managing, and flipping out-of-state properties from real estate investor and agent David Greene.

The Book on Tax Strategies for the Savvy Real Estate Investor

Taxes! Boring and irritating, right? Perhaps. But if you want to succeed in real estate, your tax strategy will play a huge role in how fast you grow. A great tax strategy can save you thousands of dollars a year. A bad strategy could land you in legal trouble. With *The Book on Tax Strategies for the Savvy Real Estate Investor,* you'll find ways to deduct more, invest smarter, and pay far less to the IRS!

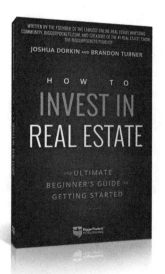

How to Invest in Real Estate

Two of the biggest names in the real estate world teamed up to write the most comprehensive manual ever written on getting started in the lucrative business of real estate investing. Joshua Dorkin and Brandon Turner give you an insider's look at the many different real estate niches and strategies so that you can find which one works best for you, your resources, and your goals.

CONNECT WITH BIGGERPOCKETS

and Become Successful in Your Real Estate Business Today!

Facebook
/BiggerPockets

Instagram
@BiggerPockets

Twitter
@BiggerPockets

LinkedIn
/company/Bigger
Pockets

Website
BiggerPockets.com